If These WALLS *Could* TALK:

NOTRE DAME FIGHTING IRISH

Stories from the
Notre Dame Fighting Irish Sideline,
Locker Room, and Press Box

Reggie Brooks with John Heisler

TRIUMPH
B O O K S

Library of Congress Cataloging-in-Publication Data

Names: Brooks, Reggie, author. | Heisler, John, author.
Title: If these walls could talk. Notre Dame Fighting Irish: stories from the Notre Dame Fighting Irish sideline, locker room, and press box / Reggie Brooks with John Heisler.
Other titles: Notre Dame Fighting Irish
Identifiers: LCCN 2021023915 | ISBN 9781629379180 (paperback) | ISBN 9781641257183 (epub)
Subjects: LCSH: Notre Dame Fighting Irish (Football team)—History. | University of Notre Dame—Football—History.
Classification: LCC GV958.N6 B76 2021 | DDC 796.33/2630977289—dc23
LC record available at https://lccn.loc.gov/2021023915

This book is available in quantity at special discounts for your group or organization. For further information, contact:

Triumph Books LLC
814 North Franklin Street
Chicago, Illinois 60610
(312) 337-0747
www.triumphbooks.com

Printed in U.S.A.
ISBN: 978-1-62937-853-4
Design by Amy Carter
Page production by Patricia Frey

Hi Mom!

CONTENTS

FOREWORD

I t was not really all that long ago that I hardly knew anything about the University of Notre Dame.

As a kid growing up in an inner-city Detroit neighborhood, I actually liked Oklahoma because Brian Bosworth was there at the time and I was a linebacker.

Plus Michigan was not far away, and Bo Schembechler wanted me to come and be a "Michigan man." They really wanted me to be a linebacker too.

At the same time my high school coach, Bob Dozier at Mackenzie High School, convinced me that my long-term football career would be better served if I focused on playing as a running back. Some of that was my size—he didn't see me playing at a high level as a 5'11" linebacker, and he was probably right.

I liked the fact that Notre Dame wanted me to run the football, and I knew Lou Holtz liked to use the fullback position in the running game.

Then, during my senior year in high school, Schembechler retired and I came to realize Michigan was going hard after a running back from Ohio named Ricky Powers.

When I went to sleep the night before I was going to announce my decision, I really did not know if I would choose Michigan or Notre Dame.

But when I woke up I put on the Notre Dame hat, and I will tell you that there was no one happier than my mother, Gladys, because she loved everything about Notre Dame.

It turned out to be a great experience, both on and off the field.

* * *

I wasn't very worldly when I first arrived in South Bend—I had barely been out of our neighborhood in Detroit. I learned a lot from a cultural standpoint during my three years at Notre Dame because it was a completely different environment than I had been used to.

And the football part was awesome because when I enrolled at Notre Dame, they were coming off a national championship in 1988 and a 12–1 season in 1989.

We were the No. 1 team in the country when I began my freshman season, and we had a chance to win the national championship every year I was there. In those three years we went into 17 different games ranked fifth or higher in the polls, so there was no shortage of attention on our program.

The players who came in with me comprised maybe the best recruiting class to come to Notre Dame, and they already had plenty of good players. Including me, we had five people from that class who ended up as first-round picks in the NFL Draft: Bryant Young, Aaron Taylor, Tom Carter, and Jeff Burris.

It wasn't as if I was the only talented running back while I was there, because we also had Rodney Culver, Ricky Watters, Tony Brooks, and Tony's younger brother Reggie. I actually didn't play much as a freshman in 1990, but Culver—who also was from Detroit—moved from fullback to tailback in 1991, which gave me more of an opportunity.

Reggie had an unbelievable year in 1992, and the two of us made it tough on defenses because we both had good speed and decent size. It was not going to be easy for anyone to tackle either one of us.

I'm still proud that Notre Dame ranked third in the country in rushing in 1992 when we were there—that's the highest national ranking for Notre Dame in that category since 1946, when they finished first.

* * *

I still remember the time Coach Holtz, Joe Moore, and Vinny Cerrato came to my house to recruit me in Detroit. I liked playing for Coach Holtz—he was an intense guy on the practice field and at games, but we were always prepared. And he always had a good way of making sure none of us got too big-headed about ourselves. He knew exactly what to say at exactly the right time.

I remember stopping in to see him after I'd been playing in the NFL for a few years. He gave me some great advice that really helped at that time in my career.

My time at Notre Dame was enjoyable and beneficial, both on and off the field. I made a lot of great friends, played in some big-time football games, and walked away a better person.

I loved the fact that Reggie came back to Notre Dame a couple of years before I retired from the Pittsburgh Steelers. It's great to come back to campus knowing you've got someone you know to connect with—after a while I'd been gone long enough that there were not many people left on campus or in the football department whom I knew from my years there.

Plus Reggie has become sort of the inside Notre Dame football guy for as long as he's been around and covering the Irish. Through his Monogram Club role, there are not many people who have been part of the Notre Dame football program whom Reggie doesn't know.

That makes him perfect to create this record of all his connections with Notre Dame football. He's not only a good friend, but he also knows all the ins and outs of what football has been about for multiple decades.

I told Reggie I'd buy his book just to see what he had to say about our three years together on the field. We had a lot of fun, and I wouldn't trade the experience for anything.

—Jerome Bettis,
who rushed for 1,912 yards for
Notre Dame from 1990 to 1992.

INTRODUCTION

Every former University of Notre Dame football player brings his own perspective to the time he spent in South Bend—whether a highly recruited high school All-American, a walk-on, or anyone in between. Former Irish running back Reggie Brooks is no different.

Yet Reggie brings to these pages a unique look at Irish football fortunes over the last three decades and even earlier:

- As a player in the late 1980s and early 1990s he played on some of Coach Lou Holtz's greatest teams. The Irish finished a combined 41–8–1 during Reggie's four seasons in a Notre Dame uniform, finishing those campaigns in two Orange Bowls, a Sugar Bowl, and then in the Cotton Bowl for his final game. Notre Dame's four bowl opponents in Reggie's four years combined for a 43–2–1 record during those regular seasons. The Irish finished second, fourth, and sixth in the final Associated Press polls after three of those years.

- Reggie's Irish teammates include College Football Hall of Fame players Chris Zorich, Aaron Taylor, and Raghib Ismail, plus a long list of all-stars including Jerome Bettis, Todd Lyght, Rick Mirer, and more All-Americans than you can remember.

- He was the star of the show in two of the most memorable plays in Irish football lore. One of those was a run against Michigan in which he was literally knocked out when he was hit a few yards short of the goal line and the other was his reception on the two-point attempt against Penn State in the famed Snow Bowl game at Notre Dame Stadium. A few weeks after that contest, the final regular season game of his career in 1992 at USC proved to be one of the more spectacular ground-gaining efforts in Notre Dame history.

After a handful of years playing professional football Reggie returned to Notre Dame, first to work in the university's Office of Information

Technology and then quickly taking on some football media duties within Irish athletics.

A few years later Reggie took on a new role with the Notre Dame Monogram Club that gave him an even greater window into what Notre Dame football is all about. In his role coordinating football alumni relations, Reggie came to know virtually every living former Irish player in some form. He hung out with the Notre Dame Heisman Trophy winners and hundreds of other former Irish players, coaches, and staff.

Reggie brings all that to the pages of *If These Walls Could Talk*. From being an Oklahoma high school football standout who came to South Bend not knowing all that much about Notre Dame, over time he became ensconced in the history and tradition of the sport at his alma mater.

He had one view as a player, another as an alumnus watching from afar, still another as a media member covering and analyzing Irish football games, and, finally, another in a role that proved a more-than-interesting conduit between the current program and staff and those who came before in the blue-and-gold (and sometimes green) uniforms.

More than anything, Reggie provides an inside look at what the life of a Notre Dame football player is all about. Even as an All-American, he had his share of frustrations, struggles, and challenges to marry with all the victories, yards gained, and accolades as his career unfolded.

As his dream of reaching the NFL came true, even that step proved more than a little complicated, and often on the same days he was making headlines for his play.

Ultimately, his story came full circle as Reggie returned to Notre Dame, providing him with a unique, long-term insider's look at many of the individuals who made Irish football a nationwide attraction.

I've known Reggie since he first came to campus—and eventually worked side by side with him for close to two decades. After the retirement of longtime Irish assistant football coaches George Kelly, Brian Boulac, and Tony Yelovich—all of whom eventually joined the athletic administrative ranks—Reggie became the most consistent presence on the Irish campus when it came to football connections.

So sit back and enjoy his take on his own journey—and the people and places that have made Notre Dame football headlines over the years.

—John Heisler

CHAPTER 1
2020: SUCCESS AMIDST ADVERSITY

The 2020 football season was determined by overcoming loss. You look at that team—it started with the players Notre Dame lost from the previous season, but also the time they lost over the course of 2020, starting back in the spring. It started with the loss of the seniors and some other players to graduation and the NFL. And when you look at the Notre Dame football team from the 2019 season, you consider the success they had there. They had a strong group of leaders at various positions and particularly on defense—really at every level of the defense.

You start with the front end, and you look at two stellar defensive linemen—who were the key to the pass rush for Notre Dame's defense in 2019—Julian Okwara and Khalid Kareem. Both those guys were drafted by the NFL and had some success. Then you look at the next level and you lost Asmar Bilal at the linebacker position, and then on the back end you lost Jalen Elliott, Alohi Gilman, Donte Vaughn, and Troy Pride Jr.—all players who played in the NFL in 2020. And that's just on the defensive side of the ball.

On offense, you lost Chase Claypool, Cole Kmet, and Tony Jones Jr., who were all integral parts of the offense and key contributors at the skill positions. You lost 50 to 60 percent of your offensive production, particularly in the passing game. When you add in Chris Finke it goes up to 70 to 75 percent of your passing offense that has moved on and is no longer on the team. That's why I said the 2020 season began with accounting for losses.

Then you move from the loss of players to the loss of time. When you lose players and don't have the opportunity over the course of the spring and summer months to gain familiarity with new combinations, it's tough to find a level of development and trust in the passing game. When COVID-19 hit it took away spring ball and the summer sessions, which you normally have for a quarterback to get acclimated to a new receiving corps and new players. You need to develop those relationships with new backs, because Jones was a key part of the offense in the running game and now he's gone. You lose that opportunity and also the opportunity to become comfortable with the new offensive coordinator, Tommy Rees, and his quarterbacks. That's a loss of time and opportunity to gain a familiarity with the play-calling and what to expect from a young coach in an expanded role.

What made 2020 so special was not so much the success that was had, but how they were able to have such success in the face of such loss. You look at this—you lose spring ball and you lose a lot in the summer, and then there's the uncertainty and lack of familiarity with players. For a quarterback like Ian Book, timing is critical, and not having the opportunity to develop that timing with new key components isn't easy. When you have a player like Kmet or Claypool coming back, there's a level of comfort that you have as opposed to breaking in an entirely new receiving corps. Then add on top of that the reality that Book was coming off some struggles at times in 2019, even with the success he had with Claypool and Kmet. There's a need for trust between the quarterback and the receivers. And you can see there's a possibility that it will affect you if you lose those pieces.

Not to say Notre Dame had it any worse than anyone else in the top programs, but Notre Dame can't afford to lose those opportunities. It affects your psyche and it affects the comfort of being able to go out and compete on that level. I can only imagine how difficult it was for Book to develop those new relationships and then not have the ability to play with them over the spring and summer as much as he would have preferred. Then you aren't in school for a while after COVID-19 hits. So not only are you not allowed to grow and connect with the guys to develop relationships on the field, but you also lose a semester of what I consider to be what makes Notre Dame a different place than any other. There's a presence on campus and there's a connectivity of being on campus that was taken away, and that affects you.

I can't say I know exactly how every one of these guys felt, but I have an inclination as far as losing all these opportunities and seeing these things happen. You can use FaceTime and Zoom and all this technology, but being physically present with all your teammates has a profound impact. You see this season and it's hard to go into the year—at least looking in from the outside—finding a lot of positives with these things occurring. How are these young men going to address this? How are they going to overcome it? How are they going to handle the loss? And then, boom, the next thing you know there's the question mark of whether they are even going to have a season.

At this point Notre Dame had been shut down in the spring and students had been sent home. Unlike most institutions that could fathom competing in athletics without being on campus or having the student body on campus, Notre Dame was not about to allow that to happen. So going through those months of uncertainty in March, April, and beyond—not being able to practice, not being able to be in the classroom, not being able to walk around campus, not being able to engage with teammates—was extremely impactful, I imagine, in a negative way.

There hasn't been enough said about the Notre Dame football program and its connection to the decision of the university and its president, Father John Jenkins, to have in-person classes in the fall of 2020. Because Notre Dame would not play football in the fall if the student body did not come back for in-person learning. That is a distinction that I feel is unique to Notre Dame, because I think other institutions would not have had a problem still playing sports while the student body was remote. I don't think the decision was made based on needing Notre Dame to play football—I'm sure it was factored in to some degree, but that was not the full decision, because for Notre Dame to be Notre Dame it needs to have in-person learning. The institution is not built for digital learning; it's built for community. And for me and so many who went to Notre Dame, whether you were a student-athlete or not, the community is about being physically present with others.

There was a lot of consternation about whether Notre Dame would be allowed to open back up. It wasn't just a decision made by the university, since we are part of St. Joseph County and the state of Indiana, so a lot of the protocols put in place dictated whether that would even be a possibility. And that's where, in my mind, the viability of Notre Dame playing a season was overlooked. So again these are all losses that this team faced even before there was a season. It was May 18, 2020, when Father Jenkins announced there would be a fall reopening in the face of COVID-19. The university was committed to the plan, but if something were to go wrong, it would have to go back to a remote situation—and the football season would be over.

You look at how things played out—and it ultimately played out well—but think about the mind of an 18-, 19-, 20-, or 21-year-old football player and the uncertainty of it all. This is how the 2020 season started. I know the guys maintained a positive perspective as a team and as a coaching staff—they had to maintain that positive thought process if they were going to have success. But I know there had to be doubt. Can we get this done? Is this possible? With the 2020 season I was struck by the level of commitment and discipline that these young men had to show. It started with assessing the loss, but it all came down to how they addressed and handled the loss that was projected on them.

The decision was made—there was going to be a return to campus. So we had this opportunity to figure out how we return to campus, how we get student-athletes back, and the timing of it all. The season was dictated by a lot of uncertainty and a lot of adjustments, not only by the student-athletes, but also by the coaches, the administration, and the behind-the-scenes efforts of so many men and women at the university to handle the unknown. No one knew when the pandemic was up, down, or sideways—whatever the case may be. There was a lot of uncertainty.

The main thing as a coach is that you want to avoid panic. You don't want to project panic and uncertainty because players feed off of that. They feed off of how you react to difficult situations. But coaches have to look at the losses. From the defensive standpoint, you lost starters, safeties, linebackers, defensive linemen who went to the NFL, and a few offensive linemen who graduated. And then offensively you've lost other key components. You've got to replace them all, yet you're not allowed to interact with your players. Everything is virtual.

I don't know how many of you play football, but football is not a virtual sport. It's not conducive to doing everything virtually because it requires a hands-on approach. To be successful you need to actually play. You need to practice. And not that we were in a situation different than other teams, but it's different for Notre Dame because of the type of institution it is. So the 2020 season started out with uncertainty and loss, and it really did take a lot to determine how to overcome that. How do you push through? This season was predicated on these aspects—on the need for discipline and great leadership to actually come through this.

Then on May 25, 2020, something happened that rocked me to my core. I am a Black male, I have Black sons, and to see George Floyd die under the knee of a police officer was chilling. May 25—just a week after the decision was made to reopen the school—was the day that social unrest across the country reared its ugly head. You see these young men competing, and just watching his death and the indifference shown to him affected so many. It was a difficult thing to watch, but it was also a lesson that so many Black men have had to learn early.

To have something like this occur created a level of anxiety for not just the Black players—because these are young Black men—but for everyone in the Notre Dame community. Coming back to campus now brought a lot of anxiety. I had the opportunity to speak with Daelin Hayes, who led and was the key speaker at the June 18 rally and walk for unity. A lot of times what you see in these situations is the Black community being outraged, but not as much outrage within the majority of the white community. But this situation—murder—really galvanized and united the entire team beyond the typical teammate relationships.

These young men shared their pain with their white teammates, and their white teammates got to see the hurt and the struggle of their Black teammates, which hadn't really happened before. I can speak to not having shared the struggles I had as a young Black man in America with my white teammates. Yet in this trying, difficult situation, it opened some eyes, and it drew the white players into the lives of their Black teammates and vice versa. That rally and walk for unity was not just about the white players supporting their Black teammates—they were there supporting their brothers because they were brought into the experience of their teammates, their teammates' parents, and their teammates' relatives for centuries.

When you are able to really express the hurt, the pain, the fear, and the frustration of what occurred to George Floyd and earlier to Ahmaud Arbery, the white players got to see their Black teammates in a different light. It created a stronger bond than just being a teammate. When you feel a family member hurting or see a family member being attacked, you are going to defend. And to me, it created a level of awareness not only by the players, but also by the coaching staff. To have Brian Kelly, the head coach, walking with them had a profound effect on our athletics director, Jack Swarbrick. This summer had a different feel because so many times you see this outrage, but then it dissipates. This has not dissipated, and it did not dissipate through the season. It became about our players continuing to voice their disdain for police brutality, and at the same time, honoring each other and growing stronger in their awareness in taking on the hurt of their teammates. It was about saying, "I'm not only standing with you, but I'm also feeling this with you. I'm in this fight with you." And it creates a deeper bond when you are willing to do a little extra. Because when you see a teammate who's hurting, it's like an injury. When you see a teammate go down, you pick them up because you have to. You want to see them flourish and succeed. Because when they flourish and succeed, we all do. And that was the sense of the rally cry that came from the social justice movement—not just from the Black players, but from the whole team.

The involvement of the football program and the athletic department at that Juneteenth rally really sparked something greater within the Notre Dame athletic community. It springboarded into that season—seeing our football team, what occurred, and what they did to support each other. They came back right before they were supposed to start practice and they had this rally right before their workouts began. It was palpable—the hurt and pain, not the division. You want to feel your teammate made whole, and I really feel that the rally wasn't for everybody else, but it was for themselves. They spoke out as a team and as the Notre Dame football community.

It brought out some issues and it created some opportunities for a stronger bond. The rally became a rally cry—a cry for the team to bond together. I have to commend Ron Powlus, the administrator for the football program. He was already dealing with COVID-19 as an obviously integral factor in developing the plan to return. And then he had another situation that hit him, and he had to adjust and adapt. There was a sense of, "Hey, how do we support these young men who are dealing with the hurt and pain of this injustice?" And that had to be a part of that return to practice and return to some sort of normalcy.

You're looking at loss, you're looking at anxiety, and you're looking at hurt and a deep pain that's been inflicted. How do you maintain and keep the team together? How do you deal with all these instances of struggle? Part of the key, to me, of this team was having discipline and strong leadership. With all the loss and uncertainty and all the things that happened, this is what defined this team—the strong leadership on both sides of the ball and from the staff.

You had to work through the notion of, "We didn't have this, we didn't have that. We weren't able to do this, we weren't able to do that." Those things test your mettle, but that's where success comes from. Hayes on the defensive side of the ball, Book on the offensive side of the ball, Kyle Hamilton on the defensive side of the ball. And then you have Ben Skowronek, Kyren Williams, and a lot of other guys stepping up. Aaron Banks, Jarrett Patterson, Liam Eichenberg, Myron Tagovailoa-Amosa. It required guys to step up. Drew White, Jeremiah Owusu-Koramoah—these guys had played in the past and played well. But you saw guys rise up and take up a stronger leadership position to replace those losses first and foremost—but also to define the identity of this team. And part of that was needed. In defining the team, how do you handle adversity and how do you handle difficult situations? And I'd say the 2020 team had to go through more adversity than any team I can ever recall at Notre Dame. Just the compounding issues from one moment to the next and from one moment of uncertainty to the next.

The social justice issues never really left because there were more issues of police brutality—plus other incidences of the pandemic really having an impact. In the midst of all of this, you are trying to build a team, bringing together a group of impressionable young men to do something significant. On the outside looking in I won't say it was impossible, but it was difficult at the very least. And to see these young men step up and fight through the adversity, fight through the loss, fight through the difficult times, and build those bonds was something I was extremely impressed by because they overcame the limitations.

There were limitations on who could be in the locker room at certain times, so this was a team that stretched further than the 100 or so people within the football program. It extended far beyond that list, and it required a team effort and a commitment that stretched beyond the Guglielmino Athletics Complex. It required more of others, and the community, which is what sets Notre Dame apart, came into play. You don't get to where this team got in 2020 without other factors, other groups, other teams, and other administration beyond the football administration building and supporting that community to provide the young men the success that they had this season.

The one thing that stood out to me most was the level of discipline it took to handle the different protocols in place and to overcome the adverse situations that occurred. You are going to have some positive COVID-19 tests and you are going to have some continued adversity. But to do that over a 12-game season was impressive to say the least. And all these things occurred before they even had a practice, before they even played a down, and before they even played a game. All this adversity and struggle and strife and uncertainty and pressure just continued to come at this team, and they just continued to step up, and little by little you saw them figure it out.

The season started in a way that was a tough deal. The schedule changed, the opponents changed, and they didn't even know if they were going to have a season at all. The students still hadn't returned, but the team had already come back and was practicing, yet was at the mercy of a virus that they couldn't see—an enemy they couldn't really define. They were wading through difficult situations, finding their way through, feeling their way through—and these difficult losses were requiring this new group of players to step up and be accountable. Unproven young players and unproven veteran players thrust into new roles, all while processing difficult situations and difficult struggles that have been thrust upon them. And they were looking to elevate their game in the middle of all of it.

CHAPTER 2
THE SEASON UNFOLDS

Thee 2020 season started with a home game against Duke. So who were going to be the individuals who would step up? You had the known commodity in Book, but over the course of the last few years, he had some struggles and there were questions about which players were going to step up and be his receivers. Who would be the go-to guys for him? He had been the second-leading rusher in 2019, and none of the other running backs in play for the first part of the season had much game experience.

Tommy Tremble had flashes here and there as tight end, but the question was about where the offense would come from for this Notre Dame football team. What type of identity would they have? Early on, the breakout kid of the year started right out of the gate—and that was Kyren Williams, coming in and rushing for 110 yards and 93 yards in receiving in the Duke game. You saw this young man blossom into a star. Weeks later I had the opportunity to talk to Autry Denson, who had recruited Williams, and he talked about how special the young man was and how he came on the scene like gangbusters. I've got to admit I was shocked, but watching him run and seeing the tenacity with which he runs, his physicality, his explosiveness, and his ability to make cuts, I was impressed. There were a lot of expectations going into that first game, but a lot of question marks too. As strong a showing as Williams had offensively, there were still questions about Book's performance, how he would play under a new coordinator, how that relationship would work, and who the receivers would be. You found a good dynamic when you saw the pieces there, but the ability for them to come together was still in question. Then you get a potential star in Williams and his playmaking ability, and you see Book still finding his way and trying to find the rhythm you need as a quarterback.

It was a solid game for Book (19 of 31 passing for 263 yards), mostly a tight end–centric game as far as throwing the football. With the running backs you started to get a formation of what this offense was going to be. A lot was predicated on the strong offensive line play and the running game and really good tight end play out of the gate. You had a sense

Quarterback Ian Book gets his arm game-ready.

that was what it was going to be—to me, Notre Dame has kind of been Tight End U, producing stellar tight ends over the years. The running back situation was answered loudly by Williams, and you got a sense that freshman backup Chris Tyree would help too. But Williams established himself as a force to be reckoned with right out of the gate.

Defensively, Owusu-Koramoah set the tone for a season that led to All-America and All-ACC honors—he stepped it up and started off with a bang with a sack and nine tackles, plus a forced fumble against Duke. The things that stick out most about Owusu-Koramoah are his speed, his aggressiveness with the football, and his willingness to hit people. And you saw that with this team right away. There were struggles with some missed tackles early on, but they found their rhythm. There was just striking athleticism from the players—Kyle Hamilton looked good, plus there was an impressive showing from some of the linebackers you really hadn't seen before, so you got a sense of what type of defense this was going to be. I remember the year before, the big question mark for this defense was the experience of this linebacking corps. Right off the top the tone was set by these linebackers—White, Owusu-Koramoah, and Bo Bauer. You saw these guys really step up and show more presence from the defensive standpoint. You get through that game, a 27–13 win, and you see the formation of things to come.

Going into that second week is when Notre Dame stepped it up and established itself. The Irish dominated South Florida to the tune of a shutout (52–0). Book was efficient—he took care of the football—and you saw the backs and the tight ends as more focused recipients of the passes. There was not a lot of passing in that game—19 throws by Book and 45 rushes—yet the running back and offensive line established themselves (281 rushing yards). The identity of this football team was going to be physicality, running the ball, play-action passing, aggression, and efficiency with the football—all while defensively flying around and making plays.

This is where the depth of this Notre Dame football team showed, particularly at the linebacker position. You had two or three linebackers who didn't play in that South Florida game and you had third-team linebacker Jack Kiser step up, win a game ball, and establish himself as worthy of being in that rotation and playing at that middle linebacker slot. You sensed the depth, and you had some pieces in play for the linebacking corps. I'm a big Clark Lea fan, and seeing his presence—he was the primary coach of this group of linebackers—you got to see him step up in a big way. You had Kiser and White getting it done—and you saw the versatility of this defensive front. On the edges you had Adetokunbo Ogundeji and Isaiah Foskey, and you have Tagovailoa-Amosa up the middle establishing himself. Notre Dame was a run-stopping team that really set the tone in the first two games with 181 combined allowed rushing yards.

Around this time, there was a hiccup. We wound up having to postpone a game because of a COVID-19 scare. When you're talking about 18-, 19-, and 20-year-old kids, getting some cases really affects the team. There was another situation when we had to forgo the next game, against Wake Forest, too. It really left us wondering if we could get through a season with such uncertainty in regard to the virus.

You've got these young men who are fighting through and trying to stay as committed and as safe as possible, but they are also going to class and there are opportunities for mistakes and incidents to happen that put the team at risk. It was kind of a make-or-break situation over that two-week period, and it all had to be brought back under control. I was extremely impressed with how the leadership on this team stepped up and said, "We cannot afford to let this slide—we cannot afford to give up because we have a special group here." They rallied around each other and held each other accountable. The level of accountability in this situation really showed itself in a huge way coming out of those next two weeks.

While other football teams were having weeks of high COVID-19 cases, it was very impressive how quickly that scare was brought back under control. It was through the leadership of this team and that connectedness and football community. They rallied around each other and set the tone for the rest of the year by saying, "We're not going to cost ourselves a season." They had to make the determination about who they were going to be.

A couple of weeks later we wound up beating Florida State at home, and though there were a few mistakes here and there, it was a pretty dominant performance against a program that was rebuilding its team under a new head coach. It was the usual suspects—Owusu-Koramoah, Hamilton, Ogundeji—who continued to step up defensively. When I talk about the guys who were considered leaders, one guy who was struggling early on was Hayes. He did not have a lot of huge numbers. He didn't flash, and what I mean by flash is making plays around the ball. That's what you saw with Owusu-Koramoah and that's what you saw with Hamilton—these were guys who were showing up around the ball. Foskey, Owusu-Koramoah, and White were guys who would flash. They may not have made the tackle, but they were guys who were in the vicinity, rallying to the football, and who had a presence about them.

Offensively, Book was still having a solid game (201 passing yards on 16 of 25), but the team dominated again on the ground with 353 yards rushing. I'll say this: the backfield was reminiscent of the teams I played on—they were very physical, dominated the line of scrimmage, and had some very explosive, powerful backs who could make plays. Williams shined again with a stellar performance of 185 yards and Tyree had 103 more. Two backs with more than 100 yards—in this offense that's not common, but that's a credit to Rees and the style of play-calling that he had. It was very reminiscent of an old-school pound-it-out, grind-it-out play, with the quarterback being the efficient individual he was, not turning the ball over, making plays, and making plays with his legs.

Book gained some confidence in his receivers. This was the first game in which we saw the receivers having more of a presence, such as Javon McKinley with five catches for 107 yards. Braden Lenzy was also involved, with three catches and a touchdown. Little by little and quietly, the receiver who caught my eye this season was Michael

Mayer—a true freshman tight end who continued to show up game in and game out. He had two catches in this game, and three earlier this season in the Duke game. This team continued to build its identity of who they were going to be and how they were going to get it done. They dominated Florida State. The execution was not as crisp as they wanted, but they found a way to win.

The next game was probably the biggest scare of the season for Notre Dame, and that was against Louisville. It was more than a little surprising, to say the least, how poorly we played. There seemed to be a lack of fire and tenacity in that game, and it ended up being much closer (12–7) than what it should have been. Williams had another 100-yard game (127), but it was not as big of a win as many expected. They got through it and found a way to win by playing well defensively. The same guys at the top of the leaderboard—Hamilton and Owusu-Koramoah—continued to show themselves as leaders on this defense.

The game at Pitt was a much better performance from this team, and maybe the best performance from Book up to this point, with 319 yards passing. Pitt made the decision that it wasn't going to allow Notre Dame to run the football, and that was fine. The thing I liked about this game was that Rees was committed to the run. We still rushed it 50 times without getting the outcome we usually get, but it forced them to step up and that created opportunities for our receivers, Avery Davis, Skowronek, McKinley, and Mayer. They were starting to step up and make plays on the outside, and it was no longer falling mostly on Book, the tight ends, and the running backs. Boom!

By the time we played Georgia Tech, Notre Dame had moved up to No. 4 in the country—and this was another really solid performance offensively. Williams had 76 yards, averaging over five yards a carry and leading this team. But this was the game where you saw Hayes step up and become a leader rather than just when he was off the field in practice. He had five tackles, two sacks, and two forced fumbles against Georgia Tech. He really showed up in this game, and this was right before we played Clemson. He stepped into his role as a leader and did it with his performance.

It all showed in a big way, and it was very much perfect timing that would lead to what was a season unto itself going into that Clemson weekend. The hype was all there. We needed a massive defensive performance, and we needed all of our top players to really mind their p's and q's defensively if we had any hope of winning. They stepped up, had a great game, and it was a strong performance by Notre Dame offensively. But defensively we found another key to the puzzle, which resulted in a dominant defense all year long. I'd put that defense as one of the best with its athleticism, physicality, and playmaking ability, compared to any other defense in the country. And it came at such a vital time. The Clemson game—that was it. Going into that game we needed everybody at the top of their game if we were going to have any possibility of coming out with a win against such a superb team with talent like you wouldn't believe. We needed all of our defensive guys hitting on all cylinders—and that's what we saw. Coming off the Georgia Tech game, this game gave us exactly what we needed to have the opportunity to do something very special, and it solidified Notre Dame as one of the key forces in college football during the 2020 season.

From the very beginning I've always felt that Book was the key to success for this team—the key to getting in and out of the pocket and finding team success through his ability to run. I'm not saying he was a dominant, dynamic runner, but his ability to move running lanes was critical to his success because it allowed him to get into a flow. If you know anything about football, especially offensively, getting into a rhythm and flow with the ball is critical. Leading into the Clemson game the hype was everything it could be considering we were in the middle of a pandemic. As I watched the season unfold, I saw the importance of Book being a critical part of the run game. That's when he was at his best and when Notre Dame was at its best—when he had success both running and throwing. His running opened up his ability to find receivers and opened things up for other players. It was also important that we got more from the outside receivers—Davis, McKinley, and Skowronek. They weren't always as much a part of the success offensively. With the passing game it was more the tight ends and running backs. From time to time you'd see an outside receiver have some success, but it wasn't until the Pitt game, when Book had his strongest performance as a passer, that you saw the outside guys having more success.

Going into the Clemson game we needed to be firing on all cylinders because they were going to be successful offensively—they were too strong and too explosive to be shut down. As good as our defense was, it was vital that our offense stepped up in that game. In the two games prior to Clemson you had notable games by Davis, McKinley, and Skowronek—and that was a good sign.

We knew the key components going into the Clemson game. Williams had established himself as one of the top backs in the country—and this was a game when he would establish himself as a premier player with pass protection who was capable of coming out of the backfield. Then you had Tyree and C'Bo Flemister, but the improvement of Book getting back to some semblance of his 2018 season really showed itself in this game. Outside of the turnover down by the goal line, he played his best game. The stars showed up. People don't always give credit to this group, but the offensive line was phenomenal this year. Jarrett Patterson at the center—you started with him. Inside out with the continuity, Banks was a key part of it. Eichenberg, Robert Hainsey, and Tommy Kraemer—they made themselves into a tremendous group. They deserved to be up for the top offensive line honors for the year. What made Notre Dame successful was its identity, which was rooted in physicality and started up front. They established a presence about themselves—in some sense it reminded me of the line from my senior year. You looked around and it was one guy after another playing at a high level, stepping up, and dominating people.

You had all the hoopla, but there were doubts about Notre Dame and who the team was. That game solidified Notre Dame as deserving of being considered one of the top teams in the country and validating that top-five ranking. There was always a question mark, yet I go back to what they lost and had to overcome. There was a mind-set in that locker room and a lot of it started from the spring and culminated in the Clemson game when everybody said Clemson was going to dominate. Notre Dame had established itself, yet people did not give Notre Dame any credit coming into that game. Notre Dame was undefeated, playing at home, and was still an underdog. That's not supposed to happen. But the last thing Notre Dame ever receives is the benefit of the doubt when it comes to football. We get scrutinized more heavily in a lot of circles. There seems to be a higher standard for us, as if Notre Dame is not as good as it shows. We were facing an undefeated Clemson, and everybody was counting Notre Dame out.

Somewhere along the way we kind of lost that home-court advantage. We lost the advantage that people would not want to come play at Notre Dame. Clemson came in early to experience the Notre Dame campus, and I don't blame them. But they came in like it was some sort of Walt Disney experience—and they seemed to be saying, "We'll take care of business in the football game."

Book had a strong game both running and passing, and it felt like we had that rhythm and had developed a level of consistency offensively. Owusu-Koramoah was having a phenomenal season—and so were Hamilton, Foskey, Jayson Ademilola, and Shayne Simon. This team had found its groove. But the uncertainty of whether they could finish out the season kept football in jeopardy, and it was entirely out of their control. Consider the mind-set of the players and coaches. Having all of these things happen and not having the ability to change anything was difficult. But the energy of the students at home games was great. The leadership that was needed and the personal and internal fortitude necessary to block all of the uncertainty out and home in and focus—that really resonated with me and made this 2020 season so special.

Then boom! Clemson's top player, quarterback Trevor Lawrence, is out, and there wasn't a lot of immediate knowledge of his backup, though you saw him have some success the week before. There was a lot of belief that was necessary to compete when everybody was telling them that they didn't have a chance. You could sense the confidence in the players. They put it all together—even with the turnovers and mistakes. They found a way to win. The key guys stepped up.

Book at least gets a first down if he doesn't fumble into the end zone. We were about to punch it in down on the goal line another time and got a penalty. Those two plays could have been a 14-point swing. To me this game was not close. Notre Dame dominated physically, running the ball, making plays, and creating turnovers. This was the game that set the tone for what they would do the rest of the year. This was the culmination, the validation, and why Notre Dame was and is a top five team. The win resonated—the energy was palpable. The game lived up to everything.

Clemson played well, but we put the hammer down on Travis Etienne (18 carries and 28 yards)—how well we defended him was the key. Then we established the run and were dominant overall in the run game (208 yards to Clemson's 34). That was one of the best games called by Rees because of the synergy with Book and the rest of the offense. I have to think Rees gained some confidence with the success the offense had that night. Lea's defense and its confidence, and the belief that each group had in the coaches and the coaches had in the players set the tone for the success. They were going through so much that they'd never been through before. Talk about grit. The social unrest, the pandemic, being part of the ACC for the first time—a lot of firsts. And to see them react in this game displayed why the 2020 team was successful despite the outcome of the last two games.

Notre Dame finished the regular season by winning on the road at Boston College (45–31), beating a very good North Carolina team in Chapel Hill (31–17) with a dominant second half, and then rolling over Syracuse (45–21) at home in early December. The Carolina result was especially impressive because they shut out the Tar Heels in the second half and held a team averaging 43.3 points per game to only 17. This team earned its way into the College Football Playoff.

* * *

2020 was a year like no other. We all dealt with the struggle of the virus and we all dealt with the issues of racial injustice. I would have to say with all these things going on, I was quite impressed with the level of play and the strength this team displayed. It was not the outcome we would have liked at the end—losing to Clemson in the ACC Championship and to top-rated Alabama in the Rose Bowl CFP semifinal—but it was definitely a great season by Notre Dame. In that respect, speaking as an alum and an employee of the university, I was very grateful that we actually had the season at all, considering all the obstacles that could have caused it to not come to fruition. It speaks to the uniqueness of Notre Dame and the strength of the program—not only for 2020, but it also established an opportunity of what could be and the possibilities for the future. And it established the strength of the program. This season challenged the locker room like no other.

Going back to the locker room in the 1950s, when the first African American players played at Notre Dame, I've heard so many stories from Wayne Edmonds about his experiences. There were so many who went out of their way to make him feel like part of the team, including Father Ted Hesburgh. Coaches come and go, players come and go, but there's a common thread through the years: the connectedness of the locker room. This brotherhood and sense of belonging transcends different time frames. Different issues always rise up and this culminated in 2020, pinpointing what makes Notre Dame special and how you gauge team and individual success. Football is the consummate team sport, but it goes beyond the games and the practices. This year spoke to the strength, mental perseverance, and physicality it takes—but it also spoke to the emotional struggles that occur and the emotional connectedness within the team.

It is all about leadership, discipline, and the strength it takes to overcome the trials and tribulations as young men. That's what will stand out about this season—the sheer magnitude of the challenges they faced even before they played one snap in the course of the season. You saw the strength of team—the importance of all members and their ability to be greater than the sum of their parts and how they fit together. Any little nuanced challenge could have easily torn them apart, but they found a way to work together and stand strong and believe in each other. There were injuries, which you will always have, among other setbacks, but they faced challenges from within as well as externally—including the unseen virus.

As football players we see things in terms of structure, with rituals about how to do things and game plans that you execute. You adapt to the unforeseen circumstances, and yet I can't imagine how challenging this was. You have Black players and white players forming all different communities, and you are forced to address social injustice as a team and see how that forges a bond between teammates. White players stood up for Black players at a time when it was difficult, to say the least. To see Banks and Eichenberg stand together and Kiser and Williams stand together—opposite sides of the ball, but a common goal. White players saw Black players in a different light.

This also happened with former players, even though they could only get together virtually. It was so impactful to see players from different eras coming together. It was called Rally House and it happened on every Saturday Notre Dame played. The camaraderie of the 2020 team affected not only the current team to stand strong, but it also resonated with so many of the former players. I was blessed to be at the forefront of this community, which really showed me that Notre Dame football is still strong and this strength transcends time—those bonds still overcome difficulties years later.

We had teammates from different eras talking to each other. Brandon Wimbush talked to Rocky Bleier and Allen Rossum talked to George Goeddeke, showing the depth and breadth of the Notre Dame community. The Rally House became a locker room for the ages. Preston Jackson and Luther Bradley, Jeremy Akers and Kapron Lewis-Moore, Jerry Tillery and Ross Browner—we all got to see each other beyond the playing field in a different light, and it was remarkable.

Victor Abiamiri, Louis Nix, Tom Thayer, Bob Crable, Vagas Ferguson, Rick Naylor, Mike Townsend, Robert Blanton, Marc Edwards, Bert Berry, Steve Beuerlein, Allen Pinkett, and Shawn Wooden—all players who did not play together but still made a connection. Mike Whittington and Darius Walker—a linebacker and a running back—had their own unique connection because Whittington played in the USFL with Walker's dad.

Joey Getherall, Jerome Bettis, Kris Haines, Rick Mirer, Tyler Newsome, and Ricky Watters—week after week the bonds strengthened. Alohi Gilman, Theo Riddick, and Jarron Jones—week after week there was somebody new. Jim Lynch, George Kunz, Wes Pritchett, Wayne Bullock, and Rod Smith. This Notre Dame epitomized what Notre Dame is all about. Terry Hanratty and Stephon Tuitt, Shane Walton and Tony Rice, Jimmy Clausen and Chris Zorich. Manti Te'o and Derrick Mayes. This is Notre Dame—it doesn't matter when you played or who your coaches were, you find the common ground.

Notre Dame has an opportunity with these struggles with social justice. Notre Dame is not immune to the issue, but it's in these bonds that you find the commonality to get through the difficult times. The focus on Black and white versus the focus on teammates. To find that common ground and see it happen when guys from the 1960s and 1970s connect with guys from the 1990s and 2000s. Players from the East Coast, West Coast, North, South, and Midwest all finding brotherhood and common ground. This team's greatest success was putting Notre Dame in a position to overcome some of the challenges the university faces—with football at the forefront—and to stand for something and stand against something as heinous and as un-American as racism. We are challenging those norms and demanding better of ourselves, and it's inspiring to see how this flowed all the way back to the 1960s. It gives me hope for the future to see how these young men—Shaun Crawford, JD Bertrand, Griffin Eifert, TaRiq Bracy, Simon, and Jonathan Doerer—stood together as a team in 2020.

Notre Dame's legacy is not so much that they made it to the College Football Playoff, but that they overcame adversity that no other Notre Dame team has experienced. It shed a light on a period of time that has haunted our country for decades. We saw the growth, fortitude, and level of commitment to each other when we said we're going to overcome racism, the pandemic, struggles, strife, and injuries, and we are going to stand up for each other. It was about the far-reaching impact this season had on so many players who came before them. It's a testament to the power of the 2020 team and the power of the locker room—to keep focus, stay committed, stay disciplined in the face of those struggles, and know there are generations you helped bring to a better end.

CHAPTER 3
GOODBYE TULSA, HELLO SOUTH BEND

Growing up in Tulsa, Oklahoma, I never truly considered playing football at the University of Notre Dame as a possibility. Frankly, I had no real concept of where Notre Dame was—or that it even existed.

I played football, ran track, wrestled, and played a little basketball—I had a very diverse sports background. But I was very much focused on all things Oklahoma. I thought I was going to go to Oklahoma or Oklahoma State to play football or run track.

Knowing and understanding what it meant to play football and the opportunities that it presented was foreign to me because I'd never been out of the state of Oklahoma except to run at track meets. There was no thought of attending a university like Notre Dame.

My own recruitment really started with the recruitment of my brother Tony, who signed with Notre Dame two years before me. He received a lot of attention, was the No. 1 player in the state of Oklahoma, and was getting a lot of looks from coaches all over the country.

During that time recruiting was very regional in a lot of respects. Our reference points for universities were limited to Oklahoma, Nebraska, Oklahoma State, Texas, Texas A&M, SMU, and maybe LSU. The focus of our understanding of college football or college athletics was geared around the Big Eight and the Southwest Conferences.

When you are being recruited at a high level like my brother was—he was receiving letters and telegrams from all over the country—and when you are so inundated with offers, you try to narrow things down. A lot of those letters get tossed to the side and you tend to focus on the schools that are giving you the most attention. A lot of times it becomes about schools that are within your region or in the area because you are more accessible to them and they are most accessible to you.

As Tony was getting recruited, I was back in the wings, two years younger, just watching how it was playing out. I observed him going through his stacks of letters every day—and I thought it was crazy how many items he'd receive on a daily basis.

One day as we were going through them, there was a letter from Notre Dame. Tony said, "That's nice." But it didn't register with him. Tony was going to toss it until my dad saw it. That became our first real introduction to the University of Notre Dame.

My dad started telling stories about Knute Rockne and "the Gipper" and the historical significance of Notre Dame that he knew from his upbringing. He was born in 1925, so he was around listening to Notre Dame on the radio in its heyday.

At the time of Tony's recruitment in the mid-1980s, Notre Dame was struggling a little bit. Oklahoma had the opportunity to play for the Big Eight championship and go to the Orange Bowl—there was a lot of hype locally. Notre Dame was not doing all that well—for a long time they weren't even an afterthought.

As my dad was telling us about Notre Dame and we started to hear more about Frank Leahy and the teams he had back in the day, Tony's interest was piqued. The recruitment process went on for him and he heard more from Notre Dame and about local alumni who were from our area. That was kind of an eye-opener to see the number of people from Tulsa who were Notre Dame graduates. Coach Lou Holtz was just now getting to Notre Dame and starting his recruiting.

I would see the coaches who would come to our house—and every now and then I'd peek at one or two of Tony's letters to get a feel for what recruitment was like. As I continued to get interest from schools when I was starting my junior year and having some success, I thought, *Okay, there's more to this recruiting thing than Oklahoma.*

I was still a big fan of Oklahoma and Oklahoma State. But Tony was getting more and more recognition for the success he had, and going into his senior year—the start of my sophomore year—we started to hear even more from Notre Dame, and we started to see more of the influence Notre Dame had in our area. There were a number of very successful individuals in Tulsa who were alumni of Notre Dame. So we started to become more and more aware of the influence, depth, and reach of the University of Notre Dame.

At the time, Vinny Cerrato, Notre Dame's recruiting coordinator, was a real bulldog on the recruiting trail. He trailblazed a lot of things from a recruiting standpoint that were light-years ahead of where other schools were. I watched how he recruited Tony—how he came in and the things he was saying to my mom and dad—and I saw the alumni in our area. At that time, hardly anyone had left Tulsa to go play football, outside of going to Texas or Nebraska or somewhere in the Big Eight. So when Tony started getting that interest from Notre Dame, that turned some heads.

Watching that whole process play out, seeing the stress involved and how tough it was for my brother, definitely helped me home in on what was important for me. I realized he was 17 and making a lifetime decision based on playing a game. I saw how it wore on him, and it opened my eyes to the business of college football. Just like anywhere else in Oklahoma and Texas, football was everything. I got a taste for what being recruited was like prior to my senior year, so I was able to think about what was really important to me.

My brother Tony decided to go to South Bend. He was one of the first players from North Tulsa that I knew who went to the University of Notre Dame—it was a big deal to spurn the University of Oklahoma and Oklahoma State. To tell them no was extremely difficult because you had some dynamic coaches—Pat Jones at Oklahoma State and Barry Switzer at Oklahoma. Leaving the state of Oklahoma and being the No. 1 player in the state was big news. Seeing some of the backlash he received for making the decision to go to Notre Dame affected me. It was like, "Wow."

I wasn't yet on the level of my brother in terms of recruiting. I wasn't ranked that highly in the state as a recruit, but coaches got to see me my sophomore year when I got to play. Then my junior year I was able to do some more things and have some success.

Going into my senior year I was pretty hyped up, and I set a few records in preseason games to put myself in a position to be more highly recruited. I had gone to some different camps locally and really showed well. So a lot of those area schools were pretty high on me.

It was going well, and my brother was at Notre Dame. But I was thinking that was his thing—I didn't want to define myself through what Tony was doing. I wanted to say, "Hey, what's important to me?" because we were pretty different people. I ended my junior year strong, so I was listed as a top recruit and a top player in the state of Oklahoma going into my last year of high school.

In the kickoff classic games that we had—like halves of games—before my senior year at Booker T. Washington High School, I was averaging over 15 yards a carry. Then in the last game we were playing I rolled my ankle pretty badly on the turf at the University of Tulsa. I was thinking it was just an ankle sprain, but it was swollen pretty badly. I missed the first few games, but then I started to play way too early and wound up twisting my ankle again. I played one more game that I shouldn't have played but then just stopped, so I wound up having a terrible senior year.

I was thinking that nobody was going to recruit anyone with a bum leg. But I was still able to go and visit some schools that I had never considered. I was also thinking this was going to be tough because nobody was really going to want me.

Early on, I thought Notre Dame was recruiting me just to appease my brother because he played well and wound up starting during the 1988 season. I was thinking, "Man, this is just kind of a handout." In my mind, I wondered why anyone would recruit me when I was injured and didn't really play my senior year and didn't really play a lot my junior year until the end of the season?

I thought, "I'll take some visits, I'll make the most of it, and I'll take my chances at one of the smaller schools." Well, that wound up not being the case. I was still being recruited pretty hard, particularly by Oklahoma State, Tulsa, Texas A&M, Arizona State, and UCLA. I also ran track, so there were some opportunities in that sport—I received some recruiting letters to run track at Florida and Tennessee. My mom was a big fan of me running track, and I was feeling a little better because letters were still coming.

I actually came up to Notre Dame to watch my brother play a few times during my senior year because I was hurt. We'd go to my high school game, even though I couldn't play, and after the game we'd pack up and make the 13- to 14-hour drive overnight to South Bend. I got to spend some time on campus and see what Notre Dame, the community, and the people were like, not as a recruit but as a fan.

I ended up visiting Oklahoma State, Notre Dame, Wyoming, and Arizona State. My trip to Oklahoma State really was an unofficial visit because it was so close—I didn't use an official visit for that. I went to Wyoming because they were recruiting one of my best friends from high school. I didn't really think I'd go there, but I had a blast, by the way!

Arizona State was the best visit I had—more because of the scenery and the people there than them really being a power on the football scene. At Oklahoma State, Barry Sanders was still there, but he was going to end up leaving early and going to the pros, so they were selling me on the chance to be the next Sanders in Stillwater. They recruited me the hardest of the schools, and I really enjoyed it. I had a lot of teammates from high school who were at Oklahoma State, and I loved their offensive system. I thought I could step in and start right away.

I took all my visits, and that was when recruiting started to get intense. I feel for young men and women who have not gone through the process and do not really have an understanding of who they are. I didn't know who I really was—I thought I would just get a handout because my brother was a good player, and I was riding his coattails. So when people are saying this and that, if you don't have a good head on your shoulders, there are going to be opportunities to make some big mistakes.

During my visit to Oklahoma State, I got to sit down and talk to Coach Jones. Some of the assistant coaches also came in, but I was all by myself. I think it's imperative that young men and women take their parents on recruiting visits because there's so much you don't know as a 17-, 18-, or 19-year-old kid. The coaches were pressuring me to make a decision, and I left there crying because I just felt attacked. I also felt additional pressure because there were some potential opportunities at Oklahoma State for other players on my high school team. If I made this decision it could benefit them as well.

I went back home and told my parents what happened and that I didn't know what to do. I didn't want to talk to anybody. My parents tried to give me some guidance, but unless you've been through it, it's hard to give perspective. My brother, having gone through the process, was valuable in helping me weed through issues because a lot of the things he went through definitely helped me.

I kept watching Notre Dame. They had a good season my brother's freshman year, but during his sophomore year they were steamrolling through teams. They played at such a high level that they ended up winning the national championship. I kept looking at the players they had in the backfield.

Being a running back—and I didn't know it at the time, but their expectation was for me to play defense—I saw that my brother was in the backfield, along with Rodney Culver, Anthony Johnson, and Braxston Banks, and there was Ricky Watters who played flanker but also got some time in the backfield. I kept thinking, "there's no way I can compete with that group." Once again, I was thinking they were just recruiting me because I'm Tony Brooks' brother.

We traveled to Phoenix for the national championship game at the Fiesta Bowl, where Notre Dame played West Virginia. The thing that always stood out to me was the camaraderie within the Notre Dame team—how those guys played and worked together. It was very much something that I had growing up in North Tulsa.

I made the decision, after my official visit in January, to commit to Notre Dame. Again, there was some backlash, even within my high school. People didn't leave Tulsa to go to other schools when Oklahoma and Oklahoma State were doing so well in football. One thing that may have helped me make my decision was that, at the time, Oklahoma State and Oklahoma were both on NCAA probation.

After I decided to go to Notre Dame I felt good about it. But, I will say, during my visit to Notre Dame the cold weather really hit me. I was not ready for that. I didn't have a coat—I just wore a sweater. The other times I'd been there during the fall for Tony's football games it was usually nice and around 60 degrees.

But I was still all set to take that next step in my life's journey to attend the University of Notre Dame.

CHAPTER 4
ON THE SCENE
AT NOTRE DAME

When I arrived at Notre Dame for my freshman year the first week of August in 1989, it was pretty exciting.

I was looking forward to competing and being a part of the Notre Dame football team. With the Irish having just won a national championship in 1988, I was thrilled to have the opportunity to compete and play as a freshman. I came in all bright-eyed and bushy-tailed and thinking, "I got this."

I felt like I could really do some things to help the team when I got there. Then reality set in.

That first week was rough sledding. I felt like I was a physical player, and I was in good shape, but it started out really tough. I was one of only two running backs in the freshman class—along with Dorsey Levens— and at that time Coach Holtz was big on running the football.

Back then the freshmen came in a week before the upperclassmen, which made things manageable because we were competing against other high school players. I felt like I had some decent skills and was a solid player. But practice was grueling—learning the plays—and it was hot, so it was a real adjustment. We were having two-a-day practices, and it took some time for me to really understand what that meant.

Levens and I were the only ones running the ball. We also played a defensive position, so I worked at cornerback too. We had a lot of ath-letes—good athletes who could play multiple positions. Craig Hentrich, another freshman, was a great kicker, but he was a darned good safety as well. He was physical, he would hit you, and he was tough.

We were all 17-, 18-, and 19-year-old kids competing against each other, and this was the top recruiting class in the country. I was compet-ing against the best. I was going up against defensive players who were top of their high school positions. Brian Ratigan and Demetrius DuBose were the linebackers—and then I was going up against guys like Junior Bryant on the defensive line. Another physical guy at outside linebacker was Karmeeleyah McGill. These guys could flat-out run. I was fast, but these guys on the defensive side of the ball could really move.

After transitioning in for that one week and just as you are starting to get your bearings, the upperclassmen come in. The following week you are back at it again, and you are already beat up a little bit. Once the upperclassmen come in, it's a completely different dynamic. And you are still feeling like you are fresh from high school—you're green.

When the upperclassmen came in, oh my lord, the practices seemed like they were ratcheted up times 10. There was no, "Okay, we'll work you in slowly." As the veterans came in a lot of freshmen transitioned to being the scout team players for the first-team defense. I went from going against guys like Bryant, DuBose, McGill, and Ratigan to experienced guys like Chris Zorich, George Marshall, and George Williams on the line, plus linebackers Michael Stonebreaker, Ned Bolcar, Wes Pritchett, Arnold Ale, and Andre Jones. Keep in mind these guys had just won a national title and gone 12–0.

I'm thinking, "I'm not horrible," but I realized really quickly what it's like when you are coming up against the likes of Jeff Alm, Bob Dahl, Bolcar, Scott Kowalkowski, and Devon McDonald. McDonald actually scared the crap out of me. This dude had 3 percent body fat, was chiseled, and could flat-out run at 245 pounds and 6'4"—and he just looked mean and menacing. And these were just the front seven—not to mention the back end, where we had All-American Todd Lyght, plus players like D'Juan Francisco, Stan Smagala, and Pat Terrell. These were the guys I was competing against when I was on the scout team on a daily basis, and they would just pound on you.

You're just coming in there and trying to figure it out as you are going through practice—and often I was just literally running for my life. As a scout team player, you're getting hit running through the holes. And many times I was just running to get away and survive. The practices were tough—so physically demanding. I didn't ask questions. I just tried to make it through from one day to the next.

It wasn't like the guys were mean, it was just how we practiced. This was way more challenging than what I was expecting in terms of the physical and mental demands. Then you would have injuries and you have to be able to process that side of it too.

The upperclassmen knew the lay of the land and how things operated. But as freshmen, we'd be sitting at lunch and wouldn't really want to talk to anyone. Your body hurts, your mind hurts, your pride hurts. But you aren't going to show it because you can't show weakness. Adrian Jarrell and Will Pollard were freshman receivers, and they were realizing how difficult it was going up against Lyght, Smagala, Francisco, and Terrell, and how physical the safeties were. Dorsey and I were worried about trying to block McDonald and Jones in one-on-one drills.

Things became more troublesome when I found out my brother was not going to be allowed to play that 1989 season. He was going to leave Notre Dame, go to Holy Cross College, and have to work to get back into Notre Dame. He was one of the major reasons why I decided to come to Notre Dame, and that source of support was now taken away.

Expectations at practice were high, and understandably so, given that this was a veteran football team with a lot of very good players coming back and expecting to have another great season. And Coach Holtz was not especially patient with guys who messed up. You don't screw up in a Coach Holtz practice and not hear about it. I was battling through this—but what was helpful was that the guys were very supportive. I could sense the team dynamic and the importance of the team being together and just putting their arms around me.

The other players understood it was a loss because my brother had been one of the leading rushers from that national championship team the year before and had been a significant cog in the wheel. He was such a physical and vocal presence on the field and in the locker room. But I took it harder than anybody. A lot of his teammates, classmates, and guys who came in with his class two years prior said, "Hey, we got you. Hang in there."

Watters treated me like a little brother, as did Lyght, Jones, and Ale—these guys embraced me. The thing that always comes to mind is how my dad was a big influence on me throughout my playing career in both high school and Pop Warner. He would always say, "Suck it up and don't quit."

That adjustment period was extremely difficult because family meant a lot to me. My brother and I were extremely close—we've been close all of our lives—so having that connection taken away put me in a difficult spot. Sometimes I look back now and I'm still wondering, "How did I make it through?"

Camp finally broke and it just felt like, for so many reasons, a weight had been lifted. There was just something about the daily pounding—physically beating up on each other—that was really tough.

Guys were really frustrated and complaining, "Why can't we go helmets only?" because we were going in shoulder pads. If you're in full pads or just shoulder pads, there's not a lot of difference. If you are in full pads it means you're tackling for a Holtz-coached team. But if you're in just shoulder pads and shorts then you are not allowed to be on the ground. I still have not figured out how that works, but that's taking it easy on you when you go helmet, shoulder pads, and shorts. That's a light practice in the Coach Holtz era.

Having some injuries coming in and really not being considered one of the guys who was going to play, I played special teams. But I was not thinking special teams was really okay—I didn't have an appreciation for that phase of the game even though Coach Holtz preached the heck out of special teams and that was a major part of a lot of our success.

I just never looked at it as being something of a big benefit to the team. Not having that mind-set, I was just thinking I was not good enough. I was a little down on myself, not having that confidence in what I was capable of doing. I just continued to kind of plug away and struggle through, just trying to maintain on a daily basis. I was in survival mode.

CHAPTER 5
THAT 1989 IRISH TEAM

The 1989 Notre Dame football team was the best collection of talent that I have ever been part of. Those guys played at such a high level, and it was a valuable experience just learning from such a strong group of hugely talented players.

It was interesting to see where that team went—we just missed out on accomplishing another championship. This was one of the most visible, dynamic teams in college football, in my mind, and I think of the commitment, the toughness, and the grit. This was a team that was physically dominant and had a strong mental presence. It was a group that leaned on each other and really brought out the best in each other both on and off the field in a lot of respects.

It was one of the most remarkable seasons I've ever been involved in. Being on that team really helped me grow, develop, and see what it meant to be successful—the importance of getting outside of myself and learning how to be a part of a team. It's amazing how we overcame different types of adversity and challenges. We had a lot of young guys in my class who really had a lot to learn. But we figured out how to do it, and a lot of it had to do with the leadership on this team. This set the tone for my four years at Notre Dame and the success we had over the course of those four seasons.

* * *

The first game we played was the Kickoff Classic, almost like a mini bowl game, against Virginia—and we played in Giants Stadium in East Rutherford, New Jersey, where the New York Giants played. I was traveling, so I was thinking, "Wow, I get to go to New York." This was my first game, and it was going to be on the big stage. It was an exciting time, and I actually got to play.

One of the things I always appreciated about Coach Holtz was that he'd always have you prepared to deal with the media. He would have professionals come in during two-a-days, and you would go through mock interviews. Coming out of high school you didn't think you'd deal with the media early on. But everything was so much bigger and promoted so much more because it was Notre Dame. You had to be prepared for that aspect of it because the spotlight was always on you, whether you were a prominent player or not. Being a member of that team, not to mention a team that had just won a national championship, the spotlight was always there. He was adamant about us being able to handle that spotlight—whether in good times or bad.

I was just glad to be going on the trip—seeing the sights and being a part of the team. That was one of the first times I felt that level of connection, being on my first college road trip in a big city with a lot of media coverage, taking it all in, and just trying to be a part of this team.

We got there, and Coach Holtz would always have us do pretty much the same regimen. We'd go through individual and team meetings, special teams meetings, then relaxation, visualization, and lights out. Routine was really a key part of the success that we had because Coach Holtz was big on doing things the right way and being consistent in those things. He wanted to present the same energy and flow that we would have every game. Being the most prepared that we could be was always a prominent part of our trips. Our practices were part of that preparation—that readiness to go out and be successful on the field.

It was a great experience to see the camaraderie and the pageantry of an away game for the University of Notre Dame. Another thing I appreciated about Coach Holtz was that the experience went beyond just going to the hotel, going to meetings, and then going to the game. We got to visit some of the sights in New York, and it all seemed so seamless how we moved from one place to the next.

The game turned out to be a rushing clinic. You watch our offensive line in practice and you really don't get a sense of how good they are until you watch them in a game and see how they just knock guys off the ball and take control of the line of scrimmage. The 36–13 score was not indicative of how our offensive line dominated against Virginia.

We led 33–0 at halftime and had outgained them 333–60 in total yards. Rice was named the MVP, Lyght had a couple of interceptions, and we scored five touchdowns on the ground just in that first half. I got in the game late and had two rushing carries.

I was just glad to be able to make that trip to experience something outside of the dorms and campus after three and a half weeks of fall camp. Having the opportunity to go and play another team and to physically go out and punch somebody else in the mouth instead of your own teammates was pretty cathartic for us, to say the least. I was enjoying watching our backs just running up and down the field—Watters, Culver, Anthony Johnson, and Rice.

Rice was a leader on that offense and on that team, and guys would follow him because he was such a tough, tough guy. He would get into the fight with you. Johnson—one of the most underrated running backs I've ever been around—was a humble individual. His leg drive and his ability to run in traffic were second to none. As I think back on that team, that collection of talent was outrageously good.

I played against our defense every week in practice—yet I didn't really appreciate how good the guys were until I saw them in action other than chasing me around the field all day. It also gave me a sense of satisfaction knowing how good our scout team was because we had to prepare our defense on a weekly basis to face some really good teams. In that year alone, we faced seven ranked teams, and it started the second week in Ann Arbor, Michigan.

* * *

After the opener we literally had to recalibrate our schedule to get back on track. We had a week off—if that's what you want to call it—because we didn't play a game the next weekend. But we didn't really have a week off because it was just more of us beating up on each other and the physical toll that came from that. It wasn't two-a-days, but Coach Holtz made sure we got in the work we needed to get in.

I cannot say enough about the guys I played with—they were going through the same tough practices, and it was very helpful that they would reach out and make a point of making me feel like part of the team.

We were ranked No. 1 and No. 2 was Michigan, so this second game was a big deal. Notre Dame was used to playing Michigan early in the year, often to open the season, but this was another level in terms of the hype.

The game was at the Big House. That was one of the toughest places to play because it's more than 105,000 strong and it's almost like the fans are sitting on top of the field. It's built similarly to Notre Dame Stadium, but they have some of the rowdiest fans you'll ever see. And

Tony Rice checks in with Coach Holtz on the sideline against Stanford.

they don't particularly like Notre Dame. So for early September, this game was a big attraction.

Coach Holtz had a good time all week talking about the Michigan coach, Bo Schembechler. We'd get toward the end of team meetings and he'd say, "Well, fellas, I called Bo and I said, 'Hey, Coach, our guys are tired; they're beat up; are you going to take a break and go shorts and helmets only?'

"And Bo said, 'Oh, no, Lou. We're going to strap it up that first and second practice, and we're going to get after it.' I tried to talk Bo into taking it down a notch, but he wouldn't do it, so, fellas, we're full go."

This went on all week. He tried to act like, "I'd love to take it easy on you guys, but our opponents aren't taking it easy—they're getting after it."

But maybe it worked. Raghib "Rocket" Ismail ran two kickoffs back for touchdowns that day and that had never happened against a Schembechler team at Michigan. He ran the second-half kickoff back 89 yards and then did it again in the fourth quarter for 92 yards.

We ran the ball 27 times to start the game, and we only completed one pass and attempted two all day long.

We finished out the game running the football, the final score was 24–19, and Ismail ended up on the cover of *Sports Illustrated* the next week. Ismail had been a major contributor to that '88 championship team even as a freshman who had never really been a receiver before. He was never that comfortable in the spotlight—I think he felt like the older guys should have been getting the attention. But there was no turning back after that Michigan game.

* * *

We then came back and played our first home game against Michigan State, and that's always a physically demanding game. You aren't going to come out of that game without scars, bumps, and bruises, whether you played in the game or not.

We won it 21–13 with another big rushing day—257 yards. Watters scored twice in the first half, and Johnson got the game-winning touchdown with about eight minutes left. We held them to 75 yards on the ground and got a huge fourth-down stop by Bryan Flannery in the final quarter.

Then we went to West Lafayette to play Purdue, and we were just physically dominant. It was 34–0 at halftime, and it ended at 40–7. Rice had a really nice day with 270 passing yards and another 67 rushing. He completed 12 of 15 and Derek Brown had a 100-yard receiving day. It turned out to be the biggest day of my freshman season, with seven carries and 20 rushing yards.

Purdue had eight turnovers, five in the first half, and the yardage at halftime was 344–93. Their only points came with 33 seconds left.

Next we headed to Stanford to play our fourth game on the road out of the first five—again, physically, we set the pace up front with our offensive and defensive lines and we got the win (27–17). A lot of our success came from how we imposed our will on other teams—and that all started at practice. It was just a weekly deal of competitiveness. You've got to suck it up and find a way to get back after it and come back out the next week because you are going to face another tough opponent.

The Stanford game was tied at 14 in the middle of the third period, and Stanford set a Pac-10 record by throwing the ball 68 times. Terrell intercepted a couple of passes, Hentrich kicked two field goals in the final period, and Johnson scored a third-period touchdown that put us up for good.

* * *

We then went into a stretch where we played three ranked opponents in a row. It started at Air Force—they were ranked 17th, but we beat them 41–27 at their place.

Our running game, again, was the main difference with 332 yards, and Ismail ran a punt back for a score. We were ahead 21–0 before Air

Force had a first down and it was 35–14 at the half. It was a strange game because Dee Dowis threw for more than 300 yards for an Air Force team that had been averaging about 440 on the ground.

When you go to Colorado Springs the air is a little thin there—just jogging around you are a little out of breath. But that was one thing about our team that really showed throughout the season, that mental toughness to overcome the smallest things. It's the little things that count. That was something Coach Holtz always stressed in our preparation.

We were always prepared to go play four quarters every week—week in and week out. We went straight through. After the Kickoff Classic we had that weekend off, but then when we started with Michigan, there was no bye week after that. You just went one Saturday to the next, pounding, grinding, and getting after it.

That's one of the reasons I think this was one of the more talented and gifted teams—just because of the toll it takes to play and what it takes to get yourself up to play at a high level every week for 11 weeks straight. I still say that's a remarkable feat to this day.

* * *

That year we played No. 9 USC at home and, man, that was one of the most talented opponents we had in 1989. They had a lot of people back from the 1988 team that had been unbeaten coming into the end of the regular season against Notre Dame the year before.

You look at our starting secondary that day—all those guys were league ready. Lyght was a two-time consensus All-American, Terrell went on to play professionally, Smagala played in the league and was one of the fastest guys on the team, and D'Juan Francisco and Rod Smith both also played professionally. You're talking about physical guys who competed at a high level. Our secondary was one of the fastest in the country. We didn't always get the props for that, but I knew how fast they were because those guys used to chase me around practice all week long.

Just being part of that game was a great experience. I was watching their receivers—John Jackson in particular—run these patterns and give guys like Lyght fits. I'd really never seen a receiver take it to Lyght like that. Jackson ended up with 200 receiving yards.

Todd Marinovich was their quarterback—a left-handed gun-slinger—and they came in pitching and catching. Ricky Ervins ran for almost 1,400 yards that season—he was running the heck out of the ball—and we were down 17–7 at halftime. That was the first time all year we were playing from behind to any extent.

That was also the game when we got into the pregame fight in the tunnel with USC. A lot of people say Notre Dame was blocking the tunnel and blocking USC from getting back into the locker room. We had a ritual that we did every week where we went through warm-ups then finished off with a punt and punt coverage where the guys who weren't on the field lined up in the back of the end zone. That day, USC decided to go through us instead of going out and around the end zone area.

I have to say this—I'm so glad they put in the minitunnel when they did the renovations of Notre Dame Stadium in 2017 where they put in a separate entrance for the visiting team to come out. We had a set ritual—this is our house and you're not going to come in and do whatever you want to do. We weren't going to start anything, but we sure as heck were going to finish it. You come in our house, there isn't going to be any disrespect. Not in our house, baby—not in Notre Dame Stadium. It will not happen.

That really set the scene for the football game—but it also probably caused us to come out a little overhyped. We made so many mistakes to start that game, and the fact we were able to find a way to come back is still surprising to me.

We had five turnovers, three of them on special teams—we fumbled a kickoff return and two punt returns. We put them in great field position and then had fumbles by Johnson and Rice as well. To have five turnovers against a football team like that? The fact that we were only down 10 at half was phenomenal—that was a testament to our defense. They were getting after us, but our defense kept coming. That's the thing that set our team apart—the tenacity. There was no quitting. We never got discouraged. Even on the sideline, the scoreboard was never an issue of, "Oh, man, we're down, we're losing." It was, "Okay, what do we have to do to figure this out and find a way to win this football game?"

I was playing against these guys on a weekly basis. Lyght, Zorich, Terrell, Alm, Dahl, Jones, McDonald, Donn Grimm, Bolcar, and Francisco—you can go down the line and keep naming guys. These guys played at such a high level. They had that receiving corps at USC that was tough. But I really feel that at halftime, going into the locker room, we were able to compose ourselves, and that's really one of the traits of a Coach Holtz team. He's not always yelling and screaming at you. He's a psychological master about what his team needs to self-correct.

We went into the locker room and addressed the issues that we had. A lot of it was just to calm down. We played as poorly as we could have played, yet we were still in it. The theme coming out was that we just made every mistake imaginable in that first half and were down 10. We came back out and right out of the gate it was a completely different dynamic. We started to focus in a little more—we were a lot calmer. We were still fired up, but there was a sense of urgency there to do things and play within ourselves rather than trying to make something happen.

We came out for the second half and we dominated USC. We scored three touchdowns in the second half. We found a way to win, and a lot of it was because we dominated the line of scrimmage in that second half. Our offensive line kept pushing—kept driving. Johnson, one of the best inside runners in my mind to ever play, was hitting it up in there.

Rice was making big runs and some big throws—one big completion to Ismail for 41 yards really got us going on the touchdown drive that won the game. Rice scored on the next play from the 15 with about five minutes to go. USC had been giving up 35 yards a game rushing and we went for 266 overall—99 from Tony.

There was something about that USC game, not just from the standpoint of coming back and winning, but the psychological edge that it provided us going into the rest of the season. It didn't matter where we were or what we were doing, we were going to find a way to win. We were almost on autopilot—we played and practiced at such a high level physically, and the tone was set by the starters because our practices were so intense as we went through that season.

We found a way to make enough plays to win that game and, at least in my mind, I figured we'd go undefeated. We were at home four weeks in a row.

We came back and absolutely annihilated No. 7 Pittsburgh (45–7). Pitt hadn't lost a game yet and actually scored first to lead 7–0. We only completed one pass, but the running game was solid again with more than 300 yards. Terrell ran an interception back for one touchdown, and Ismail went 50 yards for another score.

At this point, we were sitting at No. 1 in the country. You don't think you're feeling yourself, but we definitely were.

The Navy game ended up at 41–0. We ran for another 400-some yards, and we won easily, even with only one pass completion. That's how dominating our run game was. Our defense allowed only 166 yards from Navy, and just about everybody got to play.

The last of those four games in a row at home was against SMU, and it was about the same result. We won it 59–6, with SMU's program still coming back from its NCAA probation. We fumbled away more than we should have, but it didn't matter. We scored 35 points in the second quarter and ended up with 572 yards.

At some point we did not need any more points, so after the game everybody wanted to talk about the idea that Rusty Setzer actually went out of bounds on purpose instead of scoring.

I didn't make the next trip, to play Penn State at Beaver Stadium. I watched the game, and again Notre Dame just dominated the line of scrimmage. Guys told me later that it was one of the coldest games they every played in. But when you are No. 1 and you are sitting on top of the heap, life is good.

Penn State came in with the top scoring defense in the country, giving up an average of only 9.2 points a game. But we ran for 425 yards and won it 34–23. It was the most rushing yards allowed in Penn State history. Rice gained 141 yards on the ground, and Watters had 128—this was especially a big game for him since he's a Pennsylvania guy and we had never won in State College.

Coach Holtz had a great line about this game: "I wouldn't have expected to run for that many yards in a marathon."

* * *

We ended the regular season with a huge game at Miami. There had been a groundswell of negative press from the incident at the USC game that kind of seeped into the narrative for the Miami game. We were really subdued for that Miami week, even though we were going to play a No. 7 Miami that was known for its swagger and bravado. It was almost like we were deflated going into that game because of outside forces that dictated what we were allowed to do.

I remember the bus ride to the Orange Bowl—fans literally attacked our buses. People were yelling, throwing stuff at the buses, and cussing at us. It was crazy. I distinctly remember one person in a wheelchair, just yelling, giving us the finger, and screaming all kinds of obscenities toward us. It was one of the most vulgar scenes I've ever been a part of—the whole environment was unsafe. It's one thing to think college athletics is about rivalries, but this was way over the top.

Everything about that event and the environment seemed designed to try to intimidate us. Coach Holtz had set the tone by telling us, "Do not respond; do not say anything." So we were trying...but we were back on our heels, and seeing our team not come out and play with the same focus and intensity was disheartening. We didn't come out with the same vigor and confidence.

It just seemed like Miami's energy definitely trumped where we were coming into the game. They were the Hurricanes—they were the U. And they had that bravado going before the game even started. We felt like we were not allowed to show what our team was made of. When you don't come with the same fire and drive that you had all season long, it makes for a long night. That's the one game—the one time—that we did not respond in a manner in which I was accustomed to being a part of this 1989 football team.

We struggled a little on offense and only managed one touchdown. Miami got an interception right before the half that led to their go-ahead score. Then they manage to convert on third and 44 in the third quarter, and that led to a touchdown drive that lasted more than 10 minutes. It was the end of our 23-game win streak, which is still a Notre Dame record.

We had a whole month to stew over this loss and it did not sit well. It did not sit well with us at all. We were going to go back to Miami to play in the Orange Bowl against the No. 1 team, Colorado, and that was really going to be something. We felt there was unfinished business. We found a way to go in and get the win, but it's one of those things where sometimes you barely remember the wins. There are certain losses that stick with you throughout your career that you reflect back on and think, "What if...?"

Over the course of my four years on the team, we lost only eight games and tied one, but that Miami game is the one game that still hovers over me. That has always stuck with me even though I was not a prominent contributor that season. That was the one week of the 13 games we played when we were not ourselves. And it showed, as we lost 27–10 against a really good football team. They did not see the best Notre Dame team, and it cost us in the long run.

* * *

Colorado had been playing inspired football for one of their fallen players, Sal Aunese, their quarterback who had died from cancer that September. They were scrappy—a really good football team. This was the first time I'd been part of a bowl—the first couple of days there's no curfew. Coach Holtz wanted us to go out and enjoy the festivities and the different aspects of what bowl pageantry is about.

Then, as you get a couple of days in, you start ratcheting it up and really locking in. That was the thing about this team that always stood out to me—the ability to manage and calibrate that edge and preparation even though we were there for a whole week. You're not in a normal environment. You're at a bowl game and there is a lot of hoopla and some joint team dinners. I was always intrigued by the ability of our teams to focus and get mentally established for what we needed to do to win. Winning is just as much of a mental game as it is a physical game.

We went out, and we really got after them. It was a hard-fought game, but there was never a time we felt like we were behind. We really laid the groundwork early. They had success, but there was something about our leadership that always stood out in teaching us how to win at Notre Dame. When you play for Coach Holtz, you learn how to win. There's a process to it—you don't just come in knowing these things. You develop it—you've got to develop that cohesiveness as a unit, and that's what I saw over the course of my time with that team.

You had a lot of talented guys, but these talented guys learned how to play together as a unit and learned how to mentally lock in and do everything they needed to do just a little bit more, just a little bit better than the guys they were playing. Colorado was fast, Miami was fast, USC was fast—not that we were slow—but we were not only fast, we were also physical. And we were mentally sharp. And we just had an energy—a symbiotic energy that flowed through the team that said, "Okay, someone needs to make a play, someone needs to step up." And it wasn't a forced thing—it was natural. We had natural leaders on this team and natural playmakers because we developed that sense of urgency—we developed that sense of focus and the ability to zero in.

A lot of that comes from watching guys do it—watching the ability of someone like Pat Eilers. He was a starter because this guy could lock in better than anybody I'd been around. He had this almost robotic, zeroed-in focus to go out and get a job done. We had some dominant blockers, not just the offensive line, but our tight ends—Brown, Frank Jacobs, Rod West—they got after you. Ismail and Eilers, they were not big guys, they were not physically dominant guys, but they would block your behind downfield like nobody's business.

If you were going to be on a Coach Holtz team, you were going to know how to block—running back, tight end, receiver, offensive line, wherever you played. Rice could block. It didn't matter. That's what set us apart in a lot of the games we played and against a lot of the good teams that had just as much talent but not necessarily the same razor-sharp focus and attention to detail that was mandated from Coach Holtz on a daily basis—and I do mean a daily basis.

So we came out and got the win. The game was about the line of scrimmage, because the two teams combined for only nine pass completions all night. Neither team scored in the first half, but Colorado had some turnovers and we had one memorable goal-line stand. Then we had three really solid touchdown drives after the half. We ran for 279 yards and Ismail made an amazing play, scoring from 35 yards out on a reverse. And that's after Watters got banged up early and only had two carries. The last touchdown drive was 17 plays, all of them runs, and we controlled the clock for almost nine minutes. That clinched it.

One of the best things about the bowl games is that after the game you get to stay up and party. We definitely did, and Miami was a pretty fun place to do that.

I ended up playing in seven games and carrying the ball 13 times. We ended up second in the final Associated Press poll, which still feels like a disappointment.

But this was a complete football team. We ended up ranked in the top 14 in the country in rushing, scoring, total defense, rushing defense, and scoring defense. Those are indicators of a pretty good all-around team.

We beat teams that were ranked first (Colorado), second (Michigan), seventh (Pitt), ninth (USC), and 17th (Penn State). Our schedule ended up ranked as the most difficult in the country by the NCAA.

Rice was a Heisman Trophy finalist—and he, Lyght, Zorich and Ismail were all named first-team All-Americans.

I wasn't there in '88, but it was a rather amazing two-year run for Notre Dame football.

CHAPTER 6
FINDING A NEW ASSIGNMENT

After the end of the 1989 season, I realized I was not as prepared to make that jump from high school to college as I thought I was. I learned a lot from it all. And as the second semester began, I found out there was a transition in the works—and it involved me switching from offense to defense, going from running back to defensive back.

A lot of that had to do with the number of running backs that we had and the lack of defensive backs on the roster. But it was not something I wanted to do. I hadn't played defensive back since freshman or sophomore year in high school. I didn't really think that was the best spot for me.

I was actually brought into Notre Dame as an athlete. That was something Coach Holtz was really big on—bringing in athletes, guys who could play multiple positions, play both sides of the ball, play well, and get coached up. The coaches wanted to get me moved over there sooner rather than later but going into workouts I was just trying to keep my head above water. It really hit me hard—but it was just one of those things where you suck it up and deal with it. I was never comfortable making the transition. I never completely bought into it.

But looking at the offensive side of the ball, in 1990 we had my brother, Watters, Culver, and Levens coming back in—and the recruiting class coming in included Bettis, Burris, and Setzer, though Burris ended up on defense. So the offensive backfield was stacked. Plus Ismail was playing running back some at that time too—so the chances of playing my sophomore year as a running back were pretty thin. I really wanted to play and have that opportunity—and so you do what you have to do to get yourself on the field.

Meanwhile, the secondary was comparatively thin—the main guys back were Davis, Lyght, Smith, and George Poorman. You do what's asked of you—you try to do the best you can—and for me that was making the move to try to appease the coaches and get the opportunity to play. Granted, the 1990 class of defensive backs that was coming included Greg Lane, Tom Carter, John Covington, Burris, and Willie

Clark—but they were just going to be freshmen, and that was a tall order to come in and play in the secondary as a freshman.

Barry Alvarez left to become head coach at Wisconsin after the 1989 season, so we were switching defenses. There were a lot of changes taking place, and this was my first experience with winter conditioning. We'd get up early in the morning, work out, and then go to class. We'd get in a lift in the afternoon, but we'd get our running done in the morning. Thank God we had the indoor facility, the Loftus Center, because South Bend in January and February can feel like the frozen tundra.

Notre Dame had a track around the indoor field, and at first I didn't really understand why there were trash cans around the field. But we found out real quick. Our workouts were so intense that guys would go to the trash can, throw up, and get back in line, ready to go again. It was like everything was in short bursts. Each station was so many minutes and you were going boom, boom, boom, boom, boom.

Jerry Schmidt was the head strength coach—a stocky dude with a buzz cut. Real old-school guy. To this day I have nothing but respect and love for Schmidt and the paces he put us through because what prepares you for Saturday afternoons is the work you do in the spring and the wintertime.

My first winter conditioning was something that is still seared in my brain—and yet these are times when the bonding is at its best. I developed a better connection with my teammates. I started learning how to lean on my teammates—holding each other accountable by not letting anyone quit. That was something that stuck with me. In those difficult times you find out not only what you are made of, but also who's got your back.

One of the more pronounced things was how tough and driven the upperclassmen were. There was definitely a survival mode to winter conditioning, but there was something more to it—the willingness to fight through, to pick other guys up. I was not a rah-rah type. I just wanted to do my work and get through it. You had some guys who liked to talk—the energy guys. You needed those energy guys to kind of rally the troops, and we had some on both sides of the ball.

Transitioning from an offensive mentality to a defensive mentality, I started to gravitate toward more of the defensive guys—Davis, Lyght, Poorman, and Andre Jones. Not that I distanced myself from the offensive guys—you just tend to fall in line with the group you are going to spend the most time with.

When I was playing offense, I was competing against the defensive guys and running for my life from them. When I switched over and started playing defensive back, I learned how to fight off blocks and twist my hips. One thing our secondary coach, Chuck Heater, was on me about was my weight. When I came into Notre Dame I was about 190 pounds, but I was told I could not be any heavier than 185 as a defensive back. My body fat was 6 or 7 percent when I got there, so having to drop the weight was a challenge for me. I didn't have a lot of body fat to begin with, so I had to nearly starve myself.

Spring ball started, and I was at a different position. I didn't really want to be there, but I had to be there. At defensive back there's a lot of running—and I do mean a lot of running. As a defensive back, receivers are going long and you have to run with them, come back, and then get lined back up for the next play. We had some pretty darn good receivers that I was going up against—Lake Dawson, Tony Smith, Ray Griggs, Will Pollard, Sean Davis, and Adrian Jarrell. These were all the guys I watched get after our defensive backs the year before—and now I was on the other side and they did not ease up at all.

We were doing one-on-one drills and I wanted to challenge myself, so I always tried to line up against Ismail. Everyone knows how fast he is, but he also was one of the strongest guys and just so quick. It was almost impossible to get your hands on him—even when he'd come out of a three-point stance.

We'd also do one-on-one receiving drills where they were trying to block us while we were trying to defeat the blocks. And I mean it when I tell you it was a scrap. Those were some of the best battles I've ever had, going up against Ismail, bump and run—or Tony Smith, running with him and challenging myself because he was one of the more fluid route runners.

I had not done this since sophomore year in high school, and we are not talking about average players. These guys were soon-to-be-pro receivers. They were physical and that physicality we had in two-a-days rolled over into spring ball. It was not something for the faint of heart. It was a tough go. Trying to familiarize yourself with coverages and tackling—it's a mind-set, getting up there, filling the hole, fighting off a block, coming off a block, and making a tackle.

We did tackle drills—the Oklahoma drill—and it was a competition from start to finish. It definitely made me better. But at the same time, you're going up against these guys, and when you crossed over onto the practice field, there were no friends. We didn't do the brother-in-law thing where you don't get after each other—we competed every time, and that was the mentality of this team.

At Notre Dame, under Coach Holtz, you're going to compete. You're going to come after each other, not in a menacing or vindictive way, but it's like, "I'm not going to take a butt-whipping from anybody. I'm going to come at you just like you're going to come at me—we're going to get after it."

I definitely got better, and as I came out of spring ball I was the backup at boundary corner behind Rod Smith. I was hanging out with those guys now. I still have a strong relationship with a lot of those guys, and it started with how we competed and in the classroom. Lyght is a guy with a strong, strong football IQ—I cannot thank him enough for helping me through that transition. He was a consensus All-American, and he embraced me in the film room, as did all the other guys.

It was a tight-knit group and it helped me build some confidence with the switch. They were a different bunch than the running backs. Maybe it was because there were so few of us, but we had to really hold each other up and hold each other accountable because there really weren't a lot of options coming out of spring ball.

CHAPTER 7
THE 1990 SEASON

The 1990 season kicked off with another barnburner against Michigan. Home night games at Notre Dame Stadium didn't happen that often, and I remember them bringing in the portable lights. There was a lot of hype around them—a lot of energy and a lot of new faces on both sides of the ball for our team, so it was definitely a challenge.

Going into that first game I wasn't expecting to play a whole lot. We were the No. 1 ranked team coming out of the season before—Michigan was No. 4. It was like the game of the year right out of the gate. This was a transition to a new team from 1989 to 1990. We lost some heavy hitters on both sides of the ball from that 1989 team, so it was a bit of an unknown.

When the freshmen came in—Carter, Lane, Covington, and Burris—we had some new guys at defensive back who were in backup roles right out of the gate. I was playing a new position, and I was doing it because I wanted to see the field—it's about doing what you have to do to get on the field. I was running through drills, competing, getting after it, and getting to the first game of the season—and here comes Michigan rolling into Notre Dame Stadium. You are talking about serious hype. It was electric. Coming out of that tunnel the bright lights are on and it was so infectious—just the hype and energy coming out of that locker room. I was loving every minute of it.

I'm like, "This is it. This is it." This is what you sign up for—to play games like this against an opponent like Michigan with guys you've competed with over the course of the spring and the summer. We were like, "We got this."

Michigan came out and started running a no-huddle offense, and their running back Jon Vaughn just lit us up on the ground. You think you're coming out of fall ball and in shape, but there's something about running a no-huddle offense from a defensive side that's just exhausting—especially from a secondary standpoint. They were just running guys down the field, and we'd have to turn and run—and run the ball.

Their receivers would just roll off, and they would have another fresh receiver come out to run go routes.

It was a track meet—we were not prepared for that no-huddle attack and it gave us fits. I still remember when I got out there—you come back after a series, the defense comes and sits on the bench, and the starters come and communicate what you're seeing out there.

Guys were flat-out gassed from the word go. Michigan was just rotating guys in, and it really wore us down. I wound up having to come in for Rod Smith because Desmond Howard was lighting us up too. He was really giving us the blues at the boundary corner position. Meanwhile, Vaughn was just running up and down the field even though he fumbled on the second play of the game. He rushed for 201 yards—it seemed like he was unstoppable. He just kept rolling and rolling.

But we always felt like something was going to happen and we were going to win. That was the mind-set of the team, even from the previous year. It was Mirer's first start—he drove us down there and Jarrell scored the go-ahead touchdown with less than two minutes to go.

Then Elvis Grbac overthrew the ball in the fourth quarter, and it came right into my hands. The pass was intended for Howard, who had 133 receiving yards that night. That pretty much sealed the deal, and we won 28–24.

And I'm the guy who really wasn't expected to play defense.

This time it's Mirer on the cover of *Sports Illustrated*, and the headline says, "Golden Boy."

* * *

We went up to play Michigan State in Spartan Stadium the next week— they were ranked No. 24 at the time. And I was in the starting lineup.

We snuck out of there with a win—again, they really played us tough. When you play Michigan State it's going to be a physical, hard-nosed game. It was a lot closer than what I felt it should have been. We ended up winning 20–19, but it was one of those games we felt like physically we were beat up.

We were down 10 and had to score two touchdowns in the final period to pull it out. We were pretty fortunate because Mirer's late throw bounced off a Michigan State defender right into Jarrell's hands. Culver went in from the 1 with 34 seconds left and we won.

We came back and played Purdue at home next—we won that game fairly handily (37–11). We gave up a bunch of passing yards, but Purdue only ran it for 24 yards and that wasn't going to be good enough. Plus we forced two fumbles and had seven tackles for loss.

We led 27–3 at half and Purdue had only one rushing yard. We had 500-some total yards and ran it 62 times for more than 360 yards. I ended up with four tackles.

Then came Stanford—every mistake we could make that year, we made that day. That was where we were a little too confident—too nonchalant—and we did not take Stanford as seriously as we should have. That was the game when I learned I did not want to be a defensive back, especially if I was playing one-on-one with Ed McCaffrey. He's 6'5", and it was a clear mismatch. That was something that I will never forget.

I'm 5'8", maybe, and we were in man coverage and he was big and strong. They gave us the blues—we just couldn't stop 'em. They kept finding ways. Not only did we not stop them, but we also made mistakes offensively—three fumbles on punt returns—to keep putting them in positions to score quickly. We scored 31 points, but at the same time we did not do ourselves any favors in terms of stopping them.

Their back Tommy Vardell scored the winning touchdown with 36 seconds left, but we still ended up having a chance, but Derek Brown couldn't quite hold onto the ball in the end zone on the last play of the game. We lost our 24–7 halftime lead, and Vardell scored four times.

We wound up losing 36–31—and it was a shocker. We did not see that coming at all. And it ended our 19-game win streak at home. I was credited with six tackles, but it was hardly any consolation.

* * *

We had Air Force come to South Bend and then No. 2 Miami—the last two of four home games in a row. We rolled 57–27 against Air Force after leading 31–7 at half. Mirer threw for 253 yards and we gained more than 500 overall. Ismail also had a great day, with 172 receiving yards.

We were hyped up for the Miami game—it was the last time our teams would play each other for a while. Jimmy Johnson was gone, and, fortunately, there were no incidents in the tunnel this time. We came out prepared to play, and Ismail ran a kick back 94 yards for a score. Hentrich kicked five field goals and our defense forced four turnovers.

Their receiving corps was really good, and I think we held our own—but at the same time we were definitely challenged. Miami had been second in the country against the run, and we had 305 yards on the ground in the 29–20 win.

We then went on to play Pitt—and I don't think we were as sharp. We won some games like this that we shouldn't have won, and we still found a way to gut it out and get the victory (31–22). Ismail had a 76-yard touchdown run in the middle of the final period that turned out to be enough.

We gave up 384 yards passing, but that's mostly because not many people were running the ball much against us.

We beat Navy handily in Giants Stadium—the final score was 52–31. It was tied at the half—Navy was controlling the clock and we had to score 42 points in the second half. We went back to No. 1 after that game, but we shouldn't have been giving up that many points.

Next we went down to Tennessee and had a real nail-biter there. If you've ever been in Neyland Stadium, you know how rowdy and loud Tennessee fans get. But it was one of the most hospitable places I played in, and it definitely worked out well for us. Watters had the best day of his career with an amazing 66-yard touchdown run and 174 rushing yards.

We won 34–29 against the No. 9 team in the country. It was a hugely entertaining back-and-forth football game with six lead changes, and a road win that proved something to us. There were big plays by both teams all day long, and Rod Smith's interception at the very end put a bow on it.

We came back home to play Penn State and got shocked again, even though Penn State was a very good football team and ranked No. 18. We weren't as sharp as we needed to be and made some mental errors—we weren't locked in. I won't say we were arrogant, but we should have been better than what we were.

We had 292 yards at halftime and led it 21–7. But they won it 24–21 on a field goal with four seconds to go. When you're playing a good team, you can't keep going to the well and think you're going to come out on top. We only gained 22 total yards the last four times we had the ball—they got us.

We finished the season at USC, playing in the Coliseum, and we snuck past them again, 10–6. It was great because any time you beat USC, that's a beautiful thing. It wasn't a beautiful game, but it was one of the first times we won a low-scoring contest.

Our defense had been maligned at times based on the points we allowed, but that wasn't the case, with USC managing only two field goals. My brother scored the only touchdown, late in the third period.

* * *

We played in the Orange Bowl again, and again, the opponent was Colorado—and they were still No. 1. The game came down to one play—and it was the worst call ever to this day. I still don't want to think about it.

This ended up being a big defensive struggle all night long between two teams that knew each other very well. With less than two minutes left Colorado punted, so we were going to have one last possession. Why they kicked the ball to Ismail, I have no idea. But he ran it back 91 yards for a touchdown, and it looked like we were going to beat the top-ranked team in a bowl game for the second year in a row.

But they called Davis for clipping. You can watch it 10 times and you'll still be debating whether it should have been called. He hit the guy in the side and, again, you can argue all night about whether the Colorado guy would have had a chance to make the tackle. We lost 10–9.

But it didn't matter. We still had a good year—not a great year—but it certainly did not end the way we wanted it to.

It also was Zorich's last game at Notre Dame, and I still remember him sitting on the bench after it was over with his head in his hands. Then he got home to Chicago to find out his mother passed away.

CHAPTER 8
BACK TO THE BACKFIELD

As we headed into winter conditioning after my sophomore year, Coach Holtz still felt playing defensive back was the best opportunity for me. I had some success, but I also had some struggles playing that position. Maintaining a weight below 185 pounds wasn't easy for me.

The reality was that a lot of the guys who came in—the freshmen defensive backs Carter, Lane, Burris, Covington—were a lot further ahead than I was at that point. I hadn't played the position in some time, and I made the transition just for the opportunity to get on the field—but my heart wasn't in it.

I decided to go talk to Coach Holtz about switching back to the offensive side and going back to running back. He said, "You're just not going to get the opportunity to play. Your best bet is to stay at defensive back."

You always wonder "what if" as you go through life. Coach Holtz always talked about how the mind controls the body—and at that time I was mentally drained. I was like, "This is just not gonna work."

At the time there were a lot of guys who were in the backfield ahead of me. Bettis was the fullback, and Culver, Levens, my brother, and all those guys playing tailback going into that spring. I had only had one year as a running back, but I was dead set on going back to that position.

Begrudgingly Coach Holtz said it was okay, but he said I was going to be way down on the depth chart. Kenny Spears, Setzer, Levens—those guys were listed ahead of me too. In spring ball I wasn't seeing very much action outside of the scout team—I didn't really get a chance to run with the main offensive unit. So I was kind of back to square one.

The one big knock against me was that I was an east-west runner and not a north-south runner. If you're going to be a running back in a Coach Holtz offense, you've got to be physical and run downhill.

Looking back, I harped on all the negatives that were besetting me during this time. Meanwhile I remember watching Ryan Mihalko, who is probably one of the most genuine guys I ever met. He always kept a

positive attitude and worked his butt off. He competed, he battled—
again, that positive attitude—and this was every practice. Never once
did I remember him feeling sorry for himself or saying he got a raw deal.

He came consistently with a me-against-the world mentality. He'd
go stick his nose in there in a blocking drill and dig a guy out. He'd go
in there and butt heads with Demetrius DuBose, Michael Stonebreaker,
and Andre Jones—he never backed down. A lot of times he was over-
matched, but he'd find a way to get it done. He didn't play a whole lot,
but to me he epitomized the team dynamic you want on your team. I
always secretly admired him for the way he went about doing what he
did. At the same time, I was doing just the opposite.

I was back on scout team on offense, so I was doing the grunt work.
I saw the guy who was recruited in with me—Levens—ascend into the
No. 1 spot coming out of spring ball. I was thinking, "This guy is the
same class as me. He's going to be the man, and I'm never going to get
the chance to see the field again."

To make it through as a student-athlete and as a football player
under Coach Holtz, the most important lesson I learned at Notre Dame
was the importance of mental toughness. Coach Holtz always talked
about the importance of mind over matter—the mind controls the body.
If you can visualize it, you can accomplish it. We did a lot of things that
focused on us being better mentally so we could be better physically. It
builds a skill set that's valuable to a lot of companies—it's the ability
to process something and mentally push yourself to a limit to accomplish that action. It first must form itself in the mind. If you don't have
a strong mentality, it's easier to quit—it's easier to give up and say, "I
can't do it."

But if you have a strong mentality, a strong work ethic, and a strong
mental capacity, you can push through a lot more than you could ever
imagine. I can recall going to the locker room and doing things almost
unconsciously because in your mind you've already pushed past that and
your body responds. We had a group of people who worked together to
be able to rise above circumstances and situations.

We control our attitudes—we control how we go into a situation, how we deal with something, and how we wake up every day. It's about constantly pushing yourself mentally and driving yourself from a mental toughness standpoint to go out and compete and to play and to do the things you are required to do at a high level as a student-athlete. I think that's something that just resonated with a lot of the guys who stuck it out at Notre Dame through their own frustrations and challenges.

Coach Holtz would say, "Momentum is always coming our way." That meant when something bad happened, we expected something good to come out of it. We expected something in our favor to happen that would ultimately help us win the game. It's in that framework—that mind-set—that we were able to drive a little more and push a little further. You do more and things happen because you've already made up in your mind that you are going to be successful beyond this bad situation. You find that mental fortitude to say, "Hey, I've been through this before, and this is how I'm going to get through it."

That's one of the things I always tell my kids: don't quit. Finding that mental fortitude not to quit—to keep pushing—even when it's snowing or you have to get up at 5:00 in the morning for workouts. Why are you doing this? Because you want to win—you want to be successful. Dig a little deeper, push a little further, and that is all mental. It all starts with your mind. And if you can see it—if you can formulate it in your mind—there's a way to accomplish it physically.

I look back now and realize all those things I had picked up along the way at Notre Dame ultimately helped me make it work.

CHAPTER 9
ANOTHER VIEW ON THE GAME

I've come to realize that football was more than just a game for me. It was about family—developing and building relationships that go far beyond the playing surface. Coach Holtz would always talk about banding together and working together. One of our winning attributes—the way we won—was togetherness. What does that mean? It means a group of young men came together for a greater purpose.

People talk about being a part of something bigger than yourself and that was what football was for me and the guys that I played with. I've mentioned some high-profile names—Mirer, Smith, Brown, Taylor, Watters, Bettis, Lyght, Stonebreaker. These guys were just as committed—just as passionate about playing—but we were more than just those high-profile guys.

At this point I had played two seasons of college football and was now headed into my junior year at Notre Dame—and I was still not sure if I was going to find my place and be able to do the things to help the team that I thought I was capable of doing. But my dad told me, "Stick it out—you made that commitment." That was the one thing that always stuck with me. My father had really pushed us to go to Notre Dame.

It turns out it was the guys I played with who saw me through. McGill, Griggs, Lamar Guillory, Todd Norman, Jordy Halter—some guys who didn't necessarily have superstar careers at Notre Dame. But they were paramount to getting me through that difficult time. That's when I knew Notre Dame was the right place for me, when I opened up to the guys I played with.

It was nothing dramatic or tear-jerking or anything like that. But I found that these same guys—Pollard and Jarrell—had their struggles too. I wasn't alone in dealing with all this stuff. That really helped me get through my junior year. That was probably the best year I had both athletically and academically. I still feel to this day that it's because of the support and the aid of my brothers. And I do look at the guys I played with as brothers. I still keep in contact with a lot of those guys to this day. They helped me through a really rough time. It's hard to put

Lou Holtz embodied a special kind of leadership that cemented us as teammates.

into words the struggles that I had. But there was no judgment and no condemnation, just, "We are here for you."

I think that connection was always there, but it took me a long time to see it. It's always been a part of Notre Dame teams that I played with—that desire to see you succeed. Not because it's going to benefit them in any way other than winning games, but it was a connectedness—a shared experience of the hard times and the struggles. Coming from different backgrounds, different parts of the country, different cultures—we had a shared bond.

We had to push through and fight through, but, more importantly, we had to uplift each other to be part of something bigger than ourselves. It was at that time that I really started to process the value of that Notre Dame experience. To see it, my eyes had to open a little bit more and it really helped me establish a level of trust that just wasn't there my first two years at Notre Dame.

In the fall of 1991 there was a big weight lifted off of me, and it had a lot to do with the support and the connections my teammates had with me. We all had a shared experience—it didn't matter your position. You were a part of the team. You were a part of that group. You were a part of that family that helped us to be better—better men, better teammates, better brothers. That was a strong message for me that helped drive me to be where I am today. To be a good father, to be a good husband—and always looking to improve because I was around guys who cared. We had a common bond.

Devon McDonald rarely said anything—he scared the crap out of me because he was huge. But he had a love for his teammates. He changed over the course of his time at Notre Dame and that built up our bond. We stood together. We worked together. We sweat, we bled, we fought, we scratched. We worked not just for ourselves but for each other, and that's where the success came from. It's not built on personal accolades, it's built on a team bond and a common goal and a shared experience that will force you to get outside of yourself and seek the best, not just for you, but for those around you.

I began to understand what Coach Holtz meant by togetherness. For a while, I struggled to understand what togetherness had to do with winning and playing football. But it has everything to do with it. Football is the consummate team sport. It requires 11 guys executing at the highest level and being on the same page to have plays be successful. You can scheme it or map it out from a coaching standpoint, but the teams that are successful have a greater understanding of each other. So you are a part of a larger whole.

You are more inclined to do your very best and go beyond that for someone you care about. It takes you having faith in someone and someone having faith in you to do more, to be better, and to work closer together—to have an unspoken bond. That translates from the practice field to the games. It's the ability for a teammate to read a situation—and then for you both to read it together.

Our offensive lines were just so dominant on every team I played on. Tim Ryan, Mike Heldt, Mirko Jurkovic, Justin Hall, Gene McGuire. Then you had Aaron Taylor, Lindsay Knapp, and Norman. Those guys worked as a unit. Teams would try to scheme, but it didn't matter what you did, we were gonna block it up. Our guys were gonna block it up front because they had a bond that started not on the playing field but off of it.

We were there for each other and that's how that togetherness came to where a play happened. The offensive line, the tight ends, the receivers, the quarterbacks, the backfield—we all were on the same page. I just remember so many times we would be executing a play where the defense knew where we were going but there was nothing they could do about it. That's the symbiotic relationship of a group of young men coming together and saying, "You can't stop us because we're bonded so well together that we are going to execute at such a high level—it doesn't matter what you know about what we're going to do, we're going to execute because we are together. We are one entity."

It wasn't 11 separate guys on the field. It was one unit. I don't know if that's something you can accomplish very easily in this day and age in sports because of how prevalent individualism is. But we were such a bonded group, especially from the offensive standpoint, and that's where I had a lot of my success—executing at a high level because we worked so closely together. I'm trusting that the guy next to me will do his job. That ability to adjust and adapt together, not as individuals but as a whole unit. I think that one of the key aspects of what made the Notre Dame teams that I played on so great is the bond that we had on and off the field and the love we had for each other throughout that said, "I'm not going to let my brother down—I'm not going to let my teammate down."

I realized we could trust and rely on each other. I learned a lot of that because I opened myself up to it during some tough times. My brothers came through for me. And I don't know if they even know the support and love they shared by just being there without me even telling them I needed it. But they just knew, "We need to rally around our brother."

CHAPTER 10
"I'M PART OF IT NOW"

The 1991 season was a rebirth year for me as it relates to my time at Notre Dame. It was at that key juncture when I was not only developing a greater connectedness and bond with my teammates but also engaging more in school.

I decided, "I'm going to stick it out and be a part of this. I'm changing my mind-set and perspective." I learned to stop looking outward at what I felt other people were doing to me and to start looking within. What am I doing to myself? That changed the whole dynamic for me when I stopped focusing on what happened to me and started focusing on how I could be part of the success that I've seen with these Notre Dame teams that I have been a part of.

While 1991 wasn't a landmark season in terms of me playing a great deal, I started to see Notre Dame in a different light. I started to participate and not just sit idly by and let this college experience happen to me. I started to engage in it and become more a part of it. It was in that timeframe that I started to see things differently and develop a greater appreciation for the people who were there.

In the spring I had moved back to running back. Even though I was third or fourth on the depth chart, I was probably as happy as I had ever been at Notre Dame. It was almost liberating. I started to engage a lot more with professors, and it was like a whole new world was opening up to me. I wasn't just participating. When I opened up I became more a part of that Notre Dame mystique—not as a football player but as a person.

I had a decent spring. Not great from a football standpoint, but I started to get back into the groove as a member of a team and felt like I belonged. While it turned out I didn't play a lot in 1991, that was the most fun I had as a student-athlete at Notre Dame. A lot of that success I had in 1992 was predicated on my response and development and openness that started the previous year.

* * *

We started off the 1991 season against Indiana, and I still remember the catch and run that Irv Smith had to score a touchdown. He literally had the entire Indiana squad on his back—he caught a pass down the seam and took most of the IU defense into the end zone with him. You talk about a will to win, a will to get it done. Irv Smith was probably one of the most affable people you'll ever meet, but the tenacity and the aggression that he played with was a thing of beauty. That's still a play you can find easily on YouTube, and every time I see it, I shake my head. It was one of the plays that really symbolized what we were trying to be as a football team.

Indiana actually led late in the first half, but Mirer threw for 200-some yards and Bettis had the first 100-yard game of his Notre Dame career. I carried the ball four times—it was nice to be a running back again.

We won that Indiana game 49–27, and it had some extra meaning for a couple of reasons. Notre Dame had always played Purdue, but it had been a long time since the Irish and Hoosiers had played each other. So that made it a big deal within the state and for players from Indiana, like Mirer.

It also was the first game that NBC televised as part of its new agreement to show Notre Dame home games. People like Dick Rosenthal and Father Bill Beauchamp from Notre Dame, plus Dick Ebersol and Ken Schanzer from the NBC side, were big parts of that happening. And none of those individuals are still active with Notre Dame or NBC, yet the relationship continues.

You don't see that happen much in the television business, and it tells you something about Notre Dame that from a business standpoint that relationship still makes sense for NBC all these years later.

* * *

We lost the next week up at Michigan when they were ranked No. 3 and Desmond Howard scored a couple of touchdowns. They really shut down our running game, and their back Ricky Powers went for 164 on the ground.

We came back to beat Michigan State the next week. We ran for 448 yards, I scored in the first quarter and my brother scored in the third quarter. It was the first time in 44 years that two brothers had scored in a Notre Dame game.

Then I remember blocking a punt later in the year in October against Pittsburgh and recovering it in the end zone.

Against Navy I had a 65-yard run and also scored another touchdown.

I was a lot more involved in that season (18 carries and 122 yards), but we did have a tough time in our own stadium. We lost our last home game, and that was the second year in a row that had happened. We lost to Tennessee—that was one of the most devastating losses, at least in my time at Notre Dame.

I still remember that game so vividly.

We were dominating in the first half and right before halftime we went to kick a field goal—and they blocked it and returned it for a touchdown. Not only did they score, but they also injured Hentrich on that play—he was the guy who did everything for us as far as the kicking game. He punted, he kicked—that changed the whole dynamic of the game. We ended up losing 35–34 because they blocked a late field-goal attempt that would have won us the game. It was like, "Wow."

I didn't travel to Penn State the next week where we lost—we were reeling a little bit with back-to-back losses. Don't get me wrong—those were good teams. Tennessee was ranked No. 13 and Penn State No. 8. But it was the only time during my Notre Dame career when we lost games two weeks in a row. We were spoiled from that standpoint.

The whole team got to travel to Hawaii for our Thanksgiving weekend game. I wasn't playing very much, but I was having fun playing the game again. The joy of football was back—I was actually excited to go to practice.

* * *

That year we went 9–3 in the regular season and ended up in the Sugar Bowl. We were so together—we had such a great time being around each other. This team was just a lot of fun. That was the season we had our only lone captain on a team that I was a part of: Rodney Culver. He was hands down one of the greatest leaders I've been privy to be friends with or play with. He was from Detroit, a year ahead of me, and he just carried himself as a big brother. He was there for everybody—offense, defense, Black, white.

He came from a rough part of Detroit and he embodied what Notre Dame football was about at that time and what I think it still should be. He made it about the team—it was never about himself—and he worked his butt off to be one of the best captains we'd had. He was the first one to step up for every drill. He didn't lead vocally—he led by example. But if you got out of hand or got out of line, he had no trouble stepping up to you and saying, "This is not how this is going to go." I can't remember anyone disliking him. We lost Rodney—he was in the 1996 ValuJet plane crash, both him and his wife, and that still hurts to this day.

We went into that Sugar Bowl game ranked No. 18 and Florida was ranked No. 3. They'd finished unbeaten in the SEC, shutting out a ranked Alabama team and beating Tennessee when it was ranked No. 4 and Florida State when it was No. 3. After we lost those two games in November, people thought Florida was going to walk all over us.

That was the most fun I ever had at a bowl game. But it was also the most fun football game I was a part of because we employed a defense that just confounded them all day. We were doing a drop eight—sometimes we were even dropping nine, rushing two or three guys—and it frustrated the heck out of their quarterback Shane Matthews. That's after they had been lighting people up—it looked like video game football with as many touchdowns as they were throwing all year. He completed lots of short passes that day against us and they kicked a bunch of field goals, but we knew he wasn't going anywhere.

Florida had the upper hand early. But then down 16–7 at halftime we decided to do what we did best: run the football. We turned it over to the guys on the offensive line and we said, "We are going to block you up. You can know where we're going, you may stop us early on, but that won't last long. We're going to find a way to wear you down."

Go back and look at that offensive line—McGuire, Taylor, Jurkovic, Hall, Knapp, Brown, and Irv Smith. Then you've got Bettis, Culver, my brother—and we just had a juggernaut. We wore you down. Watching that game play out was as priceless as it comes because all week we'd been hearing it from the Florida fans and the Gator players.

"What's the difference between Notre Dame and Cheerios? Cheerios belong in a bowl." Coach Holtz played that one to the hilt—and we got the message. And then there was the Gator chomp the whole week. We couldn't wait get to the game. That's the one thing—you don't poke the bear. The fan base of that Florida team poked the bear.

That second half was sheer domination. We laid into them and we ran it right down their throats. Watching Bettis run it right down the middle, seeing Culver on the option and Mirer running it, seeing our receivers on the edge dominating their defensive backs—it was a thing of beauty. Bettis scored three times in the second half and finished with 150 yards. They were powerless to stop him. Watching it from the sideline, I loved every minute of it.

The 1991 season was a special year for me—not because I played a lot or played a major role, but because that was the year I allowed myself to really be a member of the Notre Dame football team. It really established a lot of the relationships I have to this day because that's when I became part of the Notre Dame football program. It set the tone for the 1992 season, my senior year.

CHAPTER 11
ALL WORTH
THE WAIT

When the 1992 season began I was not really looked at as being a prominent contributor as it related to the offensive side of the ball. The focus at that time was on Bettis and Mirer and, actually, Willie Clark was considered the front-runner to be the starting tailback that season.

After the 1991 season, I just kind of found myself—found my focus. I made up my mind that I was going to try. I was not going to worry about messing up. I was not going to worry about doing something wrong. This was also the time I was making real connections, making real friendships, and being part of that program with my teammates. There was more of a drive, more of a determination to show what I was capable of.

After the 1991 season I talked to our running backs coach, Earle Mosley, and he helped me in a lot of ways. He really simplified the program, the play-calling, for me. He told me, "All I want from you is four yards. You take the proper steps, do the proper footwork, and get those four yards. After you get me those four yards, you do what you do." It was really basic, but really liberating.

That season was also when I had my best winter conditioning at Notre Dame. Winter conditioning at Notre Dame was nothing short of torture, but I no longer viewed it as such. It was a different perspective, a different focus for me. Going through the training, I was a little bit more keyed in, a little bit more focused. I felt a purpose in the training. There was now a purpose in everything that I did.

When we started winter conditioning I made sure I took the lead in the drills. I didn't take a backseat. I stepped forward and tried to set an example for the backfield, showing them, "This is the kind of group we're going to be." It really helped me find myself and, in some regards, find my voice. I was not a talker—I was not boisterous—I just went out and competed and executed.

Starting in the spring in 1992, I took on a leadership role. That spring all of my physical numbers from the weight room to the running were off the charts. I didn't really grasp at what level I was competing.

You don't see the levels of improvement you've made until down the road. It didn't seem like I was doing anything above and beyond, but I felt I was getting better.

My confidence carried over into the classroom. I started to understand the importance of communicating with my professors. I actually developed friendships with professors that endured when I returned to the university years later. Everything fell into place, but it wasn't an accident. It was purposeful. I wasn't only locked in mentally and physically, but I was also locked in spiritually—it was a different dynamic going into that year. I felt like I belonged. I felt like there was a purpose in being at Notre Dame.

Our spring practices were brutal—so physically demanding—and we just beat the crap out of each other. We would go at it. The backs would go one-to-one with the linebackers. We had some pretty talented linebackers we would compete against. It would be me, Bettis, Ray Zellars, and Lee Becton—we were the top four guys. We had a second backfield that was just as talented and just as dynamic as our starting backfield. Clark was playing on the offensive side of the ball. We went through spring practice and we were killing our linebackers—and I'm talking DuBose, McDonald, McGill, Ratigan, Pete Bercich—we were giving it to them.

I remember watching linebacker after linebacker going after Becton on a sideline drill. This is where you have a cone about six or seven feet from the sideline. You'd have to run between the cone and the sideline, and the linebacker would come up to tackle you. One day Coach Holtz made Becton go eight times and they could barely touch him. He was my backup at the time—this is how good we were from a backfield standpoint as far as depth. And watching Bettis, he had some of the best feet for a guy his size that you'll ever see.

There was never any animosity with the defensive guys—never any, "I'm going to get you." It was just good, hard competition. You competed against each other and made each other better. That spring we were clicking on all cylinders as a backfield because that unit was as strong as I'd ever seen during my time at Notre Dame.

Clark was injured, so he didn't really get to compete the entire spring. But all I was hearing was, "He's just the placeholder…Reggie Brooks is the starter, but he's only the starter because Willie Clark is not there." Not once did I take offense because that was their opinion. I was going to do what I could to be the best that I could be. My mind stayed clear to focus on taking every practice and making the most of it.

With Coach Mosley in the film room, we'd go through it all and he'd go, "Here are some little things that you could do." It was the little things Coach Holtz always stressed. We won by doing the little things the right way and being consistent in those things. I felt a consistency throughout the spring.

I was back there with Bettis who was the premier fullback at that time. A lot of the spotlight was on him—and justifiably so after such a great sophomore year—because he's Bettis. He earned every lick of it. We played very well off each other. There was never a deal where it was, "Give me the ball," or him not getting the ball.

You see one guy do something spectacular, and it encourages you to do something. We really pushed each other. It was like, "Hey, we're having fun," and that was what that season was all about—having fun and sharing it with the guys I played with.

I started to enjoy the game again, I started to enjoy being part of something bigger than myself. Another thing I had really struggled with during my time at Notre Dame was injuries—but I was finally healthy. Coming out of the spring game, I was about 212 pounds and much stronger. I was bench pressing 410 pounds—just about everything was falling into place for me.

Clark was back in the fall, and we were still going back and forth. But I still maintained my position as the starter going into the 1992 season. I was not just sharing the ball with another tailback, but the lion's share of the carries was going to be given to No. 6—the Bus—and rightfully so. That was my thought going in: "I'm going to have to max-imize every carry."

It got to the point that I was not known as a power back. Coach Holtz had said during the spring, "When we get inside the 20, you won't be in the game." We had some bigger backs, and he liked the big bruisers. So that was another incentive for me to take advantage of every carry I had. It was like, "Okay, hey, I better make sure I get this thing to the house anytime I got the ball in my hand if I break one."

I had to maximize every opportunity, and it probably didn't hurt that we had the best offensive line in the country, in my opinion. I remember very seldom did it ever happen in practice and definitely not in a game where I got hit behind the line of scrimmage. That speaks to the connectedness and the focus our offensive line had. They were coached by Joe Moore, one of the best, which definitely played a major role in the success that I had in 1992. There was nothing that was going to stop me from having the best year of my life.

CHAPTER 12
A SPECIAL
YEAR IN 1992

What a difference one year can make. Going into the 1992 season, any thoughts of playing football professionally were as far back in my mind as you can imagine. I was just focused on trying to graduate and get a degree from Notre Dame. But, as I said, what a difference a year can make.

The 1992 season started with a bang in Chicago at Soldier Field against Northwestern and ended on an extremely high note at the Los Angeles Coliseum against USC. The things that happened in between defy the imagination in so many ways.

The biggest thing about my senior season in 1992 was leadership. When I look at the guys on that team—particularly the senior class—they were a host of seniors who were determined not to share the fate of the previous two senior classes of losing the last home game. We had a senior at just about every position, and they took the lead in making sure we knew who we would be and the type of team we would field over the course of the year. Offensively, you always start with the offensive line because they are the heart and soul, to me, of what makes the offense run. That started with Knapp and Hall, our tackles, plus Norman at guard—all three of these seniors set the standard for how we would compete and dominate in so many regards.

At tight end we had one of the best tight ends to ever play the game at Notre Dame, Irv Smith. At receiver, Griggs and Jarrell were standout seniors who said, "Hey, we're gonna be a senior team that will demand greatness and excellence." At quarterback there was the incomparable Mirer, our co-captain and literally the quarterback of our team on and off the field.

I took on a leadership role at the running back position. Although I wasn't the star at that particular time, I did set standards—that we were going to be the best group of running backs in the country—for the running backs. I feel like we accomplished that in some regards. Bettis and I played well off of each other and complemented each other really well. That kind of goes to our nickname—we were called "Thunder and Lightning" that year.

But when you think about that offense, senior leadership was the standard. The reason we had success that year—we were No. 4 in the country in points and scoring average—was because we had strong senior leadership that established standards for how we would go out and compete on a game-by-game basis.

Defensively, it starts up front. Our defensive ends—McGill and McDonald—were stalwarts who ran the show up there, along with Bryant. Our top linebacker was DuBose, our other senior co-captain and the heart and soul of our defense. He was a classmate who was simply outstanding through the year. Nick Smith was a backup linebacker, but at the same time he was a star because he was such an integral part of making our special teams go.

We had senior leadership at every position except in the secondary. And when you look at that secondary, most of the guys who were playing or starting came in and had to play as freshmen early on. They learned and developed the experience and the understanding of what it meant to be a top-flight defensive backfield. Carter, Lane, Burris, and Covington may have been juniors, but they played like seniors, particularly that year.

And then we had a senior kicker/punter, the do-all guy in special teams, in Hentrich. I didn't look at him as a kicker—he was an all-around athlete. Coach Holtz had to stop him from running down on kickoffs because we couldn't afford him getting hurt, because he would go out and lay you out. He definitely would have played as a defensive back had he not been such an outstanding kicker.

* * *

In Chicago going into the opener against Northwestern, I really didn't go into the game inked in as a starter. It was more like my name was marked in pencil. But I think after that first game against the Wildcats, I sent the message that, "Yes, this is my senior year and I'm going to be a leader on this team—and not only a leader, but I'm also going to be a playmaker." I let it be known right out of the gate.

I knew Bettis was going to get the lion's share of the carries right out of the gate and rightfully so. He had earned that. And, let's be honest, defense was going to have to devote some focus to Bettis and that was potentially going to benefit whoever played tailback. So coming in, my whole mind-set was to maximize my opportunities.

In that first game I had nine carries, 157 yards, a 72-yard touchdown run, and another 45-yard run. We wound up winning 42–7 against Northwestern. But it was kind of a coming-out party and, with that game—I hadn't quite gotten it to full-blown ink or a permanent marker—it was definitely a little more than pencil markings of my name on the starting position at tailback. It was going to be a lot harder to erase my name after that game.

This was also an opportunity to get Bettis going and then say, "Hey, nobody's really going to be looking at me if they're focusing on Jerome. So I've got to make sure they know he's not the only weapon on this offense."

It really helped him because he went on to have 19 carries, 134 yards, and a touchdown in that game. It was a coming-out party for me, but it also established that he was a beast at the fullback position because he was that good. You knew what you were getting. Teams knew what they were going to see. They were going to have to try to stop Bettis and Mirer. But they just realized, "Hey, now there's somebody else back there we have to deal with."

Our defense held Northwestern to a touchdown and really got after them. McDonald really showed up and had three sacks. Seniors led this team, and it showed from start to finish.

* * *

We started the season off playing four Big Ten opponents in a row—Northwestern, Michigan, Michigan State, and then Purdue. The Michigan game was our first home game and it was another knockdown, drag-out battle with both teams ranked in the top six in the polls. We wanted to make a statement. I really felt like it was a game where we were not nearly as sharp as we needed to be. We made far too many mistakes—three fumbles and an interception. We didn't give our defense a chance. The fact that we were going into the fourth quarter down 17–7 really let us know that while we didn't get the outcome we wanted in this game, we could beat anybody anywhere. It just required us to be at our best and in focus.

In this particular game, every time you looked around we were turning the ball over, fumbling, botching exchanges, poorly reading, poorly blocking. This was probably one of the more heartbreaking games for the simple fact that we had this game in hand. We were dominating for the larger part of the game, we outrushed them by more than 100 yards, and we controlled the clock. We controlled the line of scrimmage. But we gave them too many opportunities, and it wound up costing us.

Going into that game I was pretty amped up. There's nothing—and I do mean nothing—like running out of that tunnel in front of the 59,000 standing-room-only fans we had every week. To run out that tunnel as a starter my senior year, knowing that I only had so many more of those opportunities, really told me that any time I touched this field I had to come out and give it my all. It was not just me who had that mentality, it was the mind-set of the entire team.

We ended up tying this game, scoring with about 5:30 left. Bettis scored a fourth-quarter touchdown and Hentrich kicked a 32-yard field goal. Then we had to intercept Elvis Grbac deep in our own end with a minute left. It shouldn't have been that close. If we took care of the football, we knew what we were supposed to do. It's clearly a game we should have won hands down. It cost us because we struggled.

The one thing that everybody but me remembers about this game was the first touchdown. It was in the first quarter, a 20-yard run. I did not remember the play until I saw it on film the next day. Even I was impressed with how it played out. It was an option play—Mirer came down the line and pitched it. I saw Corwin Brown, No. 20 (later to become a Notre Dame assistant coach), and he had me dead to rights.

I managed to make a spin move off him, avoid a couple more tackles, and then I just got smacked three or four yards from the end zone. The thing I always remember about watching it was the fact that I changed hands with the ball. This was something my dad always taught me—always switch the ball to your outside arm away from the defender. I could just hear that voice playing in my head because I was out—I was out cold. But I switched the ball and face-planted in the end zone. That was it.

I can remember that my shoulder—well, literally, the whole left side of my body—was numb from head to toe. I was moving my arm, but I was just trying to get the feeling back into it. They took a real shot at me, but I didn't feel it at the time because I was unconscious. But after seeing it again—ooh, that was a good one, wow.

The biggest thing about that game is that it was such a disappointment because at that time you didn't have the overtime rule, so we ended in a tie. As hard-fought as that game was, ending in a tie was so unfulfilling and frustrating. I really feel that we had recaptured the momentum in the fourth quarter. I was still like, "Hey, let's get out and play another four quarters."

To this day I still think we never got closure for that game, and I guarantee you the guys from Michigan feel the same way. Grbac and his crew? I'm pretty sure they are saying the same thing. We should have finished that game. Tyrone Wheatley and Ricky Powers (they went on to combine for 2,000 yards that year)—Michigan always had a tough backfield. They had a great receiver in Derrick Alexander, and the tight end Tony McGee was another guy I always respected. It was one of those games that ended in a tie, but it's still something we talk about. We needed somebody to win that game.

* * *

When you break down the numbers in the 1992 season, it's pretty clear we had a dynamic year rushing the football. I definitely had one, but a lot of the success I had was intertwined with the success of Bettis.

We were being called "Thunder and Lightning," and when you look at our statistics, that's definitely a valid statement. I was known more for the big plays, but it was his grinding, his physical runs up the middle, that created those opportunities for me to make plays.

That season we averaged 280 rushing yards a game and, of those, I averaged 122 a game and Bettis was at 82. We both averaged about 15 carries a game. When you look at other running backs during that time, you had guys like Marshall Faulk at San Diego State and Garrison Hearst at Georgia who were featured guys who got the bulk of the carries while Bettis and I were splitting carries.

Just think about that. Put one of us as a featured back on a team where we are averaging 20-plus carries a game, and you can see the potential production that was definitely there. So one of my main focuses was taking advantage of every opportunity. Because you never know when they are going to come around—especially with someone like Bettis and also Burris playing in the backfield some. In addition, Becton and Zellars were two dynamic players who came up as our backups in that 1992 season.

I rushed for more than 1,300 yards on about 15 carries per game. It was a pretty special season statistically because we had such a dynamic team both on the ground and in the air. This team averaged 37 points a game. By the numbers, we were a very potent offense. Bettis and I accounted for 23 rushing touchdowns and three receiving touchdowns— and numbers don't lie. The production definitely played out on the field with the success that we had.

In a lot of respects, we physically imposed our will on teams running the ball. We sent a message early on that we were going to be a physically dominating team, and part of that was predicated on that offensive line and the success they had. It was important that we run downhill. Looking at that year—and the differences with my previous years with Notre Dame—it was something I give credit to Coach Mosley because he really helped me going into that season.

There was no pressure on us—we just had to go out and compete. But something more important than that was the importance of running downhill. Very seldomly did Bettis or I or any of the backs get knocked back. We played forward. And what I mean by that is we played behind our pads. We were very physical. I remember Coach Mosley bringing in the gauntlet. And, man, that year the skin on my arms—when I went through the gauntlet—was gone. Ripped off every week. Because this was something we did every day. It really forced us to run with leverage, get behind our pads, and run downhill if we were going to make it through that gauntlet. We'd do this during individual drills—we'd run our footwork during handoffs and part of that was finishing the run and going through the gauntlet.

You had three or four arms on each side—the top four at shoulder level and then you had some that were around the knees. We'd go through there regardless of whether we had pads on or not. It was pretty intense the first time because we really didn't know exactly what we were getting into.

It got to the point that we were talking about how to dismantle it—take those arms, unscrew them, and toss those suckers away. Those arms were not made of a soft substance. They were a hard plastic or some sort of foam. I actually credit that machine for forcing me to play forward as opposed to the side. The other thing about the gauntlet was that it required you to get your feet up, get your knees up so you could drive through there and push through. So by learning to run through the gauntlet, I learned to run with great pad level and explosiveness but also downhill and with great leg drive.

I would have loved to have seen our yards after contact numbers. A lot of that was the gauntlet and going back to that mental toughness to battle it every day. It really set us on edge. I guarantee if I was to see a gauntlet—if they call it that today—it would definitely trigger me. My numbers were a product of the grueling practices, the determination, the physicality that the offensive line played with, the running backs we played with, and the tight ends.

You wouldn't think the quarterbacks had to do it too, but, no— Mirer, Paul Failla, Kevin McDougal—they had to run through the gauntlet just like we did. That's why I have a healthy respect for the athleticism and the physical toughness Mirer and the other quarterbacks had during my time at Notre Dame. Because going through that gauntlet was not fun. I know several times during the course of my seasons at Notre Dame I'd see our quarterbacks taking on linebackers and defensive backs and not running out of bounds. They would take some shots and deliver some blows. As Coach Mosley said, "Be the hammer, not the nail."

I remember every little saying and directive that came from Coach Holtz and Coach Mosley that year. It was all about physically

I broke off for a 73-yard touchdown against Boston College.

101

dominating the team and mentally preparing yourself for that battle on a daily basis. You go through and the numbers bear themselves out—we were successful not because we just rolled out our helmets on Saturday and came to play. It bore itself out over the course of the regular season, two-a-days in the summer, and workouts in the spring.

The team was always first. But I still feel to this day that had Bettis not been injured, missing the Navy game and being banged up for both the Boston College and Penn State games, he would have definitely rushed for more than 1,000 yards as well. That would have made a good case for being the greatest backfield in Notre Dame history from a production standpoint. You hardly ever see teams play with a fullback these days, but Coach Holtz's teams made a living doing that year after year.

Every practice, every game was a chance to do something special. That was kind of a driving force for us, and I think it really filtered down to the other running backs. The next year it was no accident the success the 1993 season produced with Becton, Zellars, and McDougal in the backfield. A lot of that was predicated on how we practiced and how we competed with each other on a daily basis during that 1992 season. You saw a lot of the transfer of leadership taking place that year and filtering into that '93 season. The success they had was definitely a joy to watch.

Setting the standard was something that was extremely important and something Coach Holtz was always adamant about. That '92 season for me was about setting a standard—a standard of competing at a high level through the course of that season. You had to exhibit that toughness, that competitiveness, saying, "You aren't going to keep me down—you aren't going to hold me down."

I had 205 yards when we beat Purdue. I remember I got banged up in the Stanford game and was limited to a degree in the Pitt and BYU games. But it was about saying, "Hey, we've got the mental fortitude to fight through pain and fight through adversity." It was all about how we win. How do we win together? How do we be there for our teammates?

And there were definitely some gaudy numbers over the course of that season.

I still had 112 yards in that BYU game, and I came back with 174 yards and two more scores versus Boston College when they were ranked No. 9 and we throttled them 54–7.

I was definitely blessed to be the first back under Coach Holtz to rush for more than 200 yards in a game and to be able to do it in two games was definitely something I will always remember. We had five games when we rushed for more than 300 yards as a team. And, again, people knew what we were going to do, but it didn't matter. Yes, you can know what we're going to do, but do you have the will to stop us?

We dominated that season, and that is something I will have for the rest of my life—to look back and say I was part of something special. It was particularly special for me because it only took one year. What a difference one year can make if you put in the effort.

CHAPTER 13
TWO PLAYS
TO REMEMBER

The 1992 season marked a better year for me and kind of etched my name in Notre Dame lore and history—specifically based on three games that season and two specific plays.

The first play happened in the Michigan game. It was definitely a bittersweet game. I mentioned before how frustrating that game was because we didn't maximize the opportunity that we had. We made too many mistakes. Starting fast was something we did a solid job of, but in that game we didn't finish.

But a lot of people go back to that one play—first-and-10 at the Michigan 20. We were moving the ball—this was still the first quarter—and we ran the option. It's one of our standard plays, but it really became a play of lore and mystique from that game. It was an out of the ordinary 20-yard run and, as I've mentioned before, I did not recall the play after the game. I didn't really realize what happened until after I saw it Sunday during our film session and team meeting.

It would be considered a read option today, but it was basically a read for Mirer and a fake to Bettis up the middle. It's an I-formation look, with me as the trailing running back. On the option, you're always taught to be five-by-five yards from the quarterback. You're responsible for maintaining the pitch relationship. As the play developed, Mirer did a nice job of pressing the edge and really forcing the end to take him and pitch.

The other thing that always sticks out to me is vision. You have to be able to see what's coming, not just to avoid it but to know how to attack it. On that particular play, Mirer pitched and I saw Brown—he was the Michigan safety and he was filling the alley. I saw him coming, Mirer made the pitch, and I'm one-on-one. This was something Coach Holtz, Coach Mosley—anyone who played or coached the position as a running back—taught us. You've got to make one guy miss. That's the very least you can do as a running back.

Watching the play, I took the pitch, I saw the alley defender, the receivers were blocking downfield—so that was my guy. It was plain and simple—that was the guy I had to beat. I was known for the spin move and I was off-balance, but I took a shot and maintained my footing. That came from running through that gauntlet on a daily basis—you have the feel to regain your balance as quickly as possible.

I was able to bounce off, fall forward, and I was at about the 7-yard line going in. The defensive back came across from the opposite side and I was stumbling, trying to maintain balance, but going forward I took a shot on the side of the helmet and it was just like, "Bam." It was at the base of the neck—the bottom of the helmet. Today he probably would have been ejected for targeting, because I was basically defenseless. It was a helmet-to-helmet shot, one that I normally would say I would never forget—but I did.

I got hit around the 4-yard line—it was just momentum and determination to get the ball in the end zone, and at the same time to switch the ball from my left to my right hand was all unconscious muscle memory. You always get the ball to the outside arm roll—get it away from the defender.

I didn't think anything of it. Okay, you made a play. There was a level of luck there. Had I been three or four yards farther away—had I been around the 10- or even the 8-yard line, that probably would have been a fumble. It was kind of crazy that I was wrapped around the 4-yard line and was able to get more steps and that my momentum got me into the end zone. Like I said, it was a great play, but at the time it was just a play that you made because that's what you do. That's what we did.

Opportunity played a major role in that particular game. We went on to tie that game, but we also made a lot of mistakes and I was part of a botched exchange on a reverse. So you tend to remember not so much the great things but the things you didn't do quite as well. That game is a tough one to swallow because it had a far-reaching impact on our chase for a national championship. This was senior year, and you fight and scratch and scrap, and you don't quite get it done—that was the case there.

That play ended up being voted the national play of the year, and they presented Notre Dame with a large framed piece of original artwork showing the play—it hung in the athletic administrative hallway of the Joyce Center for a long time.

* * *

The next play was toward the end of the season. I really feel the Michigan tie affected the decision Coach Holtz made at the end of the game against Penn State. This game was our second-to-last regular-season game, and there was a stretch there where we were playing four ranked teams back-to-back-to-back-to-back. This was also our last home game, so there were a couple of different things that were in play.

The first thing is that the seniors had lost their last home game two years in a row, and that was something that really stuck with us. Secondly, it was against a tough opponent, and it was also a game where we made a lot of mistakes. It was not absolutely horrible, but the footing was not great, partly because of the snow in the middle of the game.

It was another game where we had some costly errors that put us in a tough spot, and this time it came down to the very end. Similar to the Michigan game, we were down 6–3 in the first quarter, then tied 6–6 at halftime. We had two extremely good chances to score touchdowns early in the game and came away with field goals. Over those first two quarters we had one drive that lasted almost 10 minutes and wound up with a 26-yard field goal by Hentrich.

We were up 9–6 after three quarters, but Penn State kept battling. Our defense really stepped up—we were really getting on them defensively, just not capitalizing on opportunities. We had snow, we had sleet, and then toward the fourth quarter the sun came out. Every type of weather you can imagine we had at some point during that game.

We fought our way back, but we had yet to score a touchdown that entire game. We were a really good football team, but we could not punch the ball into the end zone for three quarters. We did not score a touchdown until the fourth quarter. I still struggle with that. How could that happen? We got down there multiple times, well within the red zone, and still only came away with field goals. That is something that just pains me to think about to this day.

Penn State was up 16–9 in the fourth quarter. We were driving down, and there was just a calmness in the huddle. No panic, no fear of failure—just determination and a complete confidence that we were going to figure this out. We were going to find a way to make this happen.

We drove down the length of the field. We scored, but we actually used our two-point conversion play for the touchdown. It was a fullback pass where Bettis blocked and then leaked out—almost like a little screen to some degree. He came out and scored a touchdown. We were in a position to go for a tie and kick the PAT and the game mostly likely would end in another tie. But I really feel that Michigan game ending in a tie affected our thinking.

Coach Holtz decided to go for two and, again, we've already used our two-point conversion that we normally practice. Coach Holtz gave some directions to Mirer, both the basic play call and then some modifications to it. I was surprised I was still in the game—it was known that Coach Holtz didn't have the utmost confidence in me catching the football.

That was predicated on the fact that I wore contact lenses in the game, but I never wore my contacts in practice because they irritated my eyes. I never thought over the course of that year to practice with my contacts in because I didn't really like them. I wore glasses to class—I was comfortable wearing glasses. I was not going to wear the goggles—no disrespect to Eric Dickerson. I would just practice without anything, so I really struggled seeing the ball a lot of times in practice. This went on for four years.

I was nearsighted, so things far away were hard for me to pick up. In football one of the things you talk about with catching is that you focus in on the point of the ball or the front half of the ball as it's coming to you. But, being at a distance, everything was blurry. So I struggled picking up the ball in practice many times. It would get up on me, and it was more of a surprise.

I was really the decoy on the play, just trying to clear it out. I lined up with trips left, a single back who was a single receiver, a tight end on the right. We were basically running multilevel crossing routes, with Bettis trying to create an opening for Irv Smith underneath.

They thought the same thing—thinking they didn't need to cover him—so I made my way across. I was the inside receiver on the trip side. I tried to pull the linebacker to safety and nobody went with me. As Irv Smith was trying to weave and come back out, the safety and linebacker sat on him and there I was. Mirer was flushed back to the left, he lobbed it up to me—and the rest is history.

Those were two distinct plays—both in that south end zone, southwest corner—that made me a Notre Dame legend in a lot of respects.

CHAPTER 14
FINISHING IN STYLE AT THE COLISEUM

The best game of my college career was also the "sickest" game of my college career—and you can define that word a couple of different ways. Unlike the Michigan game, when I was knocked unconscious, I was awake for every play I participated in during this event.

It was against probably our most heated rival—USC. It came on the last regular-season game of my senior year, against the No. 19 Trojans at the Coliseum. It was extra special because it was against USC—any time you can have a hand in beating USC as a Notre Dame player it definitely adds to the magnitude of what the game means. To have my senior season culminate in that type of game, that type of atmosphere, was beyond icing on the cake.

Going into that game, the season had been kind of up and down. We were coming off the win against Penn State where the senior class got to leave on a high note in the last home game of the season. Not only that, but it was also a great opportunity for my family to see me since I have a sister who lives in Los Angeles. Even more special, my mom and dad drove out to California from Oklahoma to catch the game. To end a season like that in that type of atmosphere was electric, to say the least. I was really looking forward to it, and I had a great week of practice leading up to it.

At that point in the year you're generally pretty banged up, nicked up, yet I was as healthy as I had been all year. I was excited to play in that game and have the opportunity to both compete and compete one more time with my brothers. Of the guys I played with at Notre Dame, I really enjoyed my senior class. These were the guys I bled with and competed with all year.

To end there in that type of situation with something at stake was great. At that point we weren't necessarily going to have a chance to play for a national championship, but we were playing for a New Year's Day bowl. Success there would set us up to play a highly ranked team somewhere in a bowl game on January 1.

Going out to California, we'd always leave a couple of days early due to Thanksgiving. We had several players from California, so their parents would come to the team hotel and we'd have a Thanksgiving meal there. Having the opportunity to get a home-cooked meal for Thanksgiving was outstanding. We had a special teams meeting, offensive and defensive meetings in the hotel the next day, and then a team meeting—then we did our relaxation period that Friday night. It was a normal preparation—a normal week of practice.

Going into the game, there was a lot of talk about USC's secondary and its defense as a whole. Willie McGinest was by far the most recognizable guy on that team. Their secondary was considered one of the fastest in the country, led by safety Jason Sehorn. They were known for their speed and their ability to get out to the passer.

Coming into that game we knew it was going to be a tough, tough task offensively and a challenge to say the least. But we were definitely up for it. On Saturday morning we got up and did our regular routine—had breakfast, kind of hung out, went to meetings, ate a pregame meal that afternoon, then went back and got ready to go. Again, everything was as normal as can be.

After the pregame meal, I got on the bus and my stomach started to feel a little funny as we were leaving the hotel—but nothing too bad. By the time we got to the stadium, I was not feeling good at all. There were four of us suddenly struggling with what ended up being the stomach flu—I thought maybe it was food poisoning—including Hentrich, our do-it-all kicker, and a couple of other guys. Hentrich being out would have been a tougher pill to swallow than me.

We got to the locker room, and we were changing, and I just was not feeling well at all. It was one of those illnesses where you're kind of sweating, so I had the chills. I wound up not going through the pregame warm-ups because I was throwing up and just not doing well at all. I was really struggling, and it all happened so quickly—from that pregame meal to the ride over to the Coliseum. I mean it went south on me quickly, and I wasn't the only one.

I got my pads on and went out for pregame, but I didn't do anything. I just stood there and was not able to participate. I remember going back in and Coach Holtz stopped me and said, "Can you go?" It never really dawned on me that I might get that question. I didn't really think about it. I said, "Yeah, I'm going to play, Coach."

At the time I was somewhat doubtful because, if you know the Coliseum, it's a real hike to get from the locker room to the sideline. There's a full 400-meter track around the field—an Olympic track, for that matter—and you have to cross that and go all the way down through the tunnel. It's a jaunt. At this point, I couldn't keep anything down. Anything I put in my mouth was just coming right back up. I went back in the locker room, and our trainers Jim Russ and Mike Bean were talking to me. "How are you feeling?" Not good. It was questionable whether I would participate.

There was no way I couldn't at least go out and try. So I somehow went out there and played the best game of my career at Notre Dame, bar none. The game against Purdue in 1992 was great. The game against Boston College had some really big rushing numbers. But this one was almost magical. And when I say I was sick, I mean I really couldn't hold anything down. I just got weaker and weaker. Water was the only thing I could keep down. They were giving me potassium pills, electrolytes—I couldn't keep any of it down.

I would get in the huddle and execute a play, and after the play I was back to this horrible feeling. But during the course of the play it was really surreal. I didn't feel anything—it was just go. It was really almost an out-of-body experience—just weird and hard to describe the feeling I had while I was running. Whenever I had to run or make a play, it felt like it wasn't me doing it.

I had some huge runs, a lot of success, but when I got to the sideline I basically collapsed. Going into halftime—when we were trying to make adjustments—I spent all of my time in the bathroom, throwing up, spitting, dry heaving. It was horrible. But by halftime I was over 100 yards rushing, had two touchdowns, and had two big runs.

We came out for the third quarter and, boom, I had another big run for a touchdown. Everything just seemed to be moving in slow-motion. I remember one play when I had a run down our sideline and got knocked out and fell into the arms of our trainer. I just went limp. And that was kind of how things went. I'd go play, but when I stopped, everything was out of me. But for some reason I was able to keep going back in. I would line up and play and it was like a switch flipped—I was back in it and competing again.

So this went on throughout the course of the game. I ended up not playing the entire fourth quarter. After one play I just had nothing left. And, in normal fashion, Bettis came in and finished them off with an eight-yard score. USC got the ball back and our defense just hammered them. McGill got two sacks, Carter clinched the game with an interception, and we wound up winning the game.

I ended up with 19 carries for 232 yards and three touchdowns. I had scoring runs of 55 and 44 yards. We rushed for 332 yards as team—USC threw for 302 yards. We won it 31–23—and it was our 10th straight victory against USC.

I never really had the chance to enjoy seeing my family. We got back to the hotel room after the game and I saw my mom and dad for a minute and my sister came by—then I was just out. So many people got sick that we canceled the normal trip that we would take on Sunday to Disneyland. There was no way we were going to make that.

To this day, when I watch that game, I marvel at what I was able to do. I cannot accurately describe how bad I felt but yet how good I felt during the course of each individual play. When I was on the field and competing it was so different from when I was on the sideline. I was out of it when I wasn't in the game, but when I lined up and the play was called, the whistle blew, the ball was snapped, and something happened. Whatever it was I still don't know.

I still can never quite grasp why I was able to play the way I did, at the level that I did, against a very good team. It all comes back to the fact that you've got to be there for your team—playing for something bigger than yourself and realizing that guys know they can count on you. From the beginning of the season, I was going to be there, and I was going to compete. I was going to do my part throughout the year to give us the best opportunity to be successful.

That game was the culmination of a season like no other. I know there are other players who have had dynamic seasons and rushed for more yards. I don't know if anyone has finished a season of that caliber against a team like USC at that level, being sick, and then playing so well. A lot of it has to do with the guys I played with—I learned to really enjoy the game and being around the guys. From a football standpoint, this is your family, and you do whatever you can do to be at your best for your family.

CHAPTER 15
SOME NIFTY ACCOLADES

After the 1992 regular season, things really heated up in a way I was not prepared for. After having such great success and leading up to the bowl game, it was pretty hectic. The accolades that came with the success that I had, I have to say, they went to my head—and not in a great way, unfortunately. It was the different opportunities that presented themselves—a lot of the All-America honors and a little bit of Heisman hype—that started to take hold in a lot of respects. Then came that game against USC.

I was not prepared for the pressures and commitments that came along with that type of recognition. I'm not a very public person. I was adept at the interviews and the various media appearances because we were taught very well how to handle those things. But I hadn't had any success to this degree during my previous three years at Notre Dame. I would see the media attention that Bettis and Mirer and some of the guys who were successful on defense would get. And I was very comfortable keeping to myself. I was kind of sheltered because when you have guys like Bettis and Mirer, the majority of the media focus went in their direction.

At the end of the season you kind of tally it all up. I was looking at Garrison Hearst and he had almost 230 carries, more than 1,500 yards, and 19 touchdowns—a darn good resume. Marshall Faulk—with 260-some carries—led Division I with more than 1,600 rushing yards and 15 touchdowns. I never really thought about me being in that echelon. I had considerably fewer carries than those other guys, but I did rush for more than 1,300 yards. It was favorable for me to be mentioned in that same breath as those players.

Hearst and Faulk were the first-team All-American running backs, and I was second team—and I didn't have an issue with that. The numbers speak for themselves. I was just grateful to be considered in the conversations for those honors. I was glad to be part of this team and the success that we had.

I ended up fifth in the Heisman voting, which was a little bit of a surprise. I was Coach Holtz's first 1,000-yard rusher. The only other Notre

Dame guys who had done that were Allen Pinkett, Vagas Ferguson, and Al Hunter—some pretty good company.

I ended up setting a Notre Dame single-season record for average yards per rush at 7.6, breaking the previous record held by Don Miller, one of the Four Horsemen. I finished seventh in the country in rushing, and, as a team, we were third at 280.9 yards a game. We also ranked fourth in the nation in scoring and ninth defensively against the run, and we only allowed 16.2 points per game.

I actually got an opportunity to travel and be part of the Doak Walker Award celebration as one of the three finalists. It was televised on ESPN and was a really nice event. I even got to meet Hearst and Faulk, both great guys—you really develop new respect for guys when you have a chance to be around them. The biggest thing that struck me about Faulk—a young guy at the time as a sophomore—was his football IQ. He had a really strong understanding of the game, and when you were talking to him you definitely had to respect his knowledge and awareness of his capabilities.

We learned we were going to be playing in the Cotton Bowl against Texas A&M, so there was a lot of hype around that too. Notre Dame has a long history of playing in the Cotton Bowl. Plus, it was down in Texas and close to my hometown of Tulsa, Oklahoma, so I knew I would have a lot of family members interested in coming to the game.

I was definitely pumped and psyched—especially after finishing third in the Doak Walker Award voting and finishing fifth in the Heisman. I was excited to say, "Let's go down to Texas." Being from Oklahoma, whenever you have a chance to beat a Texas school, it's an added bonus.

CHAPTER 16
COTTON BOWL FINALE

We were going to play Texas A&M, and they were ranked No. 4 in the country. They were known for their "Wrecking Crew" defense, so we were constantly being asked questions about going up against that group. Sam Adams was their All-America defensive tackle and Patrick Bates was the All-America safety who led them in tackles. They were talking about what they were going to do to us, how good they were, and how Notre Dame hadn't seen a defense like this.

At the time we were ranked No. 5 in the nation—we were certainly one of the top programs in the country. But it was just all this noise. They thought they were going to smack us in the mouth. But the crazy part about it was that no one had done anything like that to us all year long. That was not going to happen. We were not going to let anyone physically beat us up. That was the marquee aspect of our team—our physicality—and we loved it. We went out and competed every day— that's who we were. If nothing else, we were going to be a physical football team.

That's another aspect of bowl games that is sometimes a little frustrating. There is just a lot of time, a lot of media, a lot of people talking instead of playing. During the season you don't see the other team at any point except on Saturday, whereas against A&M, we had joint functions in the evenings, so we were seeing them pretty regularly.

Conversations were being had about who's going to do what to whom, and so you are hearing this on a firsthand basis as opposed to in the media. That was one of the things Coach Holtz was adamant about—we don't talk in the media. Plus, you had to be conscious of what you were doing and how you were doing it, being very mindful of the brand—not only the Notre Dame brand, but also your own. You represent Notre Dame, and a lot of times people are watching, waiting for you to slip up.

I'm thinking, "Let's get to the game. We'll find out real quick how good you are and how good we are." I knew the type of team that we had. I knew the people who were on our team, and I knew what we were capable of.

When it came down to the game, I knew early on what type of game it was going to be. We would run a simple off-tackle play, and an A&M guy would come up and make the tackle and jump all around after a five-yard run. I was thinking to myself, right after that first hit, that I knew we had this from the giddyup.

Early on we had success, not only on the ground but also in the air. It was a tough battle—we were feeling each other out. It was our physicality on offense against their toughness on defense. That first quarter there was not a lot happening. I fumbled twice when we were in the

Rick Mirer won well-deserved MVP honors in the Cotton Bowl.

red zone—and had I not had those slipups early in the game, that game might have been a runaway.

I caught a pass toward the end of the second quarter, and Lake Dawson had a 40-yard touchdown reception. But even before then we were moving the ball. This game was no different—we were led by the rushing attack and we definitely had success. It was not only Bettis and me—Mirer had a strong rushing game, with 13 carries. We knew because of the weather and the rain that we were going to run the football, and we did that to the tune of 245 yards. Bettis scored three touchdowns—two rushing and one receiving. After one of the touchdowns, Bates tackled Bettis in the end zone and Bates got up whooping and hollering as if *he* scored a touchdown. They did not score a point until a field goal in the fourth quarter. And our defense was really mad because it didn't get the shutout.

We dominated that game from start to finish, and it was not as close as the score made it out to be. We won 28–3, but the score could have easily been 42–zip had I not put the ball on the ground twice while we were marching down. They didn't really stop us at any point—the only times we didn't score were when we made mistakes, and two of those mistakes were mine. That was the first time I fumbled all year, in those last two games.

We dominated Texas A&M and did it in a way that was so like us. We were geared for that type of game with the weather being cold and damp. You expected a physical, well-fought game. They were ranked higher than we were, and they were talking a lot of noise. It was somewhat reminiscent of the Florida game in the Sugar Bowl. But this was so much sweeter because it was our senior year. You go out on such a high note, dominating a team in such a fashion I felt only we could with the conditions we had.

They weren't comfortable out there in that type of weather. But we were because that's what we were used to. We ran the ball down their throat. We only had to throw it three times after halftime, and at one point we ran the ball 34 straight times. I finished with 115 yards, and Bettis had 75 yards. Mirer had two touchdown passes, about 120 yards—not a lot of passing yards, but he ran the team.

Mirer was the MVP and rightfully so with his two touchdown passes and 55 yards rushing. He was the leader—our captain—who led us start to finish. To this day I have the utmost respect for him and what he accomplished. I know very well the scrutiny and pressure that come with being the quarterback at the University of Notre Dame—and he handled it with such grace and composure all year.

For us to go in and handle them the way we did—it's too bad our defense didn't get the shutout. We let it be known early on that it was our house. Our offensive line delivered a virtuoso blocking performance in that game because the holes were enormous. We silenced that "Wrecking Crew" defense that they had. The only wrecking that took place was the Notre Dame offense and defense, all game long.

CHAPTER 17
DECISIONS TO MAKE

After the 1992 campaign, I had now had a successful season and a successful bowl game. I was being courted by multiple agents, and my draft stock seemed to be getting better. I finally had the opportunity to play professional football. Playing in the NFL was always my dream. My brother was playing in the league, several guys who I played with prior to my senior year were going into the league. But even while I was going through the interview process and working out to prepare for the league, it still hadn't hit me. It still didn't feel real in a lot of regards.

I continued to train, and I started preparing for the draft and particularly for the NFL Combine. That January I made the mistake—and I regret this greatly—of deciding not to complete the spring semester of my senior year at Notre Dame. There was a level of ignorance—you think you know this, you think you know that, you think you're grown. I turned 22 in January, but I was still naïve about a lot of things that were part of that process.

That's one of the reasons I was so adamant in my former position with Notre Dame in encouraging young men and women to make sound decisions relating to enjoying their time in college. As that season progressed and my success continued, I really didn't have a lot of people telling me or directing me on some really basic things—remaining humble, remaining the person you were, and continuing to do the things that had provided the success you had.

So much of this process was unknown and unfamiliar to me. And a lot of these things you don't learn in school—like basic financial management. I decided to focus solely on the opportunity to play professionally, and I didn't really take the time to complete my degree requirements. I just let school fall by the wayside, and I started to fall away from Notre Dame in some regards, not making sound decisions or getting sound advice.

I was going to visit certain prospective agents to be wined and dined—and all the while having no clue what this business was about. I did not understand much about the NFL. As I progressed through this transition in preparing for a career as a professional football player, I was kind of feeling my way with limited, if any, direction. It was like being recruited again in a lot of ways. You've got people coming at you from different directions, which can be overwhelming. People are there to take advantage of you in some sense. They don't have your best interests at heart—that was something I was not familiar with.

I was always taught to look for the best in people. But people are telling you, "I'm going to do this for you. I'm going to do that for you." All the while they are just trying to get access to you and your ability and your talent to perform and produce money. When you're not aware of that, you start to listen to some people who don't have a love or care for you and your well-being—and that's something that's always stuck with me.

After going through that—just seeing my struggles in retrospect—it was something that still drives me to this day. I want to do better by others and always speak the truth and look for that person's best interests and give them sound advice. It's, "Hey, if you do this, think hard about it—consider all the options and reach out to people who are truly looking out for your best interests and don't have a financial stake in your success."

When January rolled around, I took some time to heal; I was trying to get my body back. I was ramping back up and preparing for the NFL Combine in February. I wound up pulling my hamstring—something I had issues with going all the way back to high school. I made the decision not to go through drills at the Combine. Looking back, I'm not sure it was the best decision, but a lot of guys decided to go that direction.

I was a little banged up, but I've always excelled when things are at their worst—when there are challenges. I'm not sure I got any solid advice to not run. I was working out, and hats off to Jerry Schmidt because he had us right. Guys were set and ready to roll, especially during our pro day.

We had a lot of guys being looked at for the NFL Draft. You had Bettis, who had decided to come out after his junior year and go into the league—plus Mirer, McDonald, DuBose, Irv Smith, Carter (he decided to forego his junior year and come out for the draft), Knapp, Hall, Bryant, and McGill. So we had quite a few guys who were viewed as potential draft picks and had had great success playing at a high level.

There was a lot of talent when you look at the team that we had. It showed when you looked at the number of people we had at our pro day and the number of guys invited to participate in the Combine. I was not really clued into what was going on—I thought I knew, but I didn't know. It's amazing looking back at what I was able to do, even being ignorant of a lot of things that related to the business side of sports.

I'm thinking now about how smart it would have been to lean on some of the guys I played with, the ones I considered friends and family. You are trying to do things on your own, and that pride can really kick in and make you do some unwise things. I went to the Combine and I was not ready. I was ready for the physical exam aspect of it, but I knew I wasn't going to be running.

The interviews and the testing? I still say to this day—and I say this to some of the younger players who come to the Combine—there's nothing that can prepare you mentally for what you are about to embark on. That experience sticks with me to this day. The number of teams, the doctors, the team staff members, the officials, the coaches, and the front office people—and that's just in Indianapolis. There are other people everywhere trying to get to you. It is extremely overwhelming, especially if you go in by yourself. And I still felt alone in that process.

I was just not mentally prepared for the doctors, the constant barrage of questions. It felt almost like I was drowning when I was out there being pulled and prodded. I hear guys talk about it today, and they are up there in your shorts, and they are measuring your hands, your arms, checking your teeth. It was crazy.

Then you have these people interviewing you who are representing all the different teams. They are asking different questions and you are coming through in groups by position. It was eye-opening to see the level of thoroughness that the NFL takes in vetting players. It's amazing the resources that they have to check into your history and your background—what you've done, where you've been.

Going into my senior season I was an unknown. You've got to understand that they don't know you. How did you get to this point? The season I had was really remarkable and to have it happen in a single year leaves a lot of questions that aren't answered. And the NFL isn't big on having unanswered questions.

They go through your history with a fine-tooth comb. The best advice I can give is don't ever lie about anything, because lots of times they're asking questions they already have the answers to. They're checking to see how you are going to handle yourself, how you are going to respond. Be true to yourself—and be yourself. But I was trying to figure out how I should answer the questions.

Then they have you take the Wonderlic test, and I did okay. You go into it with all these preconceived notions about all the things that you don't know. It's happening to you right then, and that's something that can be scary for any young man. I felt alone in a lot of regards. I was out there with these strange people and they all were asking me questions—taking me here, taking me there. This person pulling me here—well, I want to see this—asking this and that. It's so fast and furious.

I will say that because Coach Holtz's practices were so intense and we had to learn things on the fly sometimes and we had to learn to adapt quickly—that was something that helped me through that process to some degree. I was used to change—rapid change—and being forced to adapt quickly, being forced to make decisions on my feet, respond, and be prepared for anything. The NFL Combine was a lot of that—anything can happen, and anything can be asked of you. You need to mind your p's and q's constantly. You need to be on edge throughout that whole process.

CHAPTER 18
THE NFL DRAFT EXPERIENCE

A t the NFL Combine the only things I did were the interviews, and the only physical events that I participated in were the broad jump, the vertical jump, and the bench press. I was able to do 18 reps on the bench press, 9'11" for the broad jump, and 3'6" for the vertical jump.

Coming out of the Combine, I still felt like I was in a pretty good position and progressing toward an opportunity to be drafted decently high. I put a lot of emphasis on my pro day because the one thing that I was known for was my speed. After not running the 40 at the Combine, there were definitely questions. But I was legitimately hurt—I had a strained hamstring and didn't want to push myself because I was really going to go after it. But I still wonder if it would have been in my better interests to run and go through drills, because the one other knock on me was my receiving. I was not known for that, and I didn't have a lot of opportunities to catch the ball out of the backfield at Notre Dame.

Going into the pro day, which was in March, I had done my rehab and was healing up. Schmidt was extremely helpful in the process of physical development, and Russ and the training staff were outstanding in how they prepared guys to get ready for that particular draft. So coming into it I was pretty happy with where I was sitting.

You hear different things from different people, but the thing that I noticed most about preparing for the NFL Draft is that it's all about reducing your draft stock. They are always looking for what's wrong, not necessarily what's right. From the time you finish your last college game, everything seems to be focusing on reducing your value as a player. From January to April you are focused on trying to stay out of trouble and not negatively affect your draft status. It definitely creates paranoia in some respects of trying to maintain this image. You are constantly trying to improve your status, from the Combine to the pro days and from the interviews to visiting the different teams. Teams that are looking at you will bring you in to their complex to look at you a lot more closely.

As we moved closer to pro day, I was definitely nervous. I was still trying to find an agent. There's so much that goes into it from a business standpoint, yet I always wanted it to be about the game. It was something that I had played since I was a little child—but I never contemplated football as a potential career. It was something I did because I enjoyed it, and it was something I felt good about doing because it was a game. When you get to the NFL, it gets less and less about being a game and more and more about the business aspects of it.

I learned that lesson—not as quickly as I should have or needed to, but I learned it over time. As I prepared for the pro day I was doing a lot of stretching and sprinting. Those were areas I really struggled with, so because of my pulled muscles I stretched quite a bit and really focused on speed training and getting better. At the time I weighed around 210. I definitely felt strong and felt good about the direction I was headed in.

We had quite a few guys who were being looked at from a draft standpoint, so the pro day was packed. Every NFL team was there, and everybody was on edge, wanting to see how it went. At the time juniors couldn't participate in the Combine so, for Bettis and Carter, this was the first time the NFL people would see them go through all the drills and activities. Guys were ready, and that was one of the more exciting times. It was fun during this time when we were working out, and everyone was kind of doing their own thing.

We did our prep and worked together from a training standpoint. But we were all over the place because we had people coming in trying to get us to sign with them. People were coming over and wanting to talk to us. We were doing interviews. At the time I was living off campus with Adrian Jarrell. It really was a constant barrage of things and people, and I was not always real big on conversations with people. I enjoyed my time with people I trusted and had relationships with. But it was a really tough time for me because I was being forced into something that I wasn't necessarily comfortable with. I had to work on it, because it took a lot to be sociable in those regards.

We got to the pro day, and things went very well for me and a lot of guys. We had all these scouts come, and I remember the guy throwing balls to me—he kept throwing them high or throwing them low, forcing me to make some difficult catches. I was watching him throw to other people, and he was always on the money. I was wondering what the heck was going on—but it was obvious they were kind of concerned about my catching ability. They wanted to see what I could do and really tried to test me with throwing the ball. I had my contact lenses in because this was a job interview—so I was pretty keyed in. And I caught everything.

The thing I remember most about pro day was the fact that all our guys were there together and there were all these NFL people—but I was there competing with my teammates, just like any other day at Notre Dame. I loved seeing them have success and doing well. We had guys doing drills at just about every position. It was kind of nice because you got a chance to talk to some of the guys, your teammates, who you hadn't seen since the season had ended.

A lot of guys who were still on the team could come out to watch, so you got to interact with them as well. It was a lot of fun. As much pressure as it was, it was a lot more fun than I thought it was going to be. I was really nervous, and I was so afraid to make a mistake. But after the first few drills, I was able to relax and get into a flow and it went well. I ran well, and I caught the ball well—at least in my opinion.

* * *

Going into the 1993 NFL Draft, I was feeling really confident. I felt good about where I was and the success I was having and how the entire process had gone. Coming out of that pro day I was in a strong position. And on top of that, the Dallas Cowboys came in a week or so later and had a group of us work out again just for the Cowboys staff. They came in and worked out Mirer, me, Bettis, Carter, DuBose, and Irv Smith. I felt I had a really good workout for the Cowboys and was in a strong position. Being from Oklahoma, the Cowboys were my childhood team growing up. I remember Roger Staubach, Tony Dorsett, Drew Hill, and Robert Newhouse—I was a big fan of the Cowboys so it was pretty exciting to have that opportunity to do an individual workout for them.

One of the things that happens when you are going through the NFL Draft process is that you realize how extensive the vetting process is. Certain teams that have interest will bring specific players in—this was something I was not very familiar with going into it.

I was invited out to the Washington Redskins complex and went through a series of tests—actual vision, depth perception, and psychological. I met with different people, staff, and scouts. Charley Casserly was the general manager at the time—their head coach Joe Gibbs had retired, and Richie Petitbon had become the new head coach. They were in the middle of some real transition and change. But I never really thought twice about them bringing me out there.

I was still pretty keyed in with the Dallas Cowboys because of the proximity to home and from growing up a lifelong Cowboys fan. So I really dismissed the Redskins altogether as even being an option, also because they had some pretty talented running backs on the roster. Earnest Byner was a top running back in the league. Brian Mitchell was a third-down back and one of their top special teams returners and players on the team. And Ricky Ervins was on the team too. So I had no thought going into draft day that I was under consideration by the Redskins, even though I had been out to their complex. The Cowboys brought their own staff to work us out in South Bend, and I believed everything was pointing in that direction.

Eugene Parker was my agent at the time—a very reputable individual and a person who was extremely helpful to me. He was a real positive influence on me. I was back home in Tulsa and we were having a draft party, although I don't know why I had one. I had some different expectations and perceptions going into that draft because Cowboys had the last pick in the first round. I felt there was a good opportunity for me. I felt I could go anywhere in the bottom half of the first round to the upper half of the second round.

There were some really good running backs coming out in that draft. But I felt I was just as good as any of them. The Cowboys actually sent a representative to my home on draft day, and since I was kind of in touch with them I felt good about where things sat.

We got through the early picks, and it was definitely nerve-racking. I didn't know what to expect. My mom and dad were there, and so were my brothers and sisters and other family members. I didn't expect to hear my name called early, but I was still sitting there, kind of hanging out, just waiting for a phone call.

The second pick in the draft was Mirer to the Seattle Seahawks—a teammate of mine and a friend. I was really excited for him. There are certain runs that happen in a draft. The third pick was Hearst out of Georgia. He probably should have won the Heisman that year. With him going as high as three—and you had two quarterbacks go and they were at a premium—there was a better chance of me going sooner.

Bettis was the next running back, taken by the Rams with the No. 10 pick and, again, that seemed to be good for me. The next running back off the board was Robert Smith, from Ohio State to the Minnesota Vikings. At that point, I was feeling pretty good because three of the top eligible running backs were off the board early, and I was still there. I had someone there at the house from the Cowboys who I was still in consultation with, so I thought, "Hey, there's a good chance for me to go with that last pick in the first round."

Carter, another Notre Dame teammate, was selected in the first round by the Redskins with their first pick. There was no thought at all that I would be in the mix there with the talent they had at the running back position. Irv Smith was taken with the 20th pick by the New Orleans Saints. So you had Mirer, Bettis, Carter, and Smith all from Notre Dame and all taken in the first round. That was pretty neat.

I was sitting there and thinking that there was an opportunity late in the first round to be picked by the Cowboys. I figured that was where I was going to go. I was feeling pretty good and was really locked in on that last pick. Well, the Cowboys decided to trade out of the first round to pick up draft picks. From the Cowboys it was still, "Hey, you are still our guy, and this is giving us some opportunities to get some more players." So they traded down—they dropped down to the 46th slot, the second pick in the second round, and that would be their first pick.

There was a run on defensive backs and linebackers for a while. Running backs were still coming off the board—Natrone Means from North Carolina was selected by the San Diego Chargers, Glyn Milburn from Stanford was selected by the Denver Broncos two picks later at pick 43. The 44th pick rolled around and I was keyed in—the guy from the Cowboys was there and I was prepping to drive down to Texas.

We got to the 45th pick and the Redskins were on the clock. I got a call and I was thinking it would be the Cowboys saying, "Hey, we are going to take you with the 46th pick." It wound up being Don Brough, the running backs coach for the Washington Redskins. It was pretty surreal because I was thinking, "Hey, I'm going to be a Cowboy and I'm ready to roll." Instead, Brough called and said, "Hey, it's Don Brough with the Washington Redskins, and we're going to pick you with the 45th pick."

I was almost speechless. I was thinking, "What?" I was looking around—is this really happening? The guy from the Cowboys was in my parents' house and they were making the next pick. But then I got drafted by the Washington Redskins. I was in complete shock, as was the gentleman who was there from Dallas. He turned beet red. This was 1993—the Cowboys had just won the Super Bowl. They were the team. And I was really excited because I was thinking I was going to get that opportunity to play with them and it was going to be a dream come true.

I was in a haze. I didn't know what was going on. What happened? These are stark rivals—the Cowboys versus the Redskins. Everybody knows what has transpired between those two organizations for decades. The only thing I knew about the Redskins was that my uncle Tony Peters played for them. Outside of that I had no real concept of what the Redskins were about. On my visit I didn't really ask them any-thing—I was just thinking it was part of the draft process.

That was really a crazy situation. You go in thinking one thing and something completely different happens. It's mind-boggling, to say the least. They had a really strong backfield—a strong team. They were in transition as well, but I never pictured myself there. I just didn't see the need for them to pick a running back.

But that's exactly what happened.

CHAPTER 19
ON TO THE REDSKINS

Need is very important in the NFL, and most teams draft based on their needs as opposed to specific players. But later I found out from Casserly that the Redskins drafted based on the best available player. So that had something to do with my selection.

I flew out to Ashburn Village in the Virginia suburbs where the Redskins had their facility. The nicest thing was that I was not going alone. I had a Notre Dame teammate going with me, Carter, who was the first-round pick of the Redskins. We had a bit of a reunion of sorts there in DC, and it was a special time. It was all a dream come true for me since I hadn't considered the NFL a real possibility when I got to Notre Dame. I was just glad to play a game that I enjoyed—that I loved—but it was just a game. I never viewed it as something I would do professionally.

You'd see guys at the professional level, the guys I looked up to— the Walter Paytons, the Barry Sanderses, the Tony Dorsetts, the Jim Browns. They always seemed so far removed from something I would be doing. I still considered myself just a kid from Tulsa, Oklahoma.

I thought my life was going to be lived as someone who gets a college degree, gets a job, and works to support his family. But this was one of those deals where I was one of our own making it to professional football. We didn't have a lot of people from where I was from going to the league. My brother Tony went the year before (he was a fourth-round pick of the Philadelphia Eagles) and then I went, so that brought a sense of pride. I always pictured my brother being in the NFL, but, for whatever reason, I never really pictured myself having that opportunity.

It was an exciting time—it was a fun time. It was a memory I'll always have, as odd as it was with the circumstances—just having that opportunity to sit back and think it was actually happening. It was like a dream—like it was happening to someone else—even after getting that phone call. My mind was still thinking this was someone else's life. This storybook was happening to some other person, not me.

A lot of it was due to the people who encouraged me to go some-where. I thought I was going to go to Oklahoma or Oklahoma State—I wasn't planning on leaving the state. I hadn't really gone anywhere. I hadn't left the state other than to run track or play sports. Now here I was being whisked off to the DC area to play for a team my uncle Tony Peters played for in the 1970s and '80s after he played collegiately as a defensive back at Oklahoma.

It was still a real struggle for me to grasp that this was happening. I always had this fear of inadequacy—that somebody was going to take this away from me. This wasn't supposed to be happening to me. But to have my family there to share it meant the world to me. It was a special moment—a special time with people I cared about. And the people who cared about me made it even more of a blessing.

* * *

At the Redskins complex I met the front office people, the coaches, the owners—it was kind of a whirlwind deal. The team introduced me and Carter—the two Notre Dame guys—to the media, and we started to get the sense of how influential Notre Dame was, even at that professional level. Maybe we were looked at a little bit differently than guys from other schools. It wasn't about being better than anybody else. It was just that there seemed to be a different expectation or view of Notre Dame guys in the league than guys from other schools. That always struck me.

The whole deal was first class. The facilities were extremely nice. Seeing some of the football technologies and advancements in that day was impressive. It was all happening really fast. You are preparing for an entire career—a profession. It really was all so new, and I was so inexperienced and still bewildered by what had happened. I was going into a whole new culture—a whole new area—and it scared me. I was not comfortable with what I didn't know, and I was not really open to asking questions.

I went back to what always worked for me, and that was okay. I was going to put in 110 percent as a member of this organization. I was always just trying to make the team. I didn't view it as if I was one of their top picks. I was looking at the guys I was going to be competing against, and thinking that I've got to do more.

It was similar to my transition from high school to Notre Dame, coming onto the roster of a team that just won a national championship. I was feeling like I was over my head. For me, fear was a driver to not screw up. I had to bust my butt and do more because I just never really felt I belonged.

I had to find a place to live in DC because I was getting ready for training camp. You have all these agents and money managers and this and that, and I had no clue about finances. I had not a single clue—in college I had no money, and my parents were working-class people, so I just didn't know. I stayed in an apartment my senior year at Notre Dame, but it was covered through my housing stipend, plus my brother helped me out because he was in the league. I had no clue about interest rates and credit cards—I didn't have any of those.

You don't know what questions to ask, you don't know who to trust, you don't know who to reach out to. And I tended to make assumptions because I didn't want to look like I didn't know what I was doing.

* * *

The positive was that as I was getting ready for minicamp, I was as healthy as I'd ever been. I weighed about 205 pounds, and I went back to working out and preparing myself to be successful rather than just playing the game. As I got further into minicamp, it was actually a lot of fun. The plays and the concepts I was doing—they were all things I was comfortable with. I knew football, I knew how to prepare, I knew the game, and I knew what I needed to do to get myself ready. I left the other things alone and left them to people who had my interests at heart.

I was starting my life as a kid with almost no money coming out of college who now had almost $1 million dollars. And I had no clue what to do. Investments? I just ignored all that. I lost track of what was going on from a financial standpoint and focused all my energy into playing and competing and making the team.

I picked things up quickly, so the transition from a football standpoint was really good. Even the strength and conditioning program was somewhat similar to what we did at Notre Dame. I was used to high-intensity workouts, really driving and pushing yourself to your limits. I really threw myself into that. I found a condo—I picked a place close to the facility so I could stay focused on making the team. I had a bare-bones apartment because I didn't know how to pick out all the things that went into having a place of your own. I had a TV so I could play my video games, work out, come back home, and mind my own business. I was okay with that.

Before actual practice started I ended up going out to California for a Pinnacle football card photo shoot—this is what they call OTAs (official team activities) today. Bettis was there, and so were Carter, Mirer, McGinest, and Hearst. They had us dressed up in our uniforms to get action shots. It was a lot of fun, but it was also great having that time to enjoy the company of the guys you both played against and played with. It was a real blast—and nice to see the guys with a smile on their faces all the time.

Getting ready before training camp, I stayed close to the facility and would work out there. But I found out that until I signed a contract, I couldn't go to training camp—and that was a little nerve-racking. I had no concept of contract negotiations. I just wanted to play football. So I thought, "Hey, whatever they are going to pay me to play a game, that's cool. Let's get it done so I can go play."

I still had some insecurities. I was coming in as a rookie, and I picked up things at the minicamps I was a part of. But it was always in the back of my head: "I don't know if I can do this." It was more the feeling that I wasn't worthy—I wasn't good enough. When you are working out on your own or with the young guys, it was hard to measure how well I was doing from a conditioning standpoint or how much success I was having or how I was developing competitively.

As I moved closer to training camp, I grew even more nervous. I just wanted to play ball—I wanted to focus on football and the other things that come with being in the NFL. Outside of the fun stuff, I didn't want to deal with the business side of it—I kept my head down and looked at it like college. Don't make any waves and don't do anything to upset anybody. If you do that, you will be okay.

CHAPTER 20
ROOKIE REVIEWS

G oing into my rookie year, I didn't have a lot of expectations for myself. I just focused on trying to make the team. Right before training camp started, I made the decision to work out with Darrell Green. This guy is a multiyear All-Pro and was recognized as the fastest man in the NFL at one time. Several guys including the running backs in the group—Byner, Mitchell, and Ervins—and other guys on the team said you don't want to fool with that man. When he works out, he takes it to another level.

Green was a defensive back who was 10 years older than me. I was just 22 and I was feeling myself because I was working out in terms of lifts and some of the runs, and I knew track workouts could be pretty grueling and really demanding. But I know it definitely helped me in my transition from summer track to football in high school, and I ran a little bit in college.

I thought, "Let's see what he's going to do—he's not a spring chicken." I went out to George Washington University, where he worked out. This was after minicamps and after he'd been All-Pro—he had been in the league for years. He was a veteran. I've always been of the mind to challenge myself and want to compete with the best. Only a couple of guys would work out with him—Carter was a rookie, so he didn't work out with him. He didn't fool with him. Defensive backs are a little bit different—they do a lot of running. They're like receivers—they don't hit anybody, but they run a lot.

I went out there and he kind of gave me the basics of what the workout was—it was pretty much all running. Defensive backs don't do a lot of lifting, so Green was not a guy who was in the weight room. He was all about the speed. I got out there and he said, "This is how this goes, and here's the workout." He told me he was big on running hills. I didn't find this out until much later, but he used to run this hill that was basically manufactured when he was at Texas A&I.

He brought me in for the beginner's portion—he wasn't trying to hurt me. Green was a standup guy, and it was nothing malicious. We got out there, and for the warmup we did some 200s and some 400s.

He did double what I did, and that was just the warmup to the actual workout. We were running the width of soccer fields.

All this is taking place in the summer—and this is DC, so it's hot. We've done all this and then he said, "Alright, now we are going to go hit the hill." I'm already gassed from doing the track workout—that was enough. I'm thinking, "We're good—it's time to go home, right?" He had a different idea.

There were three stages to his workout. I'm a proud person, and one of the things my dad taught me was not to quit. So we went to this hill and he ran up and down the hill. He did three sets of 10, and this hill was at about a 45-degree angle and had to be 55 to 60 yards. He would sprint up the hill and run back down—that's only one set—10 times. The next set was quick feet—short, little steps up the hill and then running back down—doing 10 reps of those. The third set was backpedaling—he would backpedal up the hill and run back down. He would do 10 of those. He told me to do five each and said that when I got to backpedaling, since I wasn't a defensive back, I should go back to running up the hill. I did all this and I thought I was about to die. I did half of what he did for the whole workout—even with the workout on the track, the running across the field, and the hills.

I got through it, and I was not going to show weakness—I refused. He said, "Good job, Brooks. Good job." I knew he had to be tired, but he didn't look like it. We came off the hill and my legs were numb. There was no way I was going to be able to drive home. But I wasn't going to give him the satisfaction of knowing that. I just said, "I'm good. I'm going to get some water." I had to have someone pick me up because I could not feel my legs. I had never experienced a workout like that in my life.

I went back again—and I don't know why I went back. Maybe the workout affected my brain! I remember getting home, and I left my car there, so I had to go back and pick it up the next day. I have never experienced a workout like that in my life, and it was clearly—for Green—one of the reasons he played that long in the league. There's a

Future Hall of Famer Darrell Green gave me one of my first tastes of the NFL.

reason that he was as good as he was. He was a tenacious competitor, and I always marveled at his ability.

This workout was a little like one we actually had at Notre Dame—a conditioning test leading up to training camp. You had to pass this conditioning test before you were really allowed to participate. I learned to pace myself after that. But you can't run with Green—he runs at a whole other level. I went back because I had to learn how to run within myself. Otherwise, I'm sure I would have died if I did that again with him at his level.

That was my introduction to Conditioning 101 in the NFL. We had a minicamp before we headed to Carlisle, Pennsylvania, for training camp, about three hours away. Before we went to Carlisle, we had this conditioning test that was conducted by the strength and conditioning coach. The test was that you had to run two sets of 14 40-yard dashes within two seconds of your best 40-yard dash time. My best time was 4.3 seconds, so I had to run every one of those 40s in 4.5 seconds or faster. I got through it, but it was not easy to say the least.

Green was showing off, plain and simple. He ran 28 40s and his best time was 4.2 seconds, so he had to run every one of his 40s in 4.4 seconds or faster. After running 28 40s a lot of the guys were like, "Oh, my gosh, I can't feel my legs." And he was still out there bouncing around. He came out and dropped a 4.2-second 40-yard dash at the end of all this. This man ran a sub-4.3-second 40-yard dash after running 28 40s in 4.4 seconds or faster! To me that's showing off. I'm pretty sure on that last set there was no way I was running a 40-yard dash in 4.5 seconds.

Going into training camp I was in peak condition. Early on I was just glad if I could get on the special teams. But being a second-round pick, the NFL is a little bit different. I actually was not given a lot of opportunities to play on special teams because I had worked myself into the rotation with the other three running backs. I still didn't really know that I had done that. I was still just thinking that I've got to make the team.

But I was used to playing on special teams because if you play for Coach Holtz at Notre Dame you're going to play on special teams, and you are going to play on a lot of them. I was used to running down on kicks, on punts, on returns, so I figured, "Hey, that's going to be my thing." Early on I was in the return game with the kickoff return and fielded kicks.

We scrimmaged against the Pittsburgh Steelers in Latrobe, Pennsylvania. Pittsburgh ran a 3–4 defense and had some humongous inside and outside linebackers. You're talking about guys who were 6'4" and 250 pounds. Levon Kirkland was like 300 pounds. For our base blocking, we were sliding protection, so you're either blocking an outside linebacker who is 6'4" or 6'5" and 250 or 260 pounds—or you're blocking the inside linebacker who is 6'2" and 270 pounds. I hated practicing against the Steelers. The only good thing about it was that we didn't do two-a-days.

I got through training camp feeling good about myself and coming in with confidence. Coach Don Brough was a wonderful coach. He was very instrumental in the success I had my rookie year, and I couldn't have asked for a better group of guys to be around. You hear about tough competition, and it is definitely precisely that when you are competing with the best players in the world playing American football.

As I've said before, we had a stable of backs, but each one of those guys was extremely helpful. I thought Ervins was the last person in the world who would want to help me because he's from USC and I'm from Notre Dame, and they didn't get along. But he was a wonderful person.

I've got to say, I was not always very confident in what I was doing. We were going up against a bunch of veteran linebackers like Monte Coleman and some other stud guys who had played on the Super Bowl team. Here I was as a rookie, trying to make sure I didn't screw up too badly. That was the thing that really stood out to me. I really think that if it weren't for Ervins, Byner, and Mitchell—and I was surprised they were willing to be that helpful—helping me get through that year, I might not have made it. I really thought that was something that was impressive.

Then you have the rookie class. Carter wound up starting at the left corner position. Then offensively it was me, and we ran a two–tight end set so Frank Wycheck, a sixth-round pick from Maryland, was also starting at tight end. I believe four rookies at some point started during that season. At least in my mind, if your team has four rookies starting in the NFL, you're not going to be very good.

This team was coming off a strong performance—a couple of years removed from winning the Super Bowl. When we got to the preseason, I was ripping off runs here and there and having some success. I still didn't think I was in the mix to play significant minutes. I just continued to focus and play hard throughout training camp and the preseason, and little by little I set myself up to have an opportunity to play going into the season. That was something I was definitely shocked by, but at the same time I felt really blessed that I was in the mix that quickly.

CHAPTER 21
MY FIRST PRO SHOT

During my rookie year, each game got more and more comfortable for me. The offense got better and better, and I must say, my rookie year got off to a great start. We came out the first game of the regular season on *Monday Night Football* against the Dallas Cowboys—the defending Super Bowl champions. You couldn't ask for a more exciting time, and to start the season off with a win against the Super Bowl champs was awesome. It was a game that will always stick in my mind. Who starts off their rookie year on *Monday Night Football* at home against the Super Bowl champions?

Playing at RFK Stadium is what you dream of as a young man playing football in the backyard, especially playing against my favorite team growing up and having the opportunity to play with such a storied program and rivalry. The Redskins-Cowboys rivalry is epic, to say the least. The way the game turned out, I had a feeling we were going to be really good.

Mitchell had a really good game with more than 100 yards rushing. Mark Rypien had three touchdown passes, and I was thinking, "This is how our season is going to be." We started off very strong—very confident. We won 35–16, but with one caveat: Emmitt Smith did not play for the Cowboys because he was holding out. Knowing that I was really close to becoming a Cowboy in April, and then getting in the game and having decent opportunities and having some success running the ball—I had 11 carries and 53 yards—was a sound victory.

We jumped on them in the second and third quarters. It just felt really good—a special moment for me. My mom and dad came up for my first game as a pro. My girlfriend (and future wife) was there. That is how you dream of starting your NFL career—having it happen in such a dynamic way and against an opponent you have a lot of respect for and who you grew up watching and admiring as a child. So we were thinking that we were hitting the ground running and that it was going to be gangbusters from there. Then it just seemed like the wheels fell off.

For whatever reason, after that game it was a struggle. I always look at that season in two different ways—I had success individually, but as a team we were not there. Knowing the Redskins were a couple of years removed from winning the Super Bowl and being a playoff team, it became more of a tough pill to swallow as the season progressed.

It also allowed me to see how dynamic the NFL was in terms of every game being different. You are talking the best of the best. You go from beating the Super Bowl champs on *Monday Night Football* to playing the Phoenix Cardinals, and you go from scoring 35 points to 10. It was sobering to say the least. That next game I didn't play as much—I only had five carries—and it was a constant back and forth in terms of finding my role in a sense. I was developing that as I went.

I had some explosive plays against Dallas, and then coming back against Phoenix, their defensive front was massive. They played more of a nickel defense with Reuben Davis—they went 6'5", 6'5", 6'4", 6'5"— that was their defensive front, and no one was under 285 pounds. They played two linebackers and then Lorenzo Lynch at nickel back. You're talking about huge guys who really clogged us up in the run game. We really struggled to get anything going. We just flat out couldn't move these guys off the ball. And you see that stark contrast in defenses over the course of the game—it was eye-opening and a wake-up call. The size of their guys, the athleticism, the physicality early on—we lost that game, and the offense struggled to put up points.

That was the first opportunity I had to see a Notre Dame guy on the opposite team—that was Steve Beuerlein, who was the Cardinals' quarterback and led them to victory.

But that was still one of those games where you are like, "Whoa."

* * *

The next game really allowed me to set the tone for my rookie year. It was against Philadelphia—kind of my coming-out party. I had the opportunity to move into the starting lineup after that game.

I had a big run for 85 yards—again, I had some individual success— but we wound up losing the game in the fourth quarter. Randall Cunningham drove them down for a score at the end of the game, and he was phenomenal on that drive. At that time, the Eagles were on a roll—after that game they were 3–0 and they were in the catbird seat in the NFC East. And lately the road to Super Bowl had traveled through our division.

We lost 34–31, but I had 22 carries for 154 yards and I was feeling like I could help the team.

We went down to Miami, wound up losing there, and the thing that really jumped out to me was that I started to see the lack of continuity for our offense. Rod Dowhower was the offensive coordinator from the previous staff under Coach Joe Gibbs and he stayed on. But he was trying to switch to the West Coast offense, and we did not have the receiving corps or the quarterback built for that kind of passing game.

The Redskins were known for the counter trey and five-step-drop deep balls, more down-the-field routes because Rypien was a big quarterback. He could stand in the pocket and throw the ball downfield and it was predicated on play action. So trying to switch our offense to a completely different attack took us out of what the Redskins were known to do.

The next week we were playing at home against the Giants, and they just drubbed us. It was a thorough butt-kicking from start to finish. We had no answer, and their defense featured the best defensive player to ever play the game—or one of them, at least—and that was Lawrence Taylor. You're talking about a guy who could flat out run. They really put it on us.

Taylor was a dominant player, and I found out firsthand why he was—he was extremely strong, and he showed us who he was. We lost that game 41–7, I only had three carries, and you saw the offense not showing up. The defense had its struggles, but I really feel our defense was good enough to win if we could have put some points on the board and moved the ball to give them a chance.

We played Phoenix again, and they beat us even worse (36–6), this time down there. Our offense had no continuity, no direction—very disjointed. I just never felt we knew what our focus was or what we were trying to do in games. The game plan didn't seem to match what our skill sets were as a team.

The following week it was the Buffalo Bills having a run with Jim Kelly, Andre Reed, Thurman Thomas, Bruce Smith, Cornelius Bennett, and Darryl Talley. I had another 100-yard game and the most carries (24) of any game that season, but we wound up losing 24–10.

We played Indianapolis at home next and had some success. Our defense won the game, getting turnovers, forcing turnovers, and putting us in a situation to be able to score points. Rypien had two rushing touchdowns and Mitchell scored as well. I had another 100-yard game, but the bulk of that was because of our defense putting us into that situation, getting us the ball to make plays. They had more total yards, but we won the turnover battle. I was in the process of having four games in a row where I carried the ball more than 20 times, but we were not having much success putting points on the board.

Then we played in Giants Stadium—I had 22 carries and 91 yards, but we only scored six points. We never found any continuity offensively. We were not built for the passing game we were trying to employ.

Next we flew out to Los Angeles and I got to see Bettis, Lyght, and Terrell. Our defense did well, but we were unable to score points. I had another solid game—another 22 carries, 87 yards, and 5 catches. So for those who say I can't catch the ball, I can.

We played the Eagles next and lost again. At the end of the game we had a chance—we got close and then, *boom*, we gave it up. Another touchdown drive in the third quarter cost us the game. We only scored 14 points—and it was by such little margins. Mark Bavaro was with the Eagles at that point. You always had that connection with the guys from Notre Dame and we had a lot of them in the league at that time—maybe as many as any school in the country did.

We finally got our third win, 23–17 against Tampa Bay. I was having more success with 128 yards and a big 78-yard touchdown run. Right after that we came back and played the Jets at home, and we lost three to zip—no points over the course of four quarters at home. You could see our fan base starting to dwindle—we were 3–10 at this point and really struggling. We were really having a rough time. We came back home to play Atlanta and got a win, although the defense scored 16 of our 30 points.

Our last road game was in Dallas and we just got throttled. Emmitt Smith was back—he had a good day with 153 yards—and they rolled us. I had a solid game with 85 yards but, again, only scoring three points was not going to cut it.

In the last game of the season, playing Minnesota at home, we lost 14–9 and just struggled to score points. All of our points came via field goals. And that was the season in a nutshell. Individual success but not team success like I was used to coming from Notre Dame, being part of a team that won. So that really bothered me. I never felt comfortable with that individual success not coming with some sort of team success. We weren't the offense we were capable of being because we didn't do what we needed to do with the passing game on a consistent basis. We were trying to move to the West Coast offense, but it was the wrong move and it cost us. I feel like it cost us at least seven wins.

CHAPTER 22
EVALUATING THE YEAR

We wound up going 4–12 and finishing last in the NFC East. It was a difficult time, and I did not understand it. I was trying to fill a void of not winning football games and was feeling very different than I felt as a member of the Notre Dame team, where we lost only eight games in four years.

I ended up with 1,063 rushing yards to lead the team and Mitchell was next with 246 yards, but it was all kind of bittersweet.

You learn quickly that it's a profession, not a game. I think that was kind of a turning point for me. It was hard for me to come to terms with being talked about as a potential star player—an up-and-coming guy—on a losing team. I was wanting to be a part of something bigger. The organization was built on winning championships—built on community. I saw those veteran players who had developed those bonds, and I wanted that because that was something I had in college.

The more I tried to be a part of it, the more it seemed I was separated from it. Not having the understanding of what it meant to be a professional athlete was difficult for me. There was an expectation that came with being an NFL player that I was not aware of and didn't really understand, and there was no one there explaining that side of the game to me. I had to learn a lot of lessons the hard way. I found myself ignoring things that I needed to pay attention to, but I didn't even know it. Instead of asking questions, I'd figure it out on my own when I should have been asking for help.

That year I was having success on the field, but off the field I was miserable. I was never really big on partying and going out to hang out—that wasn't my scene. I was comfortable being at home. But I went out to try to be a part of the team. I never developed a comfort level there—it was all just a facade. I was being somebody I was not.

The only time I was genuine and trying to be myself was when I was on the field—when I was competing and when I was at practice. I was comfortable with that because I had developed the identity of being a football player playing a game. It was also the identity of being part of a team.

I had a teammate who was a college teammate, Tom Carter, and he had some success too, leading the team in 1993 with six interceptions. We had some rookies who did well that year. I had a comfort level with Carter, but I chose to go a different route and hang out with the offense. I always think back. Maybe had I taken more time to engage with Carter and his wife, Renee—my wife, Christina, and I hanging out with them—things would have been different. Maybe I would have learned more from Carter and the people he was hanging with.

I was an NFL all-rookie selection that first season in DC, and I'm pretty sure that was the first time the rookie backfield was all from the same school—Bettis, Mirer, and I. My man Bettis was the Rookie of the Year. The accolades were there, the recognition was there, but the awareness and direction were veering off on the wrong path.

Another consequence of losing is that teams are going to make changes. After that season we changed head coaches. I was a fan of Petitbon—I thought he was a really good coach. In my view, if we had maintained the emphasis on the downfield passing game, at the very least, I feel we would have been 8–8 or 9–7. We would have scored more points, especially with the receiving corps we had.

Art Monk was still playing at a high level, Ricky Sanders was one of the most explosive guys and best route runners I've ever seen. We had Frank Wycheck as an H-back—he would have fit well within that system of two–tight end sets and then play action. We had the backs to run downhill and handle play action—we were having decent success running the football here and there.

We were trying to infuse the power run with the West Coast offense, and the West Coast is built more from a running aspect on zone runs, quick passes, three-step throws. The Redskins offense for so long was play action off of counters and power run and throwing the ball downfield. That disconnect cost Coach Petitbon his job after one year, and that was kind of the first inkling of when I started understanding football being a business.

In DC, man, if you are with the Redskins and are doing well, you have the run of the town. They love the Redskins—the support was great. There were some opportunities from a marketing side that I didn't take advantage of. But I was looking at other things and not staying true to what got me where I was. That was hard work, competing, and staying connected with God. Notre Dame is a Catholic institution, and the one thing that struck me most there was my ability to stay grounded in Christ. But I ended up completely going away from that, and it started just a little bit at a time.

You also lose sight of those people who have been there for you and supported you before you had anything—before you were anybody. That line of who is really there for you and who is there to get something from you gets skewed. I truly lost sight of that, which caused me to pull away from the people who really cared for me. I distanced myself from people who even, from a football training standpoint, were there for me and helped me. The person I always think about is Green—his tenacity, his training, his commitment. Had I stuck with him and continued to train with him, I definitely would have played longer. I would have had a longer career, but I also would have had a better sense of self-worth.

CHAPTER 23
WHERE DO I GO FROM HERE?

T he success of my rookie year with the Redskins was definitely a carryover from what had taken place my senior year in South Bend. It was one of those years where I had some momentum going—and really kept it going. At the same time there was a definite disconnect from my senior year to my rookie year in regard to the feeling of team unity, team bonding, and camaraderie.

It's not that there was not camaraderie at the pro level—I had some very good mentors with the Redskins. But it was not as cohesive of a unit team-wise, in terms of the different positions and different sides of the ball. Then we had the disparity of ages with rookies coming in, and they were just a few years removed from winning the Super Bowl. Tack onto that the collective bargaining agreement that was initiated and that cut the free-agency aspect that came with the new NFL. With free agency you couldn't hold onto players the same way. So you did not have that bond.

At Notre Dame there was consistency as it related to the head coach and the athletic department for the program. That wasn't there with the Redskins. While I had some success individually that rookie year, we were collapsing as a team. It was a struggle for me to understand the concept of life as a professional and all that goes with it. The season was much longer, it had much tougher competition, and it was a greater grind. I always felt I could have done more. I just felt the disconnect team-wise. We had such good talent, but we were not maximizing it. We had opportunities, but they did not bear themselves out.

We had a new offensive coordinator and we had more defensive continuity because Petitbon had been the defensive coordinator. We did not have that on offense. I did not have a problem sharing the ball with Ervins, Byner, or Mitchell—I was used to not having to be a featured back. That was not a focal point for me. It was more of a struggle for me to not win. I would have been happy playing special teams if we were successful at winning games.

The further we got into the season, the more frustrating it became. It just did not come together even though guys were working their butts off. I worked mine off; I was so intense that Byner once said, "Rook, you need to slow down." I was hyped up for every game—but it took an emotional toll on me.

Not that each game was not important, but they did not carry the weight that they did in college, when if you lost the game you were out of the hunt. In the NFL, you can't invest so much. I wish I had spent more time with guys like Art Monk, Byner, and Ricky Sanders to learn the nuances of being a professional—how to manage your emotions. It's the full aspect of the game—of being an NFL player.

I remember how much of a grind it was when we lost games. It was not that we did not care, but we also had to manage our mental and physical wherewithal to complete a 16-game season. You cannot have those enormous highs every single game—it's just not a sustainable way to play and compete. I definitely did not learn soon enough how to manage playing that part of the game. I took it personally when we didn't have success. What did I not do right? That's how we functioned at Notre Dame.

I was uncomfortable being anything close to the face of the program with veterans on the team who had won championships. It was disconcerting—I did not want my teammates to feel like I thought I was better than them. There was a tension, a lot of it of my own doing. My teammates never looked at me as if I needed to watch myself or do this or that—no one put me in my place. And these were individuals who had played on the biggest stage.

I wanted to perform and win. It stuck with me and it was hard to shake. I had to find a way to win. I would get home from a game and feel banged up. I'd prop myself up on pillows, and I would go back through the game. I missed this block, I missed this play. I would beat myself up all night over things I did not do well enough. I created this tension and anxiety that I never processed because I'd hear superlatives about myself but not about my team. It never sat well with me that year.

Meanwhile, I had my head in the sand in terms of what was going on off the field, including my personal finances. I needed to learn how to say no to people. I became more cynical and reclusive in some ways, and the game became less fun. I had to learn the understanding that came with being a professional athlete. Even some of my own family members saw me as more of an opportunity than a person. It created some distance.

When things did not go well at Notre Dame I would hunker down and figure it out on my own. But that behavior was disruptive, and it made me look at people in a cynical manner and not as God intended. I started to lose perspective on how I attained that success—the work, tenacity, determination, and drive that got me to that point.

As Coach Holtz always warned, "You're reading your damn-ass press clippings." And I started to do that—I thought I was bigger than I really was. NFL stands for "Not for Long" when you do not maintain perspective. And I definitely learned that the hard way.

CHAPTER 24
SECOND TIME AROUND

My second year in the NFL was the most grueling—and maybe the worst—year of my life. It seemed like everything that could go wrong did go wrong. The writing was probably on the wall—I just did not take the time to see it. You are responsible for yourself in the NFL. Your opportunities are limited, and when you don't maximize them, they can easily be taken away and you'll find yourself reeling.

It all started with the change in coaching. With Coach Petitbon fired, pretty much the entire staff turned over. With free agency and the new collective bargaining agreement, they started to move veterans—and the Redskins at the time were a veteran-laden team.

Christina and I made the decision to get married, and our wedding was going to be in July right before camp. But our families were not on the same page. Plus I was trying to learn a new offense, figure out a new system, and get familiar with a new coach. It was a snowball effect that started and kept going. When I got frustrated I leaned on football, worked out, and ran at the complex. I knew what I needed to do to get ready. But I was distracted by my wedding, which took a toll on me.

Minicamps went well—I was picking up the offense. Norv Turner was our new head coach—he'd been the offensive coordinator of the Dallas Cowboys when they'd won Super Bowls. I liked the offense—I liked what I needed to do. I was making strides and felt good about where things were heading in football. I would go to the complex twice a day to get away from the drama with my family. It felt like everything was closing in on me, but I couldn't escape because that was life—you have to take on things like this.

I was getting more attention and publicity both within the organization and outside the organization—and a disagreement about team use of my image ended up creating a major rift. I felt the team ran an ad with my photo without my permission, but the Redskins felt they had rights to my image because I was in a Redskins uniform.

The whole matter was elevated to the level of the president of the team—and his grandson was the person handling the marketing. I did

That's me as a rookie, on the run with the Redskins in 1993.

not think this was an issue—I thought it was part of the collective bargaining agreement. But the Redskins thought I was being unreasonable as far as my representation went.

John Cooke called me into his office one day, and this was just one more thing added to my plate. All I wanted to do was play football and win some football games. It went from the marketing group to the president, and I was completely taken aback.

Our team president, Jack Cooke, always introduced me and Carter to people as his Notre Dame guys. We were the first- and second-round picks of the Redskins the previous year. But my relationship with the organization took a turn with this issue. I wasn't sure I was wanted at that point. And, as it turned out, that was the beginning of the end of my time with the Redskins.

Then at the end of minicamp I tweaked my knee in practice. I got an X-ray and found out that it was a meniscus tear. My right knee would lock up and I lost some stability. This was late June, which wasn't long before training camp. There was an opportunity to let it heal up, but I went right out and had a surgical scope even though I probably should have gotten a second opinion.

I had the scope a month before training camp. The surgery should have taken close to an hour, but it only took 30 minutes because my knee was actually in good shape. It was only a fingernail-sized meniscus tear. So now I was going gangbusters to get ready for training camp. Within a couple of days of the surgery, I was rehabbing. It was grueling every day, and I was already losing ground.

Terry Allen from Minnesota came in to help at running back, coming off two knee surgeries of his own. I was fighting to get back and be the featured back, but I should not have had the surgery—I should have let it heal naturally. I would have missed most of training camp, but maybe I would have ended up in better shape.

We called off the wedding and ended up getting married at the justice of the peace because of a combination of the family disagreements and my injury. A lot of things were spiraling, which made for a rough year.

The season was beginning, and I was almost starting from scratch. I got back and could practice and do the things that were asked of me, but little by little, I was being phased out. It was one thing not to be a starter. But special teams was not even presented as an option—I was barely being allowed to participate and it was depressing.

I felt more and more isolated. No one could give me answers as to why I wasn't being given a chance to play. I did okay with a couple of preseason opportunities, but I was not as sharp as I wanted to be. I was working the rust off. Something happened during the surgery and I no longer had the explosiveness.

I thought the Redskins believed I could get back, but little by little I was told that even special teams was not an option. I was third on the depth chart and was kept on the team. But things had changed, and it seemed as if a lot had stemmed from my meeting with the president of the organization over the marketing matter.

CHAPTER 25
DIFFICULTIES IN DC

My second year with the Redskins I found myself in and out of the lineup. I felt I was penalized for my disagreement with ownership, and that was very frustrating. It soured me on the NFL. And it opened my eyes wide that the NFL was about playing the game and making sure you didn't upset the wrong people who had a large impact on where you went and your opportunities.

It felt like I was being picked on, even if I really wasn't. I went back into my shell, retreated within myself, and did not take advantage of the help that was offered to me. I felt like I was drowning. I did not handle the expectations, and I did not reach out to the resources I could have. The lack of confidence in who I was as a person changed my perception of the league.

I lost my starting job. I tried to rededicate myself and get myself up to speed so I could start the regular season off on a better note, but it was not what I was used to. My second year in 1994 was no better—we went 3–13 and, again, we were last in the NFC East.

It was tough not winning, and I was not the only one struggling with it. The Redskins were known for winning games. It was hard not to feel like you were part of the reason the success wasn't happening. In 1994 we were throwing the ball more and still not having more success. Terry Allen took the top running back spot as I struggled to find my way back.

The entire battle made it difficult to stay there and feel part of the program. It was nothing against my teammates. When Coach Norv Turner came in, I thought it would be a chance for me to shine. When that did not happen it was disheartening. The narrative seemed to be that I was against the organization and that I was blaming everyone but myself. It created a rift, and all I wanted to do was contribute. I never understood why the marketing issue affected what we were doing on the field.

I was never one to gripe, but it seemed like it was always something negative. I would have a good week of practice and get to the game and then be told I was not dressing. It weighed on me. I was perceived in a light that was not who I was. Once Allen arrived I was just a backup. I took a few first- and second-team reps—but a lot with the scout team too. Defensive guys would ask why I wasn't playing, and I did not have an answer for them. Allen was a great player and a great guy. But I never had an opportunity to play up.

I had 92 yards in our second game of the year against New Orleans and 57 the next week against the Giants, but that's about it. I only scored two touchdowns all season and finished with 297 yards on fewer than half the carries I had as a rookie.

I played in only one game and carried the ball twice in that third year in 1995—and the team finished 6–10.

That was the end for me in Washington.

CHAPTER 26
ON TO TAMPA BAY

In the off-season I was released by the Redskins and picked up by the Tampa Bay Buccaneers. It was a new start for me, and I was appreciative of that. Tony Dungy was the head coach—I had always heard great things about him.

I was still devastated by my time with the Redskins and feeling like I hadn't had a chance to reach my potential. I was a castoff, if you will. Trying to start over with another team, trying to build a team—at least I had another chance.

By the time I got there, I had developed a relationship with Darrell Green with the Skins, so Hardy Nickerson of the Bucs took me under his wing. I was always appreciative of that because Green told him, "Look out for this guy."

We did not start out like gangbusters. We lost our first five games in 1996. We were a young team trying to find our way and early on it was tough sledding. We were not putting points on the board, so it was a rough go.

I did have some chances to play though—five games with 14 or more carries, including 26 in one game against Seattle. I gained 114 yards and scored a touchdown against Denver and gained 65 yards in that Seattle game. But the opportunities dwindled later in the year. I only had six combined carries in November and December.

I connected with some really good people in Tampa. I think the world of Coach Dungy and also Tony Nathan, the running backs coach. I had great respect for Herm Edwards, our secondary coach; Lovie Smith, who coached linebackers; and defensive coordinator Monte Kiffin.

When we played Seattle I connected again with Mirer. Carter was still with the Redskins, and we played them late in the year. As I struggled through from a confidence standpoint, I was also part of a team that was struggling to win and play at a high level. It was tough. I never quite found my place to some degree. Even though I felt more a part of that team compared to the last two years with the Redskins, it was still difficult.

Not winning made me feel out of place because it was not the environment I was used to. We won only once in our first nine games. As the season wore on, Errict Rhett came back and my opportunities to play started to dwindle. Little by little I felt like I was being pushed to the side. I tried to understand where I stood and where I was and who I was as a person. In some ways I was right back to where I started with the Redskins in terms of feeling like I was not good enough. I felt less and less like I belonged and less and less like a football player.

We limped to a 6–10 finish and that pretty much summed up the last three years of my pro career. You go from being all-rookie and considered a top player to being out of the league. That was a tough pill to

Starting over in Tampa for me came in 1996, after three seasons in Washington.

swallow. The Tampa general manager said they tried to trade me, but they were told I was a problem in the locker room. That was devastating. I prided myself on being someone who could be counted on by my teammates. The Tampa people said they found that not to be true about me, but it wasn't enough.

The time I spent with the Bucs was difficult in terms of trying to find my way back. But I felt I was part of a culture shift with the people they had coming in that year who were on the team. The leadership had definitely improved. I reconnected with DuBose, my old teammate from Notre Dame. It was telling to see differences in leadership from one organization to the next. It was a definite improvement from the Redskins, even if Washington had a greater and longer history. I saw the difference in myself from one organization to the next other and the effect on the guys I played with.

That year with the Bucs had an impact on me, seeing and playing with some very talented individuals. Coach Dungy changed the culture of the organization. There was a big difference in training camp—we practiced in downtown Tampa and there was more of a family connection. I developed some really good friendships with some really good people I still consider friends today.

Nickerson took me under his wing. Warren Sapp was a fun guy to be around. Going against John Lynch in practice was something else with his tenacity and physicality. We had a good young quarterback in Trent Dilfer, so seeing his maturation was enjoyable. Our fullback Mike Alstott was an absolute beast.

The competitiveness was fun, but not in a combative way. Martin Mayhew and Regan Upshaw were some young guys coming in and having success—plus Jerry Ellison, Alvin Harper, and Rhett. Those guys worked their butts off in forming a sense of togetherness.

There had been a changing of the guard in Washington with a lot of veteran guys released. But with the Bucs there was good leadership and mentorship and a really good mix. It was great to be a part of that. We were not just a bunch of guys in sherbet orange uniforms.

I knew I wasn't where I needed to be mentally. But it was a good change of perspective in terms of dealing with people. Coach Dungy had a care for the players that was genuine—the same with Coach Nathan and Coach Smith. We didn't have great success that first year, but it was a definite move in the right direction. You could see the confidence we gained—guys started to believe. They believed in Coach Dungy and Coach Kiffin and what was being presented to them.

I never heard Coach Dungy swear—you knew when he got upset, but he expected you to still be a man. In the NFL you are told where to go and what to do—everything is mapped out for you. It's very structured. But at Tampa Bay you did not feel like you were sequestered—you were given the freedom to express yourself and be who you were. They looked at you like an adult.

Guys in the locker room—some were religious, some were loud, but it was not forced. Guys were real and made connections and trusted each other and believed in each other. It gave me perspective on leadership—who are you willing to follow?—and accountability. That was a big thing at Notre Dame and was a big part of what made up those teams—expectations and accountability.

Coach Dungy had the respect of all the players—even from the players who weren't playing. And he demanded that players treat each other with respect. It was a real team focus and commitment, and there was a strong bond between the players that went beyond the field. I was thankful for that opportunity. I wasn't where I needed to be as a football player—I did not have the fire and determination. But I was grateful for my time there. I felt like I belonged and that I was a part of the team.

When Tampa Bay released me after my first year there, I immediately went back to Oklahoma. I did not give myself a chance to get back and try to re-sign and play there or somewhere else. I wish I would have learned that lesson sooner. I saw the championship momentum and belief-building—the young guys did a great job meshing with the veteran guys. And eventually it led to a championship. It was Coach Dungy's team even though he was not there. (Dungy was fired after the

2001 season despite a winning record. The Bucs won the Super Bowl the following season under coach Jon Gruden.) You saw the turn from that 6–10 season when I was there to a hint of what was to come. Tampa Bay went 10–6 in that next year and it just continued from there.

It set the course for me later in life. I made the wrong decision that affected me and my family, and that set the tone for the next few years of my life being in limbo. I was searching for myself and my identity. We all need others; you can't do it by yourself. You'd rather not learn it the hard way, but that's how you gain or regain confidence in yourself. It put me on a track to reconnect with my faith and rebuild my relationship with God. I regret not staying, but I don't regret the time I spent there and the lessons I started learning.

CHAPTER 27
HEADING BACK HOME

After my release from Tampa Bay I was struggling more emotionally and my confidence was at an all-time low. I did not understand the professional level of football—I made the decision to pack up my family and move back to Oklahoma. I did not give myself the opportunity to be brought back to the team. It was like I left in the middle of the night in a sense.

I struggled with my emotions and closed myself off again like I did my first year and a half at Notre Dame. It affected my outlook on myself. I doubted the game of football—the purity of the sport. It once again opened my eyes to the business of pro football. It was a different experience from the camaraderie, passion, care, and what that all meant at Notre Dame. It gave me a feel for what Notre Dame really was—those locker room moments that always come back to you. There were far fewer of those at the professional level. It allowed me to see more clearly how special my teammates at Notre Dame were and what it meant to be a college football player. It's the maturity you have to develop and the care for others—even if you do not consciously think about it.

I did not reach out to anyone in the Bucs organization to tell them I was leaving, and I really regret that now. There was a sense of community in the locker room and Coach Dungy was strong in his faith. At the time, I did not realize the level of his impact on me. He did not have to talk about his faith all the time. The guys I was around—I sensed their faith in terms of how they lived. I saw it in their actions and how they treated each other.

I didn't give myself a chance to be part of what was going on there. There was a harmony there that was very different than what I'd seen in Washington but very similar to my four years at Notre Dame. But I still treasure my time in Tampa. The people I connected with and the people in the locker room—guys with different values who still found a way to build community. Just that variation of individuals—married and single; younger, brash guys and older, seasoned individuals. Coach Dungy brought it all together.

It was a blessing, but not seeing it at the time was my fault because I went into a shell when I left Tampa. There were people who supported me—my wife tried to help me through it, and somehow I did not realize the impact my decision had on my family. I was only thinking about myself. I thought I understood football, at least the game. But the politics of it were something altogether different—that was always such a challenge to me.

I did not see what was in front of me because I was so distraught about being released a second time. I did not have a very good understanding of how I got to that point again. I felt like I had failed. How could I fail at something I was so certain of? Maybe I tried to become someone I was not—maybe I had tried to please people.

Football becomes a part of who you are—it's part of your DNA. So when you are told you cannot do this or you are not good enough, it shakes you to the core. I struggled to process what happened and how I got there. I was responsible now for a whole family. I hid behind my family instead of fighting through and listening to what God wanted for me. I did not like myself. I could not see past the pain and aggravation of my current situation, and it forced me to really dig deep.

You hurt those you love the most when you don't know where you are. You point to other places and never realize that you're not looking at yourself. I did not want to face the reality of what I had become, which carried on for a period of months. When you are fighting everyone around you, you are in a dark place that's almost impossible to get out of.

Going back to Tulsa felt like going to a place where I had to hunker down and protect myself. It was about how you were viewed in terms of getting out of the community. I did not want anyone in Tulsa to see me and think, "He's back, and he did not make it." That's the power of doubt and self-loathing and not believing in yourself. You feel like you failed yourself and you feel like you failed your community by being less than you were supposed to be. You did not give yourself the space to be more than a football player.

I wouldn't take calls from guys who reached out to support me—from Notre Dame and Tampa. They tried to tell me I should come back. "You are a part of this," they said. But I wouldn't listen. You need to have perspective and have people calling you out and demanding better of you. It's hard to find your way when you lose it. So that's where I stayed for several months.

CHAPTER 28
BACK TO SQUARE ONE

A s an athlete you always think you can barrel through, even though it's not always a physical issue. You just go to work and plow through it. That's how I was successful in athletics—when you have a setback you bear down and push through it.

But you have to live and go forward. The confidence I had gained at Notre Dame and the early days of the NFL had disappeared. It was all gone. I had a new focus and purpose. But I was running in place.

Things didn't get any better until my wife pushed me about finishing school. I had separated myself from Notre Dame in a lot of respects. But that was the silver lining of finding my way forward and living and developing my life.

There were people who cared about my well-being whom I did not even think to reach out to. There was my former Notre Dame teammate Lamar Guillory—he was always positive and looking to be a help to others—and he was from Tulsa. There were Notre Dame people like Felix Park, Bill Warren, and the Siegfried family. Park actually used to film our high school football games and send copies to the Notre Dame football office.

Finally, through those connections, I was able to secure a job with Ray Siegfried's IT data department at St. Francis Hospital. My degree was in management information systems, so it was a glimmer of light. As I connected with more individuals from Notre Dame, the power of that university network really came to light. But even then I did not fully appreciate what it meant.

We moved to Broken Arrow, Oklahoma, and lived there for about a year. I thought that there had to be more opportunities out there, and my eyes were a little more open and receptive. It was hard for me to ask for help—it was just so against how I grew up. You have to fight for yourself—that's what I believed and what I was taught growing up. A big part of why I ultimately sought assistance was more about building relationships—the human side of communication with other people.

I finally reached out to Warren and he helped arrange for both me and my wife to finish our degrees—I can't thank this man and his family enough. It was empowering. My mom had maintained a relationship with Warren beyond me and my brother attending Notre Dame. It's not about the money—this helped me understand the importance of people. Finding myself and developing a concept of who I was ended up being fed through reaching out and developing these kinds of relationships.

You hear about the power of the NFL, but for me, it was the power of the Notre Dame network. It was about allowing myself to connect with people—getting to know people and letting people get to know me. I would look for the best in others but would never let people see the best in me. I continued to look within and try to find myself, which was instrumental as I started making these connections. It was the people close to me who cared more about me than I did about myself. I started to get a foothold. But the desire to play was still there—I had not completely let that go.

* * *

Over the summer I connected with NFL Europe and realized there was a chance to get back and play professionally. In the spring of 1998 I went to Barcelona, Spain, and tried to make the Barcelona Dragons team at a minicamp. I earned a roster spot and was there for two and a half months.

I found myself injured again—I sprained my knee after having a pretty good start to the season. I just was not the same, and this all happened in a limited time frame, so there weren't a lot of opportunities. Being injured in NFL Europe was kind of a nail in the coffin. Each game mattered because it was about getting film to distribute to NFL teams.

My wife and three kids were able to come over after they got out of school, and we got to see a different part of the world. That was my first time outside the United States, and it was so enlightening.

Again, you see the importance of people. We were in Sitges, Spain, a Mediterranean coastal town. When you open up a little bit you can find out about a different culture. You take some chances and get to know people who speak a different language and live differently. I credit my wife with this experience because she pushed me out of my comfort zone. I had never been separated from my family before, and all of a sudden I was in a country that was completely different. It was amazing how much that experience elevated our relationship and opened me up more to develop relationships.

CHAPTER 29
THAT ND NETWORK WORKS

I came back from Barcelona, and I was still looking to try to make it back to the NFL and continue the dream I had growing up. It didn't pan out with NFL Europe, but it did offer me the opportunity to experience a different culture and a different perspective.

While I was in Barcelona and Sitges, I ran into several Notre Dame fans and several Notre Dame alumni. Through that Notre Dame connection we started a Bible study group for the guys there who really wanted to continue expressing their faith. One thing about Spain that was cool was that they had a ton of churches—really beautiful old churches that were basically museums.

I didn't go out of my way to try to elevate or promote my Notre Dame connections, but they were everywhere. I was in Spain and would run into Notre Dame people, and at the time I also had Notre Dame teammates playing in NFL Europe. McGill was playing in Amsterdam so I got to connect with him. There was always a little something different as it pertained to the Notre Dame guys. There was some appreciation for what it meant to be a Notre Dame athlete that resonated around the world.

The opportunity to play against some teammates and have that chance to reconnect was very cathartic. I'd still go out and play on my bum leg, but I knew a little more than halfway through the season that my opportunities to play in the NFL were really slim. I sort of shifted gears in a sense and said I was just going to enjoy and appreciate this opportunity. It wasn't as if something was going wrong. I really took the time to connect with different people, engage with people, and be a little more thoughtful in the conversations I was having. And it really set the path for me coming back to America.

I had talked to Bill Warren about returning to Notre Dame, and in the summer of 1998, I went back to South Bend to take some classes there. I was still working back in Oklahoma, but I only had a few classes left to finish. In the spring of 1999, we moved into a townhome in South Bend so I could finish my degree.

With Warren, it was all about caring for people. That was a lesson that I started to learn—money is fleeting and things are fleeting, but it's the relationships that you build that are going to sustain you through other aspects of your life. The educational opportunity would not have presented itself if not for a few individuals—my wife and her tenacity to push me and Warren, who was very instrumental. It blessed me to no end.

I am still trying to figure out how to communicate what he did and what it meant to me. He'll never know—there are no words to describe how he blessed my family and continued to bless us for years. I'm not a very emotional person, but I still struggle today to articulate how impactful that was for me. It really set the tone for how I engaged with other people and it changed my perspective. That helped me to open up more and seek out individuals who were associated with Notre Dame in my hometown and other places, which then pushed me to build, or rebuild, a relationship with Notre Dame.

In a lot of respects going back to Tulsa was a reminder of where I'd come from. It opened me up to a different world that was in my home-town and my relationship to individuals who were connected to Notre Dame. And with that, little by little, my Notre Dame family started to expand. I still wasn't ready to reach out to former teammates. I had anecdotal conversations with guys I was close to in school, but it was still very limited. But I started to imagine that there was a little more to this. And that there's more to Notre Dame than just the prestige of the name and the degree and the opportunities. It really is about the people.

What was so amazing about returning to Notre Dame to finish my degree was the fact that I started to reconnect with Chris Zorich, who was there getting his law degree. I used to be scared to death of this man because he would chase me around when I was part of the scout team. He was pretty darn aggressive, and he still was with the Chicago Bears at that time.

I was 27 years old and back at Notre Dame, and I had a better grasp of the academic material and a better focus because I was there to finish my degree. I had a greater appreciation, and I put in more effort to connect with professors. I was so much more in tune—there was a confidence from an academic standpoint that I did not have when I was in school there as a student-athlete. It was a different perspective and a level of maturity that were very beneficial.

A lot of the people in class didn't know me as Reggie Brooks, the football player. Not having that burden helped me flourish over that spring and summer to finish. In some ways I felt more a part of Notre Dame during that time than I really did as a student-athlete. That's something that will always stick with me.

CHAPTER 30
WHERE DO I GO FROM HERE?

My identity was in playing sports and everything revolved around that. When the opportunity wasn't there, I was forced to see things beyond football. That was one of the reasons I chose to go to Notre Dame—the opportunities beyond football and connecting with that far-reaching Notre Dame network. That's all you can ask for—the opportunity. Now I had to reassess, find myself, and see what I could do beyond playing football. Everything until that point had been worked around my desire to go back and play.

I completed my degree at Notre Dame, and it was a beautiful moment for me because I was able to share it with my family. I was moving in a productive direction.

I learned about maximizing opportunities while playing football. And that helped me understand the value of the Notre Dame connections beyond football—it's about people, it's about relationships, it's about networking. Originally I did not do that well enough at Notre Dame on a foundational level. It was actually the network reaching out to me. You hear about it, but it has to manifest in something tangible. You have to engage with it, and I was very passive at times in that engagement. It does not just happen—you have to help it happen. I was learning more about who I was beyond the game.

I, at least, was inquiring about what this network was about. What does having a Notre Dame degree mean? Put your head down and mind your business. But this football thing was still prevalent.

* * *

I had never thought I would do anything related to coaching. But I actually started to coach at a local Tulsa high school. This was something that kept me connected to football. I was working in IT, but at times I felt a little empty just sitting at a desk. Going back to what I learned at Notre Dame, I wanted to give back.

I thought this was a chance for me to give back and maintain a connection to something I enjoyed being around. I helped my uncle Tony Peters coach at McLain High School in Tulsa. My NFL background gave me some cachet, but I never really thought I would be doing this from a career standpoint. Still, the more I did it the more I enjoyed it.

I also connected with an NFL program designed to help former players transition to their next careers. I really commend the NFL for that. It required some work to engage, which was something I was starting to do more of. Guy Troupe was a former football player from my high school—through this program that he led I found out I was not the only one who struggled to make the transition.

They had two tracks: one for coaching and one for broadcasting. I wound up coaching in NFL Europe with Peter Vaas, whom I knew well as he was an assistant coach when I played at Notre Dame.

* * *

In the summer of 2000 I also played for a Notre Dame alumni team. Former Notre Dame quarterback Pat Steenberge put the team together and we played a game in Hamburg, Germany. It was pretty wild—I think we're the only university to have an alumni team like that go play a team from a different country. It was awesome getting that group together—getting some of these guys back together—including Dean Lytle, Terry Andrysiak, Mark Brooks, Becton, my college roommate Jarrell, Clint Johnson, Ivory Covington, Eilers (who also had played with the Redskins), Pritchett, Dave Butler, Brandy Wells, Francisco, Brian Hamilton, and lots more. It was so great to reconnect with those guys. It was such an eclectic group of guys—a bunch of old guys—but having the chance to strap on the pads again was great. And to do that overseas was a beautiful thing—it was the Notre Dame network at its best.

Only Notre Dame would be able to pull this off—take former alumni and give them gear, pads, and helmets. All we had to do was bring our own shoes. To do this required so many moving parts—I still marvel at Steenberge and what he does with his company to promote American football opportunities overseas.

It was cathartic for me to participate and play the game I love and do it with a group of guys I admired. It helped me maintain that connection and helped me understand it was not going to be my day job. It was a chance to represent Notre Dame and it showed how much people care. I was the MVP in the game, but it was not about the accolades. It was about the camaraderie—being in the locker room again. I played with guys I had never played with and I saw the commonality in the thought process—we were representing Notre Dame. We were very fortunate to represent and uphold the standards we learned while we were at Notre Dame. I was grateful to have that opportunity. It helped me start to consider the opportunities beyond the game.

The company that owned the Hamburg Blue Devils, the team we played over there, wanted me to come to Germany and work in IT and play football. That's a common thing in Europe—you have a job for a company and also play football. But my time had passed. I was committed to coming home and reassessing things with my wife and family. Where do I go from here? What's my skill set beyond football?

That game in Hamburg showed me that football was just a game, but life is more than a game. To see what my former teammates were doing was impactful. That helped me in my transition, seeing how those guys had moved on from football and made successful lives for themselves.

CHAPTER 31
BERLIN TO INDIANAPOLIS

A s I continued to coach with my uncle, I became a little more intrigued by the opportunity. I still felt a sense of loss and confusion—and I had some Notre Dame teammates who were still playing, so football was always in the back of my mind. I just could never picture myself coaching. Most of my coaches were tough and regimented, and I'm not sure that's the mind-set of younger generations.

When I got that call from my Booker T. Washington High School connection, Guy Troupe, it seemed like another opportunity. It was a think tank—a working session. The NFL did its due diligence to try to be aware of the issues and pitfalls of the transition from playing the game. And the program helped me reflect on my own transition.

When I left the league I did not watch pro football games and I did not want to hear about the NFL. But it's critical that you remember people and that they remember you. I had not spoken to Troupe since high school and now he was in a role assisting the NFL. That networking component became critical in that situation. It helped me process where I was. This allowed me to see some things and take stock of my life. You see others who are struggling and there's a little embarrassment from feeling like a failure. It's hard to move forward if you haven't dealt with those feelings about no longer being in that space of being a professional athlete.

The league program of transitioning into coaching or broadcasting was all about staying part of the game. I listened and took notes. You would coach in NFL Europe and then you were part of an NFL franchise during the preseason. My wife's constant support was critical, and I was just trying to figure this out.

I joined the Berlin Thunder team with Peter Vaas, and it was a perfect fit. He'd also been the running backs coach when I played in Barcelona, so I knew the system he was running, and I really enjoyed the experience. It was not about the money—it was the chance to be a part of something bigger than myself and to communicate that to someone else and feed into those individuals. I had a good rapport with people, and I knew the game.

That summer in Berlin was very impactful because at the end of the summer term with the Thunder, I came back and participated in the Indianapolis Colts training camp under Coach Dungy and interned with his coaching staff.

Berlin was awesome—visiting another country and experiencing Germany and seeing the divide between east and west. It was the same city, but you could see where the wall had been—there was such a difference in the look and feel of the country based on that dividing line.

How to really be a team influenced my approach in coaching and working. It was about working together to be successful. We had a rough season in Berlin, but it was successful as far as the rapport I developed with the coaches, which helped me better define my coaching style and how I communicated. I felt very much at home in Germany in that sense.

The Thunder finished 3–7, but it was a positive learning experience to understand who I was and what I wanted to do and where I was going. It presented an opportunity. It was a lesson learned in how to understand a situation when things do not go your way. Football is a consummate team sport and requires more than a few individuals being successful. Everybody has to buy in.

* * *

I then started my internship with the Colts, and I certainly had the utmost respect for Coach Dungy in terms of how he led—how he ran a team. I was hoping it could turn into another opportunity as an analyst for the team. With players like Reggie Wayne, Marvin Harrison, and Peyton Manning, this was a very good team already—obviously moving in the right direction. I spent July and August with them—another great experience.

Tom Moore was the offensive coordinator, and I learned so much from him in terms of how to construct a playbook and how to construct a practice. He had been with the Steelers for a number of years. He was a little grizzly, but he was willing to teach and that always stuck with me. He spoke to you and not at you. He was willing to listen and let you know why he agreed or disagreed. He let you know that he heard you, and he would hear you out. He did not know me from Adam—he's been around a long list of All-Pros. But he made me feel like a person who could contribute something. He knew I was trying to learn and understand, and he offered his expertise—he had plenty of that.

That training camp gave me a great appreciation for the football IQ of Manning—and this was just practice. He practiced how he played. You could not practice with him unless you knew the playbook inside and out. He was very structured. He could dissect a play—dissect a defense—and if you were not good at disguising your defense he would eat you up.

Moore would send in a play, but it had multiple meanings and it was up to Manning to process all this based on the defense. There were multiple dimensions within one play call. Manning would run the play that gave them the best opportunity to succeed. It was a very fluid system, but it was not easy. It was extremely complex in how it was run. Routes and blocking schemes were all in one play, with multiple meanings depending on the defense. Everybody had to be on the same page.

Dallas Clark was the tight end, and he came in late, so they were trying to bring him up to speed. But Manning was so far ahead of him. If you were not locked in, you could not succeed. I was talking to Manning once about something simple, and I tried to nicely suggest that maybe he was a little intimidating because of his knowledge. Understand that Manning carried a lot of weight.

I mentioned to him that you have to bring people along to get them up to speed. You have to get the info across to someone else. He did not know me, but maybe it made him think about being a little more empathetic. How do we get someone to the level of understanding he needs so he can be effective and productive on a consistent basis? So many coaches are system-oriented, but you have to be open to new ideas and perspectives.

Moore had constructed this thing with all the flexibility that was so dynamic and so refreshing and it called for some real creativity—absolutely right up Manning's alley. That opened me up to be more receptive to hear more about flexibility. His playbook was built over years. He developed it at all the different places he had been with all the different players he had coached. It was always responsive to the situation at hand, and I had never known the game to be like that—flexibility but still with continuity as a team. His playbook was a living entity because it morphed over time—he was always looking for what was next. I am in awe even to this day because it was so refreshing and open-minded. You could see all the possibilities.

Coach Dungy dealt more with the defense, but he engaged with the coaching staff as he delegated. He trusted the people who coached with him. He asked for my opinion, and that was impactful for me. At the first preseason game I watched the pregame, and they ran every single route—Manning and Wayne versus every single coverage. It reminded me of the visualization we did the night before games at Notre Dame. The Colts executed the passing game as well as anyone at the NFL level.

I was not chosen for the one analyst role and, in some ways, that set me back to square one again. I thought I had found my calling, so it was a bit deflating. But I cherished the opportunity. It was just another thing that propelled me forward. It was a learning experience that helped me develop. I was going to keep working to be better.

CHAPTER 32
A WINDOW OPENS
IN SOUTH BEND

D espite not getting the extended opportunity with the Colts, I thought I'd made a lot of strides and put a lot of energy into it—it was all about putting together a game plan, film study, and everything else that went into it.

I learned a lot in Indianapolis about how to engage with others and be open to other perspectives. Being a part of a successful team is always based on feelings of trust. It's not as much about talent, it's more about how much you care for someone else and how much they care for you. And you perform at a high level to show that with your approach. I needed to see how impactful it was to life—not about just a game and not just about me. I did not need to chalk it up as if I'd been mistreated because that wasn't the case.

Back in Tulsa I applied for a position with Union Public Schools in the technology department. They were part of a system change, and I had experience in project management. Meanwhile, we were pregnant with our fourth child.

It was August of 2003 and we had carved out a decent life, but it was not what I thought was meant for me. I was just existing—there was so much more I should have been doing, but I didn't allow myself room to grow. But you find out what you are made of when you change your perspective. You can't lie down and roll over when you are told no. You need to dig deeper, find something within, and move out and take a chance.

I was comfortable at Union Public Schools, but it still never felt completely right. The change to a new system went well, and I started to think about helping coach at Union. But eventually my wife and I sat down and talked about where we really wanted to raise our children.

I had submitted an application to the Office of Information Technologies at Notre Dame some time back, and I got a call in October, three or four months after submitting it. Notre Dame was a place we felt a connection to. There was a love for the place and the feeling of community and people who cared for us. We both felt strongly about that environment.

I got a call saying they wanted me to come and interview. Notre Dame was going from an HP system to a new one, and I had years of experience with that kind of system change. I went for the interview in January, they offered me the job, and I accepted. As we were packing the kids, I was thinking, "This is where I need to be."

We drove our U-Haul to our new apartment and I immediately felt this sense of opportunity—it felt so right to be back. When you hear people talk about being back home, this felt like being home, returning to Notre Dame.

CHAPTER 33
BACK TO CAMPUS

We returned to Notre Dame in February of 2004, and one of the first things my wife and I did was visit the Grotto. We went to campus and brought the kids to see the beauty of it all. We lit a candle and were just taking it all in. We headed back to the car, down by the old log cabin, and we ran into Father Hesburgh, the former Notre Dame president. He was taking a stroll around campus. It was so surreal to see this legendary figure all by himself—he's a national landmark personified. It almost felt like we were students back on campus.

We decided to go over and introduce ourselves. He wasn't president when my wife and I were students there, yet he remembered both of us, which was just remarkable. I did not know he followed sports that closely. It was astounding—we saw the former president of the university and he was just out and about. That sticks with me even to this day—I'm blown away that he took the time to speak to us.

He always had an air of calm and caring about him. It was not false or fake—he was genuine. He said, "We're so glad you are back at Notre Dame." He somehow knew I had taken a job here and wanted to know how things were going. It put him in a whole different light for me. He validated our presence here. This was our home—this was where we belonged.

I was on cloud nine talking to him. We were having a conversation like we were good friends, yet I'd never met him before that day. So I was floored. He made you feel so important when he talked to you. We got back to the car and wondered if that really just happened.

* * *

I started working in OIT in a building right next to the library that is now named after Father Hesburgh. The first day I was a little jittery—it was kind of like starting training camp. But the thing that came through immediately was how people made me feel. It reminded me of why Notre Dame was so special. People cared about you in a different way, even if it did not directly benefit them. You are valued—and that was the essence of what drew us back. I worked in OIT for four years, transitioning the university to a new system. I enjoyed the work and the people I worked with. I thought I was kind of finding my way.

I never went over to the football office. My time had passed—it was a new day, a new age. In some ways I kind of wanted to hide a little bit. I did not want to overstep my bounds, so I just stayed away. But about a year in, Notre Dame was looking for someone to work with Jack Nolan on its football postgame radio show. I was already on campus and it was easy because it was talking about Notre Dame football. It became my reintroduction to Notre Dame football.

It was always a great thing to be part of something bigger than myself—and that was Notre Dame football. To have that chance was something I jumped at even though I was not overly comfortable speaking in a public forum. It was touch and go in the beginning, and it took some time to find my groove. But at the same time it reengaged me with Jurkovic, one of the most beautiful human beings you will ever meet, and his wife Angie. The three of us—Nolan, Mirko Jurkovic, and myself—played off each other on the air and it worked well. We took questions over the air, but we were live outside Gate 3 of the Joyce Center. Some of the conversations we had were hilarious, to say the least. The whole experience gave me some value in my life. And to do it at Notre Dame was icing on the cake.

* * *

This was 2004 and it turned out to be Tyrone Willingham's last year as head coach. We did not have a lot of success, and it's tough when Notre Dame is not doing well. No one is lukewarm about the Irish. Still, this kind of reenergized me with Notre Dame football and Notre Dame athletics, and life was good. I had found some value in myself.

My wife went back and finished her degree and we were both finding our groove—we found some direction and made some progress. When I started doing the radio show it helped me to reconnect with and do a little outreach to the football program. One guy I got to know was Justin Tuck. He had a lot of talent, but he left a year early to play in the NFL. To reconnect with a place that helped me grow and develop meant a lot to me. I had that sense of pride, saw the hurt when they did not win, and paid attention to how they handled their opportunities.

In the transition to Charlie Weis as the new coach, it was big bravado—especially since he's a Notre Dame alum. There was a lot of talk and energy and excitement around that transition. It was a pivotal year in a lot of regards, with a new role and focus for me and a chance to reconnect with something I thought I'd lost and did not know how to regain.

CHAPTER 34
END OF THE WILLINGHAM ERA

It was a hectic year in 2004, with us getting settled in South Bend and finding our footing. Larry Williams, another former Notre Dame player and captain, left the Notre Dame licensing department to become the athletics director at the University of Portland, where Father Bill Beauchamp (the former executive vice president at Notre Dame) was the president. That created the opening on the postgame radio show. It turned out to be a lot of fun, and I really enjoyed doing it. To watch football and be connected to my alma mater was something I really appreciated.

That final season under Willingham was a rough year on the field. Having done a little coaching, I had a different perspective. The team had a lot of talent—you wanted to see them be successful—and it was tough seeing them not be able to get it done on the field.

As a former player you can get sucked in. I did not know how much Notre Dame football meant in my life because I had been gone so long. I used to watch games and keep up, but it's different when you are right there. I had no problem talking about Notre Dame as "we"—it was my school, my university, my team. I would see players around campus when I was going back and forth from work. You see them walking on campus, and it takes you back and you reminisce.

I worked with a number of different business units in the OIT transition. I got to know professors, other people in various business units—some I had not seen in a long time—and some others in academic units. I had not realized how much Notre Dame was still a part of me. There's a bit of nostalgia—you remember things like the late nights in the library or the dining hall.

Going back to the Loftus Center from time to time, being back in the Joyce Center, and being back on the practice fields once in a while—it all kind of drew me back in. I did not come back to Notre Dame to do anything with the athletic department. I had been a little jaded in some respects and lost a little of my love for football. But this new connection really invigorated my love for the game and for Notre Dame football.

It all happened in less than a year and it still meant a lot to me. It was a great opportunity to be a part of the university and regain some perspective as far as my role in OIT and my connections on campus. I saw a different side of Notre Dame as a university than I had seen as a student-athlete. I was now more mature and able to understand the value of the Notre Dame education and the importance of the people who were responsible for that.

I did not realize how isolated I had been as a student-athlete until I saw Notre Dame in a different light, seeing different aspects of the university that shaped my life going forward. I became more involved in what Notre Dame was. My perspective as a student-athlete had been limited—I gained respect for the business side of the university and the work the professors put in to create the product of a Notre Dame education and experience. I saw how all that played out together—not just in the athletic department but all the connectivity all around campus. It became very rewarding to reconnect with people I had not had contact with for years. I saw it now as a colleague—and it gave me a different perspective.

Willingham wound up losing his job, and the search was on for a new coach. I did not want to get too close to it in some respects. Charlie Weis came in and immediately made an impact. He had a great season in that first year at head coach, 2005. But I did not really know many people left in the athletic department. And I saw that was the same case with other alumni.

Coach Holtz and his staff were long gone. For so many years our connections as former players were with the coaching staff and just a few administrators. For us this connection was limited to former assistant coaches George Kelly, Brian Boulac, and Tony Yelovich—but our connection to others wasn't really broad in terms of outreach. It became a tough situation between Coach Weis and the football alumni because there was not a real good connection between the groups.

The hiring of Coach Weis was an interesting one. He was a Notre Dame alumnus, so there was an expectation that he understood how things would work on campus, even though he had never been a head coach. And it was hard to argue with his record with the New England Patriots. He, Bill Belichick, and Tom Brady did some awfully impressive things in his time there, including winning another Super Bowl after he'd already taken the Notre Dame job. He made big headlines when he came to South Bend and immediately talked about his teams having "a decided schematic advantage." That made all the sense in the world and for the first few years it worked out that way—but that phrase later came back to haunt him a little bit.

In retrospect, Coach Weis' job in New England and his position at Notre Dame couldn't have been any more different, even though it was all football. With the Patriots, all he needed to do to make his team successful was build his connection with Brady and call the right plays on Sunday. He seldom dealt with the media other than for Super Bowl media days. He could look at video from 6:00 in the morning until midnight to prepare. People in the NFL knew him, but from a general public standpoint he was not especially visible because of the way the Patriots did business.

At Notre Dame, there is so much more to it. There's a lot of media for the head coach. There are all sorts of relationships that need to happen on a campus because so many people want to connect with you and your program. I'm not sure Coach Weis ever thought he needed all those other people on his side. He probably felt like if his teams won games, the rest of it would all fall into place.

It was also a complete coincidence that the Guglielmino Athletics Complex opened in Coach Weis' first year as the new home for the football program. The facility was fabulous—I can tell you there were NFL teams that didn't have facilities comparable to that. But the layout was not particularly friendly—and that wasn't Weis' fault.

As former players, we were all used to just walking into the first-floor football offices in the Joyce Center to say hello to our former coaches and other people we knew. It was a much more intimate setting there, even if it maybe wasn't great for business on a home football Friday.

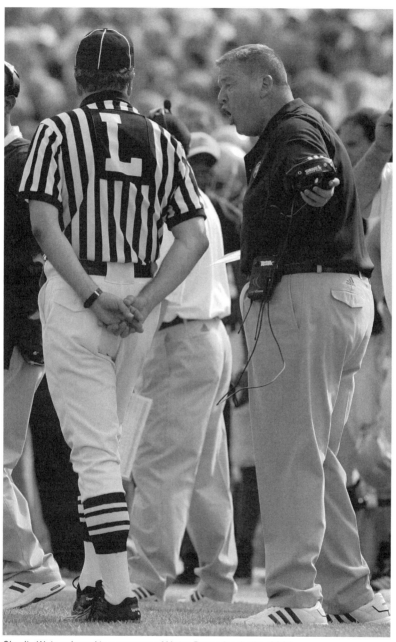

Charlie Weis ushered in a new era of Notre Dame football in 2005.

But the Gug, as nice as it was, was really closed off to visitors unless you knew someone up in the second-floor offices. You couldn't just wander through any longer, and that offended some former players who took it as if they weren't welcome. Coach Weis was worried about coaching his team—he didn't particularly prioritize alumni relations. But that eventually became a sticking point.

* * *

Anyway, it was wonderful to see how God works, even if it involved a career I was not considering. Notre Dame decided to create a role out of the need to connect and reengage with former football players. Maybe it was something everyone in athletics had taken for granted, in great part because people like Kelly, Boulac, and Yelovich were mainstays for so long. Even if you didn't know any of the current assistant coaches, you always knew that some combination of those three guys would be around and their offices would be packed with former players on Fridays and Saturdays of home weekends. Those three essentially served as the football alumni relations department for a long, long period.

A new role was built by Kevin White, who was the athletics director at the time. The thought that former players all of a sudden weren't sure they were welcome went against everything that Notre Dame was and rubbed some of those former players the wrong way. That became my reintroduction to the Monogram Club. I'd gotten my letter jacket when I was in school, but that was it. I had no other connections to the organization. But this was the opportunity for me now in athletics.

Over those previous three or four years I'd reestablished a connection with a lot of people in athletics. I did not go to practice much—I wasn't looking to do that with the current team. But the Monogram Club role was a chance to reach out to some guys from the 1960s and 1970s—and even earlier—whom I really thought highly of. I got to reach out to former players with the goal of reconnecting them with the Notre Dame football program.

The position developed as I went along, but in essence it was all about making sure guys felt welcome. A lot of these guys had been instrumental in building the program, but they did not feel a part of it any longer. These players had built what Notre Dame football was now about—it was important to find ways to engage with them. I was a good example—and Notre Dame was all about bonds and relationships.

CHAPTER 35
THE WILLINGHAM DECISION

My return to Notre Dame also coincided with a turbulent time for Notre Dame football. The last season under Coach Willingham did not go well. He started out in 2002 with the Irish going 8–0 and finishing 10–3 after losing the Gator Bowl game, ending up 17th in the final polls.

They beat Michigan at home and Michigan State in East Lansing in the final minutes, with Maurice Stovall ending up on the cover of *Sports Illustrated* after that second game. That's how anxious everybody was for Notre Dame to be good again. And they won a huge road game at Florida State with *ESPN College GameDay* there. They finished ninth in the country in scoring defense, allowing a little more than 16 points a game.

Coming back the following year and going 5–7 was a letdown in a lot of regards. There had been talk of Notre Dame being resurrected, and then not even being able to play in a bowl game the following year was hard. Losing 45–14 at home to USC, even as good as the Trojans were, didn't help the situation. The losses to Michigan, USC, and Florida State were all one-sided.

When 2004 rolled around there was talent—guys who absolutely knew how to play the game of football, could play at a high level, and did just that on a professional basis. You look at Brady Quinn, Jeff Samardzija, Ryan Harris, John Carlson, Tom Zbikowski, John Sullivan, Stovall, Victor Abiamiri, and Justin Tuck—there were some very good football players on that roster. But it just did not live up to expectations, given the talent on that team. I was somewhat taken aback with the talent they had compared to the results. They did not match up.

At the end of the year when they fired Willingham, it really hit me hard. Notre Dame was now a different place for me—coming back 10 years later, it was a different campus and a different atmosphere. But it was still Notre Dame football. I wanted to see the team do well. They went 6–6 and still played a bowl game after the decision was made on Willingham.

It was a little awkward playing with an interim coach when Coach Weis had already been hired—and the 38–21 loss to Oregon State at the Insight Bowl was probably indicative of that. We beat top-10 teams in Michigan and Tennessee and then lost at home to Purdue, Boston College, and Pittsburgh. The lack of consistency was frustrating. And yet the team was actually No. 4 in the country in rushing defense, giving up only 88.2 yards a game on the ground—and that was the best by a Notre Dame team since the 1973 national championship season.

I don't know what the dynamic was like in the locker room. Losing is tough—losing at Notre Dame is tougher because of the expectations, the history, and the lore of the guys who played before you. I was always conscious of that when I played. It's kind of a responsibility to the guys before you. It was not that these guys did not care, but they did not seem to play as a team. When I saw that, just watching them without having the relationship to come and encourage them was tough. I was on the outside looking in that first year.

And talking about losses on the radio was painful because I felt for these guys. That year they lost those three home games—when the whole focus was to take care of your house, you could clearly see the struggle for them all. They just struggled to play consistently at a high level, just two seasons removed from going 10–3 and playing in the Gator Bowl.

I was always optimistic that they could turn it around with the talent they had. As a former player you want that connection—we all bleed Blue and Gold. We felt it just as much as those guys on the field. We felt we should be better than that. The Notre Dame mystique stretches across eras, and as I saw with the guys I met from the earlier decades, there was always a connection to the guys who played before them. They had the same desire to see Notre Dame at the pinnacle—so you felt you owed it to those guys who had set the standard.

The season ended with a demoralizing loss at USC, and any time you lose to USC it's painful. Guys take it personally. I was one of those guys. The three times Willingham teams played USC it did not go well. Those were all great USC teams. They were in the top 10 every time Notre Dame played them, and they were No. 1 and unbeaten in

2004. But none of those games was close. USC won by an average of 31 points—the Trojans never scored fewer than 41 points in any of those contests and Notre Dame never scored more than 14. So that particular series really went in the wrong direction.

Notre Dame made the coaching change—it was hurtful in terms of finally having the first Black head coach at Notre Dame in any sport and then they decide to fire him after just three years. It was an unwritten rule at Notre Dame that coaches had five years of opportunity to coach the program. Notre Dame would allow the coach to play out his contract, usually given a five-year deal in the modern era. That had happened with Terry Brennan, Gerry Faust, and Bob Davie—and later with Weis.

So to fire the first and only Black head coach so quickly was a black eye on Notre Dame athletics. It was difficult to fathom and tough to see happen. It was frustrating to say the least—disappointing would be an understatement. It soured me on Notre Dame in a lot of respects as far as the university leadership went. And Notre Dame took a lot of criticism for the decision.

It also was an example of how hard Notre Dame was trying to get the program back to the Coach Holtz level. Coach Holtz's team spoiled everybody going to nine straight New Year's Day bowl games, and the struggle and frustration to regain that level of success was part of the reality and presumably part of the Willingham decision.

I started to see more guys on the team from time to time around campus. As a former player at Notre Dame I'd congratulate them if they won and was proud of them when they performed. The struggles, the limelight that's always around you, the pressures of being a student at Notre Dame—I knew how taxing it all could be. I was never a fan of people who would get down on the players. I knew what it took to play and go to class and the pressure you were under. They gave a lot—they put in a lot of time and effort and it was not always recognized.

Success is not just what you see on Saturday—it's in the classroom, at practice, in the weight room, in the locker room. Those expectations are constant. Add being at the University of Notre Dame, and it's exponential. When they did not have the success they were looking for, I was adamant about not criticizing the players. Your performance may not be what it needs to be—and I will critique that—but I would never go after a player personally. How you perform is different.

I learned that from Cris Collinsworth at NBC. He was kind of a cheerleader for me when I played, but he never got down on the players—he separated the individual from the performance. I always respected his approach. The breakdowns that occur—you call them out. But it's never personal.

There were good players on that team who had a lot of talent, but they struggled to achieve the team cohesiveness. I always start with Quinn—he had a lot of talent in his sophomore year, completing a little over 50 percent of his passes, and yet I always thought there was more to that kid than what we saw. I loved Ryan Grant and Darius Walker—they averaged 4 yards per carry and combined for 1,200 yards rushing. Rhema McKnight, Anthony Fasano, and Samardzija—you had the pieces to be successful. But the offense was stagnant at times and seemed to need a little tweak.

Defensively you saw pieces on that side too—Derek Landri, Tuck, Brandon Hoyte, Zbikowski. But the pieces just did not fit, and you saw that with some of the defensive breakdowns. That group never showed itself to be the unit you thought it would be.

I still thought the firing of Willingham was wrong because it did not honor what had been the norm for every other football coach at Notre Dame. It did a disservice to the team and also to the reputation of the university. Some of the guys with eligibility decided to leave because firing him was not the right thing to do. You go from 10–3 to 5–7 and then to 6–6. Willingham should have been given the opportunity to finish it out, especially with the talent they had coming back on both offense and defense. And, as we saw, Coach Weis benefitted early from the level of talent that remained.

CHAPTER 36
CHARLIE MAKES AN EARLY STATEMENT

The Weis years were a bit of a mixed bag. When he came in Notre Dame had the pieces in place. It started with Quinn—this guy was a stud quarterback. Coach Weis came in with the pro mentality, and the thing that stood out to me most in 2005, that first year, was the talent that was on his team and how it had not translated to consistent success under Willingham.

In 2004 Quinn had only one game with a 60 percent pass completion rate, and the next year he had a breakout year and was averaging 64 to 65 percent. Coach Weis used the talent he had around him. Samardzija was one of the key figures—one of the best receivers in Notre Dame history—plus you had Fasano and Stovall, two more guys good enough to go play in the league. Coach Weis did a great job of putting those guys in a position to be successful.

Everyone always talks about the development of the players. But there's a difference between what that meant at the college level and what that meant at the pro level for Coach Weis, especially with the Patriots. Most of their guys show up as professionals, and New England during Coach Weis' time put the pieces together very well and developed great schemes to be successful.

The things that defined the Weis years at Notre Dame? Certainly a strong offense—play-calling was his cup of tea. Defense was a bit more challenging. That offense in 2005 scored 36 points a game to rank No. 8 in the country. They threw for 330 yards a game, which was the best in Notre Dame history. But all of Coach Weis' teams gave up 23, 24, 25 points a game. Those numbers just didn't match up with the most successful Notre Dame teams. Notre Dame can outscore other teams only for so long, although they did that fairly well in 2005 and 2006.

There was plenty of offense, just not enough defense. There were some good players defensively who went on to play professionally, but they couldn't put it together on that side of the ball. Maurice Crum, Abiamiri, Chris Frome, Corey Mays, Joe Brockington, Trevor Laws, Landri—they were talented, but they couldn't put all the pieces together.

Brady Quinn was a standout in the Weis years.

If you are going to be successful in college you've got to have a good defense.

Coach Weis was an offensive coach and it showed—there were guys who played at a high level. Walker had a good year—and then throw in Harris, Mark LeVoir, Dan Santucci, Fasano, and Carlson. And Samardzija would have been a top NFL pick if he hadn't also played baseball.

This is hard for me to say, but Coach Weis was also never able to beat USC. And when all is said and done, that's the game and the series that if you are not winning, you can have all kinds of other success, but that's the rivalry that matters. When I was at Notre Dame we won 13 games in a row over USC. Then between Willingham and Weis, over the course of eight years, they never beat USC. Weis brought a swagger back for his teams, but there was still an issue with not winning in those big rivalries.

The team had success, especially in the 2005 and 2006 seasons, and went to the Fiesta Bowl and Sugar Bowl. To go 21–6 over two years and be one of the top-rated offenses in the country, you had something to hang your hat on. But you never saw the defensive productivity on a consistent basis.

When Quinn left after the 2006 season, Jimmy Clausen came in and was highly heralded, but, again, he was a freshman. I felt bad for him because Notre Dame was coming off two big years as an offensive juggernaut and then went the other direction. That certainly affected Coach Weis's time at Notre Dame. In 2007 we went 3–9—one of the worst seasons on record. It was not what Weis was used to, and it didn't fly with Notre Dame fans either.

When you win it covers a lot of things. Quinn was a real leader and had a huge touchdown-to-interception ratio. Clausen came in with a lot of swagger, but he found that Division I college football was different than high school. He had never lost a game in high school, so he did not know what that was like. On top of that, he was not completely healthy that freshman season.

We played Georgia Tech in that first game in 2007 and got spanked. Clausen was thrust into a situation and did not really have all the tools and prep to have success. We gave up 30 points a game the first five weeks of the season and struggled to put up points—the most we scored was 19 versus Purdue. So we started 0–5, and it was not even close.

Then in 2008 we lost four of our last five regular-season games. And in 2009 we lost four in a row in November. There were a lot of close games that year—nine games were decided by seven points or fewer—but there were not enough wins in there. Actually that 2009 team ranked fifth in the country in passing and eighth in total offense, but it wasn't enough.

When I came to Washington one day, Joe Theismann came to talk to me and engage with me and Carter because we all were Notre Dame football players. You had that connection back with each other. Likewise, guys did not want Weis to fail because the buzz was back with Notre Dame football after the 2005 and 2006 seasons. You are always a Notre Dame guy, especially when you go into the pros. Weis had his persona from his time with the Patriots, but when he started losing, he lost some of the goodwill that should have been built up.

At the end of the day, it all comes down to numbers. Coach Weis, like Davie and Willingham before him, just did not win enough football games. It was that simple.

CHAPTER 37
ON TO
BRIAN KELLY

The transition from Weis to Kelly was intriguing to me. Everybody had their perceptions about what Notre Dame needed, and I heard a lot of conversations around who Notre Dame should get. There was always talk of Bob Stoops, Nick Saban—names like that. People forget that there are other great jobs in the country—places that have proven they can win consistently and play at an elite level. Notre Dame at the time was still trying to get back to that level.

When you look at those years after Holtz, there were ups and downs. Davie went to the Fiesta Bowl in 2000, Willingham won 10 games his first year in 2002, and Weis won 10 games in each of his first two years in 2005 and 2006. But it just didn't happen year after year for those three guys.

Kelly seemed to be the popular choice from the beginning. He had been very successful at Cincinnati and before that at Central Michigan. He won championships at Grand Valley State, so he had been around and been a head coach for a good number of years. AD Jack Swarbrick played it very close to the vest—no one really knew what he was thinking or doing because he did not confide in anyone else in the athletic department. So if anyone else was seriously considered, no one knew about it.

There was a shift in college sports—in college football—at the time, and Notre Dame was having a little harder time keeping up, as I viewed it. You bring in a pro coach like Weis and you see the differences between college athletes and pros. College athletics are very much viewed as a business today—but for the longest time, college football was still about the community in the locker room, the team bonding, and the development of young men.

Branding is this big thing now, but it wasn't as prominent back in the 1970s, '80s, and even in the '90s. It was not about the individual brand as much as it was about the brand of the institution. While Notre Dame was still a strong institutional brand in terms of college football, it was a different vibe from a player standpoint. The focus became more about individuals as opposed to the more cohesive team. That's my perspective as I look at college football, and particularly Notre Dame—it's a transition into the new era of college football.

Notre Dame had that singular place in college athletics—you either love Notre Dame or you hate Notre Dame. But you also began to see the programs at places like Alabama, Clemson, Texas, USC, Georgia, and LSU catching up—not just in the realm of talent but in the public perception.

Notre Dame was still selling the combination of providing great opportunities both in the classroom and on the football field. And Coach Kelly did that very well—"Shopping down a different aisle" was how he described it at Notre Dame. He modernized the recruiting department—they hired people to handle social media and graphics within the football office, and the growth of Fighting Irish Media took care of the video side.

But, as Coach Holtz used to say, "The teams on the other side give scholarships too." Notre Dame could still be great, but there were plenty of other programs that were in the position to do that regularly too. And these days everybody has great facilities and great administrative support for their football program. So you can go a lot of different places to have a great football experience and get a very good education.

To be a successful team there are certain things you have to do. You've got to recruit successfully, you've got to have talent, and then you have to help the development of the players. From the 2006 season, Quinn's senior year, to the 2007 season with Clausen, you saw a high-powered offense go the other direction—going from scoring more than 400 points to fewer than 200 the following year. They lost a lot of talent between those two years and had a lot of young players, but they needed development in those guys who came in behind the Quinns, the Samardzijas, the Stovalls, the Fasanos. That made it a struggle.

That goes back to that landscape that had changed. Notre Dame wasn't the end-all and be-all as it had been in the 1960s, '70s, '80s, and early '90s. You had a shift in the focus of college football—the branding, the perception, the revenue had increased exponentially, and you had a lot more television opportunities across the board. Notre Dame was no longer unique with its NBC deal because almost all the major programs were seen regularly. And as well as Notre Dame had recruited, you've got to do it at a high level year after year—and, again, there are lots of other programs with lots of good players. Notre Dame doesn't hold a monopoly.

That being said, it is still a great place to coach football—there are a lot of things about Notre Dame that plenty of other head coaches would love to have going for them. Joe Theismann once talked about the idea that you ought to be able to bottle the history and tradition and all the other great things about Notre Dame and sell it. There would be plenty of takers.

In that first year in 2010 under Coach Kelly, it was a season that was up and down. You previously had a thousand-yard runner with Darius Walker running the ball, but Coach Kelly came in with a completely different plan. It was more of a spread philosophy—that was the thing that was really coming into play in college football. The run and shoot with a lot more of an up-tempo style of offense.

It was kind of a foreign concept to me, and it didn't look like many of the professional offenses that I had seen. I was used to playing on physical, hard-charging, run-first teams, and my perception of the new offense was, "We're going out there to throw the ball." In that regard, that was the new part of it—that transition.

So in 2010 they started 1–3, which is never easy. They lost close games against Michigan and Michigan State, and fell to Navy for the third time in four years. Then they came back and won their last four, including against No. 15 Utah, USC, and then against Miami at the Sun Bowl.

Then in 2011 all the offensive and defensive numbers improved a little bit. We won eight out of nine games in the middle of the year. But we lost our first two games of the year to South Florida and Michigan, and then lost our last two against Stanford and Florida State in a winnable Champs Sports Bowl game in Orlando.

CHAPTER 38
THAT EXCEPTIONAL 2012 SEASON

The 2012 season for the Irish was one of the best seasons they'd ever put together, and it really was a turning point in the perspective of Notre Dame football. The Irish were back.

When Notre Dame plays well and does well in college football it seems to bode well for all of college football. People will agree to disagree, but I think college football is better when Notre Dame is doing well. When you love Notre Dame, you love to watch them win—and when you don't, you love to watch them lose. In 2012 you had a lot to like. Notre Dame had not been at the top for a long time—since the 1988 national championship and the early '90s, when the Irish were consistently vying for titles.

The leadership really stuck out to me on this team. Talent is important, but there's a lot to be said for the leadership. It's not just the juniors and seniors, it's also the guys who are making the plays up front. They lead in terms of guidance but also in terms of action, not just in their voices. When all that happens it bodes well for having a good outcome for your team.

In looking at that season, you look back at the previous two years under Coach Kelly and you had two 8–5 seasons. There was nothing extraordinary about those two years, but they laid the groundwork for 2012 and the explosion that happened that year. In 2010 you ended with three November wins and then a bowl game victory, then in 2011 you finished with two losses. So those were very different years with very different experiences.

And let's remember there were some staff changes in the off-season. Charley Molnar left to become head coach at Massachusetts, so Chuck Martin came over from defense to take over the offense. Plus Tim Hinton and Ed Warinner both left for Ohio State. And maybe the key hire was Harry Hiestand, who turned out to be just about perfect for the offensive line.

I don't know if you could automatically say coming into the 2012 season that this was going to be a team that could contend for a national championship. But there were some things coming out of spring ball that encouraged me—namely the leadership on the lines, offensively and defensively. That's where the game is won. These days it's all about throwing the ball around and big plays in the passing game. But you win at the line of scrimmage. I'll always be a big fan of the offensive line. You had three fifth-year guys starting with experience—they understood the nuances of the game and they also had another senior in there with them.

Braxston Cave was the focal point because you had a young quarterback in Golson who had no real experience playing in games. So the protection calls came from the center. Cave was intelligent, keyed in, and observant. I saw him play at Penn High School in Mishawaka, Indiana, when I was coaching my son. I saw how much better Cave was than the other people on the field.

The other linemen were Mike Golic Jr., Chris Watt, Zack Martin, and Nick Martin. Nick Martin was only a sophomore, but he was very skilled. And we see what Zack Martin is doing now in the pros—he's been doing that with the Dallas Cowboys for some time. Watt and Zack Martin were fifth-year guys, and then you had Cave, Golic, and a sophomore. That was one of the best lines I've ever seen at Notre Dame in some time in terms of cohesiveness and the ability to work together. You knew you would get some direction and could protect a young quarterback with limited experience.

Then you slip over to the defensive side—Kapron Lewis-Moore was a senior, Louis Nix was a junior, and you also had Tuitt in that 3-4 defense. So you had three down linemen who were real disruptors. All three of those guys played at a high level—played at the next level. You had leadership and guidance from guys like Lewis-Moore, whom we called Kap. They took the lead right out of the gate for what was the heart and soul of that team—the defense.

It all really started with Te'o at linebacker—he was not just the leader of the defense, he was the quarterback of that unit. He really excelled on communication to the back end and when shifts were made—he just knew how to get guys lined up. Guys really believed in him. Dan Fox was the other inside linebacker and those two guys played really well off each other. Then you had juniors Prince Shembo and Danny Spond—that front seven were as good as any front seven I've seen play in some time.

You think back to some of the great nose tackles Notre Dame had over the years. When I played it was Zorich, quick and explosive. That team also had George Williams at tackle—a player like Kap. Shembo was kind of like McDonald, quick and agile. Spond was like a Pritchett. They were guys who could run, play physically, and play downhill.

Zeke Motta was the playmaker and the quarterback at safety for the younger guys—freshman KeiVarae Russell, sophomore Bennett Jackson, and sophomore safety Matthias Farley. You had young guys, but you also had senior leadership. Those were stellar players with strong leadership skills—Kap, Te'o, Motta—and it all flowed well together. It set a precedent for what we saw over the 2012 season and how they won 12 games.

The offense had two senior running backs in Cierre Wood and Theo Riddick—Riddick was also a great receiver out of the backfield. They complemented each other very well. TJ Jones and junior Robby Toma—they did not put up great numbers, but they were solid receivers. I remember TJ Jones as a kid running around my house in DC. I recall how fluid he was in his route running and how diligent he was. He will always have a special place in my heart because his dad, Andre, was like a brother to me.

We came to be known as Tight End U. And we had one of the best in the country on that team in Tyler Eifert. He could line up tight as an inline blocker and he worked well with the offensive line. But he also had the ability to split out and be a mismatch. He was very versatile and a tough cover for a lot of teams. He was a senior who put up really good numbers and had the ability to lead by his play and also in the meeting rooms and locker room. You would follow him because he was getting it done on the field.

Everett Golson was a young guy with no prior experience as far as throwing the football, but he could make plays. In some ways he came out of nowhere—he needed that offensive line and the receivers, and they stepped up and helped him. That was one time that you saw a strong team, even with the new quarterback staying within himself. Then you also had the dynamic of the backup—Tommy Rees—coming off starting the previous year.

The offensive system Coach Kelly ran was very different than what Rees originally was brought in to play. Some people the year before did not appreciate the things he did. Rees was a calming influence in the

The 2012 Irish team was stacked.

243

meeting room for Golson. Rees held up early with Coach Kelly, and it helped that his dad was a coach so he had been around the game. He was a huge help to Golson. He came from a locker room that cared about each other and believed in each other. Rees had game experience and over the course of that season, it was needed when he stepped in.

* * *

The start of that season came in Ireland with all the pageantry and excitement. Notre Dame fans travel well and that certainly happened that weekend. You look back on it and you treasure and see the power and the brand that Notre Dame is around the world.

The previous Notre Dame game in Ireland was played at Croke Park in 1996. This time we played at Aviva Stadium, which was only a few years old. It was a spectacular venue, and fans could actually walk to the stadium from downtown Dublin and the Temple Bar area, where Notre Dame had a big pregame presence.

We absolutely destroyed Navy, and it was an awesome experience. You saw the capability of this team and how explosive the offense could be, especially on the ground. We rushed for five touchdowns and almost 300 yards—108 by Riddick and 99 by George Atkinson, and they each scored twice. To start the year like that, I was enamored to be a part of it.

The highlight everyone remembers was when Tuitt rumbled 77 yards with a recovered fumble to bring the score to 27–0. Plus it was a comfortable way to start for Golson at quarterback.

It also set the standard for a stellar defense that was remarkable from start to finish. It's never easy dealing with Navy's option, but we held them to 149 yards on the ground. When you kick the season off with a game like that, it lets you know what your defense looks like. It was as solid of a start as they come. And let's remember how many times Navy had caused major problems for Notre Dame teams in the recent past. The one-sided 50–10 score sent a message, even if it was only the first week.

The team actually got to do a little sightseeing—they toured Dublin in double-decker buses Friday afternoon, and they looked like rock stars the way the fans reacted and reached out to them.

In some ways, you wish you could just be a tourist. I talked to plenty of people who came to Ireland early to play golf or whatever and others who came for the game and then stayed later. Either way, I didn't talk to anyone who did not have a great time.

* * *

Notre Dame wasn't ranked coming into the opener, but they jumped into the No. 22 spot after that first win. They came back home to play a solid Purdue team—and they were expected to win—but the game showed some weaknesses.

The jet lag after coming back from Ireland may have been a factor—the team was not as sharp as it should have been. It was a tough game, but those are the kinds of games you just have to win if you want any opportunity to succeed.

How do you handle adversity? People may not normally view a matchup with Purdue as adversity, but they came back and got right back to class and had no real rest—no real chance to recover from an international flight. Golson threw for 289 yards, but he got a little banged up late. After Purdue tied it at 17 with about two minutes left, Rees came in. He led us 55 yards, made a couple of big-time third-down throws, and we kicked a field goal with seven seconds left to win it.

You find a way to get a win—you make a way. It came down to a game-winning kick—so to Kyle Brindza, hats off to you. That saved the national championship opportunity—if you lose that game, you don't make it.

* * *

Coming out of that game we took a little bit of a hit, even though we were still ranked. We came back and played our first ranked opponent in Michigan State—they are always tough.

We found a way to win again—and that was going to be a physical game that has not changed one iota since those two teams started playing. You think back to 1966, 1988, and now 2012—Michigan State is a hard out and a hard win, and you pay for it on the back end.

But this one was set up on defense. They stepped up and shut down Michigan State with three points and just 50 yards on the ground. It was Nix and Tuitt with sacks, plus Sheldon Day, a young guy who stepped up and made some plays.

The offense had its struggles—Golson had less than 50 percent completions. But there were no turnovers—and when you do that you give yourself a chance. You come away with a win against the No. 10-ranked team in the country, and you think, "Hey, the Irish might be for real." It was kind of amazing to think that Notre Dame had lost six in a row against ranked teams and had not beaten a ranked team in seven seasons—since Weis' first year. That's not supposed to happen at Notre Dame.

* * *

Now it's Michigan and you've got to step up. The defense continued to show how good it was—giving up only six points to a strong Michigan offense. We again needed Rees to come in and bail us out, but you need that to happen over the course of the season. You need some guys to step up if you want a championship team.

So to come out of all of that with all Ws the first month made a statement. Okay, these guys have a chance. How do you handle adversity? They continued to show they could do that. They could adapt and do it quickly.

With the changing environments, this was a special group. Young talent, good talent, a strong system—a group of guys who know how to handle adversity and can make changes to be successful.

The Michigan game was a vital game because Golson struggled early, and Rees had to come in and save the day. Rees did not have a stellar passing game, but he brought them through. That opened some eyes even though things started a little shaky in that 13–6 win.

Rees could have been all sour grapes and ticked off because someone took his job. It was not an easy thing to handle after you've started and won some games. But he kept his head in the game all year—and it wouldn't be the last time he played a key role.

We'd had all kinds of problems the previous two years against Denard Robinson, Michigan's quarterback. But this time he threw four interceptions in just the first half—Te'o had two of them—and then Robinson fumbled it away the first time Michigan had the ball in the third period.

Michigan kicked a field goal with three minutes left to make it a one-score game, but the Irish offense ran out the clock.

* * *

A third of the season was down and we felt like we were in the driver's seat. Then we went to Chicago and played a tough Miami team when it could have been a home game. This was the Shamrock Series—it's just a bus trip, but it's still a road game and a foreign environment, so it's not our normal home routine.

Golson came back and had a really solid game and the running backs played well—two guys rushed for 100 yards and Atkinson made some nice plays. I liked this team for its ability to run the football efficiently and effectively.

Lighting up Miami 41–3 like that never gets old. It's not USC, but the opportunity to play at a high level against them in a pro stadium and run the ball like that was enjoyable to watch. Plus Golson connected on 17 of his 22 throws, and that's what we needed.

This looked a lot like our old teams—almost 400 yards rushing and five touchdowns on the ground. We ran it for 287 yards in just the second half. And this was our third straight game without the other team scoring a touchdown.

This was Notre Dame football, at least to me. I felt really good about the football team and what it was doing. It brought back fond memories of Notre Dame football at its finest.

* * *

Then came another ranked opponent in Stanford, and they had morphed into the kind of offense we were—really physical and tough. This was a real challenge for us on defense against a pro-style offense. It was definitely a different challenge than Notre Dame had seen the first month.

Te'o was making plays, getting after the quarterback, and just tackling the ball. The defense had a great ability to get guys on the ground and get stops. Golson had his ups and downs, and Rees came in again and completed all four of his passes.

But this was tense. Notre Dame didn't score a touchdown in the first three periods and then had to kick a field goal in the final 20 seconds to tie it.

Then in overtime we made an amazing goal-line stand—three stops after Stanford got to the 1. The fourth-down run seemed to go on forever and they finally blew it dead and then reviewed it. And Notre Dame survived 20–13, ending a three-game losing streak against Stanford.

* * *

Then BYU was another squeaker and now you are grinding. It's midterms and you've got exams—there's strain at Notre Dame. It's different. It's the middle of the season, but when are we going to have a break? We found a way to pull one out. It kept our season going, and we made the most of the opportunity of beating a really solid BYU team.

They came in third in the country against the run, and yet we ended up with 270 rushing yards. Riddick had his best day yet with 143 yards, including a 55-yarder. Wood had 114 yards, and we ended up only completing one pass the entire second half. But we shut them out after halftime, and we scored after a long march early in the final period for the winning points.

At 17–14, again, it's no work of art, but this team just seemed to have a knack for figuring these games out.

* * *

Then we played Oklahoma in Norman—and, to me, that was the turning point. To see the best of the Big 12 just eight games in and to come out of there with a win was epic. The defense stepped up and the offense did what it had to do in a hostile environment.

I grew up an Oklahoma fan, so I am well aware that's normally a very, very difficult place to play.

CHAPTER 39
NORMAN AND BEYOND

To see how Notre Dame played at Oklahoma, it was the first real game in my eyes when that team went into a really challenging environment against an opponent that was playing extremely well. The Sooners were explosive, had a strong defense, but gave up a few points—but then they always scored a lot in the Big 12. Oklahoma was the most potent offense Notre Dame faced that year. I knew how intense this game would be.

Notre Dame doesn't make it to Norman that often, so you knew the Oklahoma fan base would be rabid because it was Notre Dame. Notre Dame being undefeated was a huge deal for the whole state of Oklahoma. Even longtime Sooners coach Barry Switzer came out to the Notre Dame walk-through on Friday.

I talked to some people who were looking forward to that game because they felt like Notre Dame had not played anybody who was really good. The Irish were coming off the game against BYU, when they had a tough time establishing a rhythm.

But Notre Dame has a way of rising to the occasion and they really did it that night in Norman—they played lights out. It was tight throughout—a 10–6 lead and then a battle royale in the third period with no scoring. Then Notre Dame exploded in the fourth quarter and racked up 20 points. It was as close as it gets until that fourth quarter after Oklahoma tied it at 13 with about nine minutes left—just a dogfight.

The running backs played well—Golson ran the ball well—and Te'o led with 11 tackles (all of them in the first half), a sack, and a pick. He was Johnny-on-the-spot as the defense continued to show up at the right times. A big key was holding the explosive Oklahoma offense to just two field goals in the first half.

This was the prime-time game on ABC, so there were tons of national media outlets there that night. And, truth be told, I don't think there were many people in that bunch who thought Notre Dame could win there.

After that game I saw Notre Dame as a true contender. This win was against a really high-powered offense that challenged and tested our defense.

So what type of team could Notre Dame be? I did not know if they could run the table, given how challenging the remaining schedule was. But to see how they played in that game told you something. They found a way to win and the defense showed me who they were.

It was the ability to turn teams over, and that was a key aspect of that game, especially with Notre Dame not turning it over. It was not the most explosive offensive effort, but it was still a great complement to the defense.

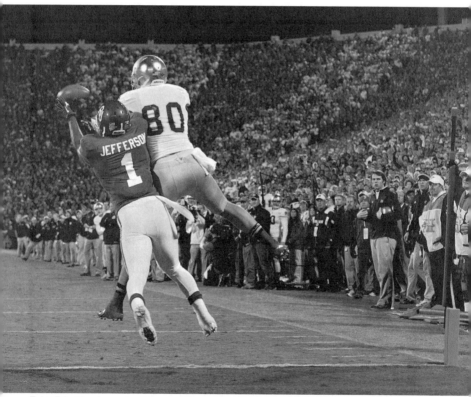

Tyler Eifert hauls one in at the goal line against the Sooners.

Notre Dame did not make a lot of mistakes on offense with a freshman quarterback, but it was critical to have a defense that took care of him and got him through games. It presaged how the Irish would finish. The bar was set higher after that game, especially the way they finished it.

Notre Dame allowed some yards, including 364 passing, but Bob Diaco always had the bend-don't-break deal. In the end they would bear down, and that started with leadership.

Te'o led the team in tackles in that game, and he was all over the place. He just said, "I'm not going to let this team lose."

You started to see the confidence level rise another notch. It was the most impactful moment in that season.

* * *

You come back after that game, and you have a little swagger about you. But you have to be mindful you do not have a letdown, which is what almost happened the next week against a solid Pitt team. You have games when you have to compete and fight hard, and it's not easy to play at a high level week after week. Can you battle back and fight when you're not at your best?

We struggled mightily. The defense played a solid game, held Pitt to just 308 yards, and the offense racked up 500 yards even in overtime. But our offense had to bail our defense out in some tight situations in this one.

Notre Dame was forced to come from behind in the fourth quarter, and it showed that we had some issues to work out—but we found a way to win. That's the nature of a successful team—rallying around each other.

We were down 20–6 going into the last period and the defense said, "We'll find a way." The offense kicked in, got it into overtime, and won it in OT. That's the mark of a championship team—to make those plays. And that's after Pitt missed a makeable field goal that would have won it in the second overtime.

It's one thing to want success, but it's another to know you can go out and execute. It's a sign of the mental and physical conditioning, and you need both to play at a high level and be consistent. It's how you overcome obstacles and mistakes and kick it in at the right time. You could see these guys had a love for each other. It showed throughout the season. And these guys showed the best defense in the country, in my mind.

Te'o said after the game that it was ugly at times and beautiful at times. That's kind of the story of the season so far. But Notre Dame won this one 29–26, and they were at 8–0.

* * *

We won in workmanlike fashion 21–6 at Boston College on the same day that Alabama lost for the first time. And then we came home and beat Wake Forest 38–0, as Golson threw for 346 yards. That was also the same day Oregon and Kansas State, the other teams ahead of Notre Dame in the polls, both lost. The Wake Forest game was a little bit of a relief and a change of pace after all the close calls.

Then it was Thanksgiving weekend against you know who—the team out west. This was the game that would make or break the season.

Notre Dame played USC and the records didn't matter. USC was struggling—they were just over .500—but you knew they were going to give it all they had. You don't just roll your hat out—it's a rivalry game and they were at home. These games matter more. This is Notre Dame's premier rival and the opportunity to upset Notre Dame's perfect season would have been gold for USC.

In that game the defense was stellar. It just showed again that we did not need Golson to be a world-beater, we just needed him to be sound and not turn the ball over. That was the difference with that season. It was not the most explosive offense Notre Dame has seen. The difference in 2012 was that we had a solid defense plus an offense that did not hurt us. The one aspect of the game was for the defense to be stout, turn teams over, make the plays that are there, and not turn the ball over.

USC scored only one touchdown, and Notre Dame for the rest of the game kicked field goals—including a 52-yarder to end the first half. Brindza again stepped up—he may not have been the MVP, but his five field goals were the difference in the football game. We'll leave it at that.

I enjoyed that game the most out of the entire season. Notre Dame had another great goal-line stand at the very end. I remember how powerful of an experience it was to win in the Coliseum and what it meant to close out a regular season undefeated. You cannot say they did not deserve the opportunity to play for a championship. Every step of the way they found a way to win, and the fact that these guys finished like that was awesome—it resonated with the alumni extremely well.

After the game, ESPN had a set on the field and Coach Kelly and Te'o came back out to be interviewed. All the Notre Dame fans stayed to watch, and it was a great scene. It's hard to explain the feeling when you know you're No. 1 and you're going to play for the national championship.

The visiting locker room at the Coliseum is really cramped. There's not much elbow room, and it's almost impossible for a coach to see his whole team when he's trying to talk to them. But after this game, it did not matter. It was pure euphoria in there. Those guys will remember that scene the rest of their lives.

And let's not pretend there's not a little pressure involved. You come that far, you're still unbeaten, and you've only got one left in the regular season. And it's a game most of the experts think you should win because USC has lost three of its last four—including at UCLA the Saturday before—and their starting quarterback Matt Barkley is hurt.

I knew how much it meant to a lot of guys. It set the tone for what Notre Dame was about, the alumni network, and how guys are there for you after you are gone. It was amazing how many people I heard from who were over the moon about the success this team had. It really did my heart good.

To see Riddick have success was neat. He was tenacious—he was the engine that made that team go offensively with 146 yards. Our running game was the gist of that success because it let us manage the game and control the clock. But, more than anything, we were a tremendously disciplined defense and it showed that night and all throughout the year.

CHAPTER 40
NO STEMMING THE TIDE

In 2012 the Notre Dame football team set a mark that hadn't been done before—they were the first Notre Dame team to go 12–0 in the regular season. In 1988 12–0 included a bowl game. This was 12–0 in a hard-fought season that will stand the test of time—thanks to discipline, focus, and resilience.

Golson didn't try to do too much—he understood his role. There was great adaptability. No one person stood out offensively, and, even defensively, you had a superstar at linebacker—but this was a team across the board.

It was a young quarterback picked up by the leadership at the offensive line positions, at tight end, and at the running back positions. They rallied around the young guy, took care of him, and let him develop his own leadership capabilities. This required others to step up and make plays so Golson did not have to be any different than what he was. That was the magical aspect of this team—guys stepped up for him and tried to minimize his mistakes. Rees handled his role—he helped Golson succeed and was a great backup as a seasoned player who had played at a high level when those struggles happened.

On defense it was leadership at every level playing for high stakes for 12 games. It told you who they were—discipline, commitment, focus, overcoming adversity, persevering, overcoming letdowns. That's how you win championships. That's what makes college football so great.

Every week requires a new focus and requires you to come out and do your best—whether it's the start of the year or midterms. You do not have the luxury of taking time off. You've got a full season, and there's no wavering of expectations. You have to be locked in from start to finish. What set this team apart was that they managed all those aspects while also being college student-athletes. You always have thoughts and expectations, but there was great selflessness too. You have to draw from a lot of things today to go undefeated.

* * *

The national championship game was not good. We were playing an Alabama team that was as close to a pro team as you could get. But, still, this was amazing for the Notre Dame football family. All kinds of guys from previous national championship teams—1973, 1977, 1988—made their way to Miami to support this team. They provided a level of spark for those guys to say, "Hey, we know what it's like to be champions, and we know what it's like to be Notre Dame football players. This will last beyond your four years at Notre Dame, and we will be there after you leave Notre Dame. You will still be a member of the fraternity."

Manti Te'o—and the Fighting Irish—just came up short against the Tide in the 2013 Discover BCS Championship Game.

The game did not end as everyone had hoped. Alabama had two great backs in Eddie Lacy and T.J. Yeldon. They also had a very solid QB in A.J. McCarron, who made it to the league, and a very solid defense. I saw Lacy take one of our linebackers and throw him down. Several times we were right there in the position to make plays, but they were just stronger and more physical than we were. They got after us physically more than any other team, and it showed.

Watching our guys come out to warm up and then watching Alabama, there was a sheer size difference. I was really struck by that. It opened my eyes. The Crimson Tide could be a pro team, with great players on both sides but especially on defense—C.J. Mosley, Dee Milliner, Ha Ha Clinton-Dix, Landon Collins. Their secondary was one of the best in the country.

Alabama ended up leading the nation in total defense, rushing defense, and scoring defense—and it showed that night in Miami. Their defensive coordinator at the time was Kirby Smart, who is now the head coach at Georgia.

Amazingly, that Alabama team actually lost late in the regular season to Texas A&M and Johnny Manziel. Nick Saban's team had been No. 1 until that defeat. And even the SEC Championship was a tight 32–28 Alabama win over Georgia that could have gone either way. But you sure did not see any weaknesses there in the national championship game.

I give Golson a lot of credit for the way he handled himself that night. It was a little bit ugly early, the Irish were down 28–0 at half, but he hung in there, made some plays, and hit some passes. Notre Dame just did not have enough firepower to make any serious inroads.

Before the game, each team was granted a set number of tickets. We had tons of requests, but our athletics director, Jack Swarbrick, made a point to provide some extra access from his own allotment for our Notre Dame football alumni. That wasn't lost on me because we got all those guys from those previous teams tickets to attend that game. That's what makes Notre Dame Notre Dame. We said, "We want our former players to be a part of this great event and be there for one another."

It's critical that we are more than a football team. It's a high-visibility sport, but those previous players stand out as who we are—part of the Notre Dame athletic family. Even current student-athletes who played other sports were there. That had great value for our guys.

The team stayed in Fort Lauderdale, and it was not the postgame party we were hoping to have. But a number of former players came and showed some love, and the current players were grateful for that.

CHAPTER 41
BUILDING ON A MOMENTOUS SEASON

After the 2012 season we thought the future of Notre Dame football was in great hands and that we'd be back in that situation multiple times. But it was not that simple because of changes after that season. Coach Bob Diaco left for UConn to become the head coach, and Brian VanGorder, the linebacker coach from the New York Jets, came in to be the new defensive coordinator.

When you look at Notre Dame and its championship teams, a common theme is defense—a stellar aspect that often set the tone for those title teams. VanGorder brought a shift in defensive philosophy that changed the trajectory of the team as it related to the success of the program and subsequent struggles in the years following.

That 2012 defense ranked second in scoring defense at 12.77 points per game—the best by a Notre Dame team since 1988. They were 11th in rushing defense and seventh in total defense, the highest ranking since 1980. That group had a lot of leadership, but then they lost the coordinator and they lost Te'o and some other key defensive players. So the team looked quite different a year later.

The two corners were back, but on the defensive line we lost Lewis-Moore. Stephon Tuitt and Louis Nix were back, and they were key components. The key loss was Te'o—I can't express enough how big of a hit that was—his leadership plus talent and production. He finished second in the Heisman voting, and it was not just happenstance that he moved to the NFL. Those two things were impactful in us going to 9–4 the following year.

Notre Dame actually was a better offensive team in 2013 in terms of putting points on the board. But the defense was not as productive. The impact of these changes carried over for the next few years, although they did win the Pinstripe Bowl in 2013.

Then in 2014, they went 8–5 and struggled at the end, losing five of their last six games in the regular season. The Music City Bowl win over LSU was a shot in the arm. But we gave up almost 30 points a game in 2014. There were some good players—Nix, Tuitt, Bennett Jackson, Russell, freshman Isaac Rochell, Day, freshman Jaylon Smith—all guys capable of playing at a high level. But the defense had regressed. They weren't reacting well enough, and they were not playing fast enough. The last seven games of the regular season they gave up at least 31 points every time—and that made it really hard to win.

In 2015 Notre Dame went 10–3, but the offense won a lot of those games—including shootouts at 42–30, 41–31. The defense was not the anchor in those years. Notre Dame is at its best with a strong defense. Quarterback DeShone Kizer played well, but there was pressure on those guys to make more plays. The only losses that year were on the road to a very good Clemson team in a two-point game that could have gone either way, a two-point game at Stanford, and then the Fiesta Bowl loss to No. 7-ranked Ohio State.

* * *

Then going into 2016 it was maybe the most pivotal season in the Coach Kelly era. They went 4–8, and it was a whole combination of things. VanGorder's defense was extremely difficult and just seemed to make players think too much. We gave up 50 points at Texas in the double-overtime opener, then gave up 36 points at home to Michigan State, and gave up 38 points in our loss at home to Duke. VanGorder was let go after the 1–3 start because of the struggles, and that tells you a lot about what happened on that side of the ball. You just don't see that happen in the middle of a season.

I give Coach Kelly a lot of credit. As painful as that season was, it would have been easy to just say, "Hey, that's just a blip. We'll be okay." Instead, it gave everyone connected with the program a reason to take a good, hard look at what they were doing. Coach Kelly spent a lot of time with Swarbrick taking stock of the situation, and he made some hard decisions with his staff. But it probably needed to happen, and it resulted in Coach Kelly sitting down with every single player to find out what they were thinking. It really paid dividends.

In 2017 Mike Elko came in from Wake Forest as the new defensive coordinator. He had no connections to Kelly or to Notre Dame, but we saw a shift. The other big change was bringing in Matt Balis as the strength and conditioning coach—it had a dynamic impact on the football team and the trajectory of where it could go after that. The big focus was making sure the team could still do the things it needed to do to physically compete at the end of the year. Because the recent record in November had not been good—four straight losses to end the 2014 season and three losses in four games in November of 2016. And, at some point, you had to say that maybe these teams just hadn't been in good enough shape to last the full year.

It's a long season. Your body takes a pounding—you need strength and endurance, and you get that in the spring in the weight room. It also benefits you mentally, because it helps you not lose focus and have those mental errors when you get tired in games. The game is as much mental as it is physical. You have to challenge yourself to get there, and you do a lot of that in the spring.

In 2017 the only November losses were the really tough one in a crazy environment at Miami and then one at Stanford, but I saw a different team. They did not struggle on the back end of things. They made a definite improvement defensively—the combination of the two losses resulted in that 2017 team finishing 10–3.

But this was a different 10–3 than in 2015 because the defense stepped up and made a lot more plays. They kept Notre Dame in games until the offense could get it going. Defensive guys were not just thinking, they were reacting. Backup QB Book came into the Citrus Bowl against a good LSU team and made an amazing play to Miles Boykin to win a game that looked unwinnable. And, boy, does a win like that change the feel of the off-season.

They went out and performed. It was great to see that reckless abandon and tenacity you need again. On defense it was Jerry Tillery, Andrew Trumbetti, Te'von Coney, Greer Martini, Asmar Bilal—guys just getting after the football when they had seemed more mechanical the years before.

These guys were more keyed in under Balis—that set the tone for the 2018 season that reasserted Notre Dame and its presence on the college football landscape. You look back at that season, and it was not the things that happened on Saturday that were the most relevant. Elko brought in that defense and brought linebackers coach Clark Lea with him and said, "I just want my players to play." You saw that in how they performed in 2018.

I also saw a different Coach Kelly—he was a lot calmer and more introspective and engaging with the players. If you want to be a great coach you have to be adaptable. He made some tough choices—he and strength and conditioning coach Paul Longo were great friends, but Kelly had to make a decision in the best interest of the team. That made a huge difference. As the 2018 season rolled around you felt something special was afoot. The guys also loved playing for Elko and Lea, so you saw some new energy and a spark in the course of a couple of years.

CHAPTER 42
OFF TO THE CFP

The 2018 season was one to remember and a lot of that was because of the energy coming out of 2017 for the football team. We saw quarterback Brandon Wimbush have a good year, and we were excited about this team because of the defense. It was fitting—there were a lot of explosive playmakers.

The season kicked off with the Michigan game—and it was apropos that it was Michigan because it was the 30th anniversary reunion of the 1988 Notre Dame national championship team. As exciting as that game was, we were not hitting on all cylinders, especially offensively. I do remember one touchdown pass from Wimbush to Chris Finke that was off-the-charts amazing.

Jafar Armstrong scored a couple of touchdowns in his first time on the field, and the 21–10 halftime lead turned out to be enough. The final score was 24–17.

We made some mistakes, we had some opportunities, but all in all we saw a solid defense that really stepped up. It was reminiscent of the formula for success in 2012 and 1988, with defense setting the stage and making plays to win games. It was a great start, and it was special that it started with Michigan, the same as in 1988.

* * *

The next week versus Ball State probably should have been a walkover, yet we struggled. Wimbush threw three interceptions, even though he also had 297 yards. You could see some things offensively; we also had some success on the ground. But when you turn it over you put your defense in tough positions and it can come back to bite you.

We had expectations for Wimbush with a full year under his belt, but he struggled, and it was hard to watch. The defense stepped in and made plays. Coney was outstanding, along with Alohi Gilman and Drue Tranquill—there was lots of defensive senior leadership. The guys who were game-day performers—Crawford, Coney, Tranquill—got things ramped up.

Sam Mustipher and Alex Bars were two great offensive linemen. Wimbush was a senior and we had Dexter Williams at running back. Then add in Chase Claypool and Miles Boykin, and you had a bunch of senior leaders. That's the formula—senior leadership playing at a high level.

Still, we had to survive an onside kick at the end, and the final score of 24–16 was a little nerve-racking.

* * *

We got to Vanderbilt and we struggled again. We were successful running it with Tony Jones, but you could see the offense was not as capable as it should have been. We snuck away with that game at home—three games in a row when we were just squeaking by. It was not where we should have been. I have the utmost respect for Wimbush—I just wish we had been able to do more to get him where he needed to be.

We got this one accomplished with 245 yards on the ground. But we gave up a 16–0 halftime lead and then had to stop them at our own 31 on fourth down with a minute left to hold on at 22–17.

* * *

The transition to Book at quarterback started at Wake Forest with no particular drama. They kept the decision under wraps all week so he was comfortable, with no real pressure to be the man. He had a stellar game against Wake Forest. We had played them the prior year and they gave us some difficulties, especially their defense. That game in 2017 was a dogfight late until we pulled away.

Book was really solid given the circumstances and with the team on the road for the first time. He connected on 25 of 34 throws for 325 yards—and with 566 total yards in a 56–27 win there's not much to debate.

It was a little bit of a similar situation to when Rees gave way to Golson from 2011 to 2012. We moved to a first-time player, and we just hit on all cylinders his first time out against Wake. The offense played great—it was a big shot in that season that got us over the hump. The offense started to click, and the defense kept getting better. For Book it was just the kind of game he needed—and it really helped everybody's confidence after a tough first few weeks on the offensive side. He scored three times himself on runs and we had six rushing touchdowns combined.

* * *

Stanford had a great back in Bryce Love, but our defense stepped up and contained him. Nyles Morgan, Coney, Bilal—these were guys who could get to the ball. Tillery had four sacks, and I loved all that about Elko and Lea's defense. They ended up outrushing Stanford 272 yards to 55 yards, and that's a big difference in the ballgame.

Tranquill had moved from safety to linebacker, and that speed and cover ability really showed in that season. The Wake game was the turning point for the offense, and the Stanford game was a coming-out party for Williams (161 yards). He was an explosive runner who added another weapon to the offense. Book threw four scoring passes, Boykin caught 11 balls, and the defense held Love to 73 yards.

Stanford came in unbeaten and we outgained them 550 yards to 229 yards. It had been a while since a Notre Dame team did that to Stanford.

* * *

Virginia Tech was next—and everybody said playing in Blacksburg, Virginia, was going to be as tough as it gets. Playing in a hostile environment—how do you handle it? We were not prepared the previous year when we got rocked at Miami. The 'Canes completely took us out of our game. Could we come out there and not be intimidated? Everybody had been talking about it because Notre Dame had never played there. It was another key point—how do you handle those difficult times?

It was a night game televised on ABC, and the place was rocking. I had heard about how animated the fans could get. But we took care of business handily. We were up 10–9 and Julian Love picked up a fumble in the second quarter and took it 42 yards for a score. At that point I knew our guys were as good as advertised. Tech came back to score, but Williams came right back with a 97-yard run that quieted the crowd. We just rolled from there. You saw the talent and the moxie this team had and needed.

It was tight for a while—a one-point game at the half—but every time Virginia Tech got the fans revved up, we had an answer of some sort. Book was 25-for-35, and once again his proficiency was impressive. He didn't make many mistakes, which gave us a chance. Boykin had a couple of scoring catches and 117 yards receiving.

* * *

Back home we had Pitt next. Coming off an emotional night in Blacksburg—we had to come off that and manage the next week. Can you come back and play the way you need? It came down to a fourth-quarter

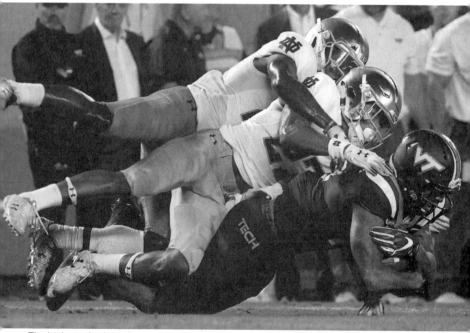

The Irish crushed the Hokies in October 2018 on their first visit to Blacksburg.

pass from Book to Boykin to win. Notre Dame never led until those two hooked up from 35 yards out with less than six minutes to play. You had to lock in and push through. Julian Okwara was all over the place defensively, but we needed every one of those plays to win it 19–14.

Next we went to San Diego, and it was actually Navy's home game. But there was a Notre Dame pep rally with 800 people at Navy Pier—it was ridiculous. Notre Dame had not played in San Diego, but it showed how engaged the Notre Dame fan base was. Williams, Boykin, and Book all had great games. Book seemed to be able to complete 65 or 70 percent of his passes most weeks, and he threw it for 330 yards this time.

It was 27–0 at halftime and it ended up 44–22. The defense held Navy to 70 rushing yards in the first half, and they can't play much better than that.

What stood out to me was that we made it feel like our home game in a completely different city. The Notre Dame Club of San Diego put on a great show. We even had former players at the pep rally—it was a special weekend that elevated the Notre Dame name. The game was hard fought—but it was never in doubt as far as I was concerned. It was another great event—the fan support was amazing.

* * *

At Northwestern we won handily at 31–21, even though it was touch and go early on. After a halftime tie, Notre Dame outgained the Wildcats 209 yards to 32 yards in the third period. Book got better and better, throwing for 343 yards this time and running it in from 23 yards in the final three minutes to finish things off. And Claypool had another nice night with eight catches and 130 yards.

Then we came home for a night game against Florida State, and it was a reunion of the 1993 game when it was No. 1 Florida State versus No. 2 Notre Dame. Notre Dame knows how to party, and it was great to see Wooden, Becton, McDougal, Dawson, and lots of other guys from that 1993 team. We celebrated another great win. It was a huge rushing performance by Williams (202 yards and two scores), with

Wimbush filling in at quarterback and getting three touchdown passes with Book banged up and out. We celebrated a great team by wearing green jerseys on a really cold night and winning 42–13.

It was 32–6 at halftime, and you just had a sense that Florida State wanted to get out of the chill and go home.

* * *

Then we went to New York to play a No. 12-ranked Syracuse team in Yankee Stadium, and our fans were phenomenal again. The defense throttled what was thought to be a great Syracuse offense. Their quarterback was Eric Dungey, and we got after him early and knocked him out of the game—it was never really in doubt.

The final score was 36–3. And this was against a team averaging 44 points a game. Syracuse didn't score until they got a field goal with 10 seconds left. Six sacks, three interceptions, and 11 tackles for losses in our win. It's all about the defense.

We played a New York team in New York, but we showed up as the home team as far as the level of play and the fan base. Notre Dame loved New York and New York loved Notre Dame. It was another electric night. By the end of the year, this team had gone from San Diego to Chicago to New York, then back to play USC in Los Angeles. I doubt another college team had done anything comparable to that level of travel.

* * *

Any chance to beat USC is music to my ears. We found a way to get a win out there. Book had a wonderful game with 352 passing yards. Williams played well—he had a strong rushing performance with 91 yards and a big 52-yard scoring run to give his team the lead. Jones scored the game-clinching touchdown on a 51-yard reception down the Notre Dame sideline with about three minutes to play. And all this came after an early 10-point deficit and with USC gaining 289 yards in the first half.

When you look back it was a mirror image of both 1988 and 2012 in some ways—finishing an unbeaten season by winning at the Coliseum over your biggest rival.

Considering the amount of traveling they had to do late in the year, plus the focus, determination, and obstacles and odds they had to overcome, all while staying keyed in, it was phenomenal. They went coast to coast with all that in a month's time—yet that's what made that team special. It was the ability to overcome jet lag and take care of business against some tough opponents.

* * *

Making it to the College Football Playoff for the first time was a major achievement for the program. But Notre Dame just couldn't keep up with Clemson in the semifinal game at the Cotton Bowl.

Trevor Lawrence, as a freshman, was even better than advertised. Notre Dame lost our star defensive back Love to a head injury, and Lawrence had a field day throwing the ball. On the other side, Clemson's defensive line just gave Book fits all day long.

In some ways, it was eerily similar to the title game against Alabama six years earlier. It was so disappointing not to be able to hang in there better after going 12–0 and feeling like you earned your way to that position.

Clemson won 30–3, Lawrence threw for 327 yards, and all we got was a field goal in the first period. It was 23–3 at halftime, and Clemson looked like the team that belonged in the championship game against Alabama. Clemson played without lineman Dexter Lawrence, maybe their best defensive player, because of an NCAA suspension—but it didn't really matter.

Clemson's defense made it tough to run the ball, and the short passing game with Book never really clicked.

It was a tough way to finish.

CHAPTER 43
COACHES TO REMEMBER

I've gotten to know multiple Notre Dame coaches over the years—first as a player and then as an employee of the university. You get a great feel for a coach when you talk to his players and to his assistant coaches.

I've talked ad nauseum about Coach Holtz and the various things he has done, his persona, and his legacy—a legacy that was built off his players and the assistants who coached under him. You had to be thick-skinned to coach under him because he was hard on his coaches. For a couple years we actually did not have an offensive coordinator because it was Coach Holtz who was really handling that.

Alvarez was only there for two years as defensive coordinator, but it put him in a great position to go to Wisconsin as head coach. I got to play under him my freshman year in 1989, and the things that stuck out the most were his demeanor and how his guys reacted to him. He had some very colorful personalities on that side of the ball, and he had to have a good understanding of the game and of people.

I was on the scout team and saw how Alvarez coached and interacted with his players. He was tough, but he was very well respected. You had "Flash" Gordon, Pritchett, Jones, and Lyght—some big, looming personalities. Alvarez coached the linebackers and those guys gravitated to him. Even quieter guys like Mike Stonebreaker wanted to be around him. He did not have an air of being unapproachable, yet he commanded a level of respect, like "I'm gonna look out for my guys. I'm someone you can come to, but do not come with any BS." He demanded that you step up, but he would listen to you and be there for you.

Those guys loved playing for him. They did not want to let him down. Even Coach Holtz did not fool much with the defense during Alvarez's time because he had a compete mastery of what he wanted to do. How he ran that defense and what he got out of them—it had a lot to do with that 24–1 streak. He knew how to prod and ride guys. He knew how to get his guys to play at a high level. He still has a strong relationship with those guys to this day—you hear that from Frank

Stams, Pritchett, and others. He carries himself with such grace, even now. They were gonna follow him, and that happened here.

Alvarez oversaw two of the most dominating defensive teams in Notre Dame history in 1988 and 1989. They would give up yards, but it was all about scoring points. Those were two of the best teams, ranking third and allowing 13 points a game in 1988—you had stalwarts across the board. That 1988 championship was won via defense—built front to back on the front line. Zorich at the point of attack—he came in as a linebacker and he added speed up front. Execution and being in the right place at the right time—this team kept things in front of them. Alvarez was very good at coaching the fundamentals of the game.

The 1989 defense rated even stronger than the 1988 defense just by the number of ranked opponents they played and the success they had. The linebackers set the tone, and those were the guys he coached. It was Ned Bolcar, Pritchett, and Stonebreaker in 1988, and those guys were on point. See ball, get ball.

He communicated to players something that was not overly complicated. It was about understanding tendencies, reading offensive formations, and diagnosing them quickly. What are they going to try to do to you based on formations? Over the course of the week you were not thinking about what to expect, because you knew what they would do—he created your keys in terms of offensive alignments.

Read the formation, read the guards, read the eyes of the quarterback. When you are in zone, here are your reads. The 1988 team gave up only 156 points over a 12-game stretch—they got after it on defense. They gave up more points against Miami than any other game all year, but the defense made the play at the end. No matter what you played they were going to come out victorious. The defense expected to make plays and that was the reason Notre Dame won.

My freshman year in 1989 we played six ranked teams that season— No. 2 Michigan, No. 17 Air Force, No. 9 USC, No. 7 Pitt, No. 17 Penn State, and No. 7 Miami, and then we also beat Colorado in the Orange Bowl when they were ranked No. 1. We gave up 14 points a game that year against an amazing schedule, and that defense was handled by Alvarez. We just had to go out and execute.

I played against those guys in practice, and they just kept coming in waves. I felt I was fast, but these guys would be in a great position all the time. It did not matter who was in the secondary, the guys stepped up. The linebackers chased us around—the aggressiveness with which they practiced was astounding. They knew where to be and how to play, and that enabled them to play faster.

USC was known to have a fast offense, but we matched them because our guys were coached up and excited to play. We never missed a beat. Look at those two years and both defenses were in the top 10 in points against—and the strength of the schedule was ridiculous. It was a remarkable thing to see.

As a person, Alvarez is someone I owe a lot to because he was someone who was approachable. He understood what it meant to be a player and a human being. I know how much he cared for the guys who played for him and the guys who worked under him. When Mario Morris became our new CFO at Notre Dame, Alvarez called and said, "Hey, take care of my guy." You know that when someone cares for you, you're going to do more to make them proud of you.

He instilled a real pride in those who played and worked for him. There's a sense of ownership—he exudes leadership—and he knew how to manage and stay cool in stressful situations. You never saw him panic. You looked to him when you needed to get something done. You could be in the trenches with him and feel good about it. He was not looking to take credit for what you did.

He was humble and comfortable with himself. It was not about him—it was about everybody's success. He understood how a team required multiple guys working together, and it was all about, "I'm going to be in there with you." He's still connected and knows what's going on with his players' families and their lives—same as when you were an 18- or 19-year-old kid.

* * *

Jim Strong was my position coach when I got to Notre Dame—he had a southern twang to his voice, but he was a salesman and he was pretty damned good at it. As the running back coach and offensive coordinator, he had a way of connecting with guys across the board. He was very charismatic in how he presented himself. He was kind of folksy—we called him the Silver Fox—but he had this energy and excitement that he brought to practices and games.

He was very passionate about what he was talking about it, and he cared about the people he coached. I was only there one year under him before he left to become the head coach at UNLV. He would always ask how my mom and dad were doing—it was small talk, but it was reassurance that he was just a regular guy. He was demanding and would get after you. He would get on my brother Tony, but even my brother had a level of respect for Coach Strong. He was a strong relationship builder.

He would know things about you that you would not think a coach would pay attention to. He was a details guy—who is this person and how can I get what I need from him? He wanted to get the best out of you. We were individuals amidst a slew of uber-talented players—with some tough successful running backs. And he coached them all—my brother Tony, Ricky Watters, Kenny Spears, Rodney Culver, Anthony Johnson, Braxton Banks. He had a way of connecting on an individual basis that was rare. Most of those guys went to the league, and you do not get there by accident.

He did not do a lot of yelling at people, but he would pull you off to the side and tell you to step it up. He was aggressive, but he managed a lot of personalities in those backfields. Johnson was a leader, but he was not a vocal guy. My brother was outspoken and drove Johnson nuts. Watters was a big personality.

What can you bring to the team and how do you fit into that backfield? There was only one football that had to keep a lot of guys happy. He got guys to understand that they better make the most of their opportunities. He knew how to connect with people and get something out of them that they did not know they had in them.

He was good at giving you what you needed at the right time—he knew when to be the stick and when to be the carrot. He made sure to get out of you what was required for you to be successful. He was an ambitious guy, and he was the offensive coordinator my freshman year. We were a running football team, to say the least, but he also had to manage expectations of the receiver group looking to showcase themselves. That was his strong suit—positioning himself between players and other coaches. He had to be a blocker for his guys and a caregiver—and he was trying to get somewhere himself.

A lot of this success came from his ability to manage relationships. He's been out of coaching for some time now. He now works in real estate in Branson, Missouri, and has been very successful.

* * *

My favorite coach I had was Coach Earle Mosley—to me he was the best, which had a lot to do with his personality. He was not a rah-rah guy, so we connected there. He was not an authoritarian or overly ambitious. He was not a lot of things, but he was sincere—he wanted the best for you. He was one of the most practical individuals I'd met.

A lot of that had to do with his time in Vietnam—he would tell us stories in meetings, and you learned real quick that he was not a guy to mess with. I can count on one hand the number of times I heard him yell at an individual. Our running back group was Culver, Becton, Zellars, Bettis, and me. All those guys went on to play in the league except Becton.

My brother was a big personality. We were in a meeting once, and Tony liked to take control—everybody knew that. This was Coach Mosley's first year, and Coach was really low-key. He said, "Hey, Tony, let's keep it down," but Tony kept cracking jokes. He stopped the film and started talking—telling us about his time in Vietnam when he slept in a tree in the middle of the jungle for two weeks to avoid being captured. He was very patient, but he was also a little mysterious about some of the things he did and saw in Vietnam. Some of it was not pretty and required a strong constitution, and it all was out of straight survival.

He was basically telling my brother to knock this stuff off or he'll come up missing. Coach was not a joker—he did not wisecrack. We got really quiet, and from that point on people got locked in when it was time to listen—eyes up and ready to go.

He brought in the gauntlet—the machine that tore the skin off of our arms and legs. He knew just where to poke and prod you to do a little more. For me, he simplified it. He got me to do more north-south running and less east-west running. And that was a simple request. His message to me was, "As a junior, just do the footwork and give me four yards—after four yards you're on your own." He coached me to a point. "After you get here it's all you." That freed me up to express myself. That was the first time someone kind of gave me an option.

He was never controlling. He'd say, "These are the things we are gonna do—this is what I need from you. I'm here to do a job and you are here to do a job. I'm not gonna be your best friend. We're not gonna hang out. I'm not selling you on something, but this is what I need you to do."

He was strong willed but not overbearing—just very matter of fact: "I will give you some directives and you either follow them or not. If you follow them, we will be okay. I don't have time to stroke your ego—we are here to work."

From the time he came to Notre Dame in 1991 through '92, my last year, we had some of the most successful backfields anywhere—me and Bettis, then Becton and Zellars right after us. He cultivated that talent. He was very instrumental in them making it to the NFL because of his approach.

I just wanted to play—I did not even think about the league. He helped me get over the hump. It was not pretentious—not self-absorbed.

Bettis was a Heisman candidate, but there was no animosity in the backfield. His attitude was, "I'm your coach—I'm not your buddy."

He reminded me of my dad—and he was like a dad to a lot of our guys. Not warm and fuzzy necessarily, but he did everything he did with the idea that we've got work to do. He was a family man—he worried his butt off. He reminded me of my dad in terms of how he did things. Just got up and went to work every day.

I'd talk to him at meetings and pick his brain. I started watching more film—he taught us how to do that. He had a way of connecting and getting guys to buy in. Who is this guy and where did he come from? "Take care of your schoolwork, we'll see you at practice. We're here to work." He had a very old-school, rugged approach. You did not want to get too far down the road with this guy.

I still keep in touch with him, and he still has that same low-key perspective. He's not trying to be your friend. He treats me like an adult versus the 21-year-old kid I was years ago. There's still this level of respect he commands when you engage with him. You know he cares and it's not artificial. It is genuine.

As a Black male he was a strong role model for me. He wasn't the biggest guy, but with the manner in which he carried himself, there was a lot of respect and admiration. What he did share with us gave a perspective of the toughness it takes to be a Black man, a Black coach, a Black person in this country. He did not complain about anything. He'd say, "Suck it up, keep your head up, and keep pushing forward."

There are a lot of lessons I learned from him. He coached me in football, but I also learned from how he carried and showed himself, always walking with pride and dignity. "Don't talk about it, be about it." That was Coach Mosley.

He had a burning passion for you to be successful, but not because it would benefit him. He wanted it for you. It was about getting you where you wanted to be. No shortcuts—he would not allow those. He would not allow you to shortcut yourself. He wanted to help you see that. It was about doing things the right way.

When you came off the field he would greet you with a high five and a pat on the back.

His deal was, "You can do this—you put in the work, you show up, you give it your all, and we'll be successful. You give me four yards and then you do you. I'll teach you the fundamentals and then you can express yourself. Be fundamentally sound, and after that, do you."

It was a life lesson in a lot of regards—he was not boisterous, just low-key.

"I've got your back—take care of your business and you'll get where you want to go. When all is said and done, give me my four yards. That's all I need."

I'll never forget that.

* * *

Skip Holtz was probably one of the most underrated coaches I've been around. He had a major impact on our offense, particularly the quarterbacks and receivers. He came in as receivers coach in 1990 and was there a couple of years when we did not have an offensive coordinator. He brought a little swagger to that receiver group, even though those teams I played on were primarily running teams.

In 1991 we did a better job throwing the football. Rick Mirer had 18 touchdowns and 10 interceptions, which was an improvement. The tight ends and receivers became a more prominent group—Tony Smith had almost 800 receiving yards and tight end Derek Brown was an NFL first-round pick with 22 catches.

Skip played a big role in the modernization of our offense. We started to use more spread concepts—it was nice to see us change it up and not be so one-dimensional. We still averaged a lot of points—almost 36 a game—with a great offensive line and a good quarterback. Skip was a big part of all that.

Skip was a young guy who could relate—he had a good rapport with players, having been a walk-on at Notre Dame. Receivers had to be great blockers because we were not going to throw it that much. Our receivers were well-rounded, but in 1991 you had a sense that we were going to open it up a little more with three-wide sets and splitting out the tight end. A lot of the influence could be attributed to Skip advocating for the receiver position and the passing game.

Mirer had a solid year in 1991, so going into our senior year there was an expectation we could pass for 2,000 yards, and that we could really have some success in that regard. Receivers started to get a look—some more real opportunities. In 1992 the Michigan State game was kind of a coming-out game—we threw a lot more and had more success with Dawson, Irv Smith, Griggs, and Mike Miller. And Derrick Mayes was a freshman on that team. The strides we made in the passing game could be attributed to Coach Skip working with his dad. The guys just had to step up.

The receivers called themselves the Afros—America's Finest Receivers on Saturday. It was about team bonding. Skip was very conservative and maybe it was a little out of his wheelhouse, but he bought into it from the very beginning.

It encouraged me to start being a little more freewheeling. Those guys had a lot of fun—practice became a lot of fun. We were focused and methodical, but it was awesome to see guys have a higher excitement level out there. We still beat the crap out of each other, but Skip brought a levity out there and he had the backing of everybody on offense.

He represented the youth and vibrancy of our offense, even though we were a run-oriented team. To see us line up in trip sets with me as a slot receiver, even though it was going to be a running play, it was a new dynamic for us. The defenses had to ask themselves, "What are they gonna do?" We scored 36 points a game and we lit it up. Skip had influence in play-calling, in formations and sets, even though Coach Lou Holtz called the plays.

Those were some of the best offenses Notre Dame had during that time. They averaged 35 points again in 1993. Coach Lou allowed a little more freedom in terms of sets and formations. Those were solid passing games, and we spread the wealth.

Skip was a guy the players could relate to—we looked at him as one of us. He understood the perspective of being a player at Notre Dame. He knew when guys needed a break. He made practice fun. When we would go seven-on-seven—the receivers and DBs going at it—Skip would be jawing and high-fiving his guys, which raised the level of play on both sides of the ball. It became a great competition. Even within the Afros group you could see the personalities of the individual guys and it had an effect on the other positions. Make it fun, enjoy practicing, enjoy playing. You don't have to take it all quite so seriously.

He would advocate for throwing the ball more, and sometimes Coach Holtz was not having it. But Skip was advocating for his guys. They broke the huddles saying, "Afros." It created some energy. I loved watching how he interacted with his guys—he was a young, white coach and all the receivers were Black. But they would get after it and he became a part of the group dynamic.

That really helped make those teams what they were. He connected with his guys and he grew as a coach at Notre Dame. The guys who came out of Skip's coaching time were required to have a strong mentality that prepared them for the tough times that would come.

When Skip came back as South Florida's head coach and beat Notre Dame at Notre Dame, I was not rooting for USF by any means. But I was glad to see him have the success he had at UConn, USF, and now at Louisiana Tech.

Skip knew how to engage his dad—and I always marveled at how he managed that. His dad was tough on him. If something went awry he was quick to take the reins.

Skip had a good awareness of the struggles of Black athletes. He had a good perspective and an open mind. He had a level of understanding and could relate—and he would have fun with you on the sideline at practice. That was just his personality.

* * *

Vinny Cerrato was not a coach, but he was an integral part of the success of the Lou Holtz era. Talk about a guy who could recruit. He was the reason for several new NCAA rules because he was such a tenacious recruiter. This guy was everywhere at all times. He knew everybody's area of the country—and he knew what it took to get the best players in the country. He recruited from coast to coast, so we had guys from all over the country—Jersey, DC, Broward County and Miami-Dade County in Florida, New Orleans, Houston, Dallas, California, Oklahoma, Michigan. He knew everybody you could imagine. He was ridiculous.

If the rule was not written, Cerrato would get the most out of any opportunity. If it did not say you could not do it, he was doing it. A lot of guys who recruited back then did not have the benefit of scouting programs and the Internet—you actually had to travel to go see players. He was on the road constantly—in Chicago, LA, New Jersey, DC, California, Texas. You name it, he was there. He was pulling top talent.

You look at the recruiting classes from when he was here—my brother in 1987, Andre Jones, Lyght, George Williams. And this is when Notre Dame was just getting back on the map—they did not have the cachet. He was really instrumental in reigniting the passion for Notre Dame. He was getting a lot of Black players to come to Notre Dame who might not have otherwise come. He got guys out of Miami when that was the No. 1 program. The Derek Browns, Pat Terrells—he hit all the spots.

He had a great formula—lots of skills guys from Florida, California, Texas. The speed guys. Then the power guys—corn-fed guys from the Midwest, Ohio, Pennsylvania, Illinois, Michigan. He could go anywhere and get guys from predominantly Black neighborhoods, and he never batted an eye. He rolled in there like he owned the place.

Bryant, Young, Bercich, DuBose, Mirer—he was the fuel to get some of the best players. Carter, Bobby Taylor, Burris—rattle off names left and right and he was likely the key figure to get these All-Americans to come to Notre Dame before Notre Dame had reestablished its name. Culver, Ismail, Levens, Bettis—we stockpiled talent and he was the key figure creating those pipelines.

When you saw Cerrato walk in you knew what time it was. He made Notre Dame a force to be reckoned with—guys came to Notre Dame from all areas of the country. He put people on notice that he was coming hard. He had Notre Dame alumni filming games and sending the videos to Coach Holtz. He leveraged the Notre Dame network in areas where Notre Dame had not recruited much at all. He went to schools and neighborhoods where white guys do not often show up.

He set a standard where you knew who he was when he came in—and the high school coaches knew him because he was great at relationships. It was a new day. Notre Dame was a white Catholic institution, but he changed that.

He made you comfortable with him because he looked comfortable and looked relaxed. He set up the visits and he knew where guys would fit—"This is what we need you to do when you host those guys." We had some stellar recruiting classes that you could put up with any in the country.

All he did was recruit. That was new for Notre Dame. In the past Notre Dame's idea was to have one of the position coaches also serve as recruiting coordinator. But Coach Holtz knew how important recruiting was going to be—and he wanted someone like Cerrato who had nothing to worry about except being on the road and recruiting. If he was in town, he'd come out to practice and help a little with the kicking game. But he wasn't kidding anybody.

Don't be mistaken—he was there to recruit. He'd be tan and looking sharp. He was the setup man for Coach Holtz, and he was the master. During the Cotton Bowl he would call recruits from the sidelines—guys would come off the field and he'd have them talk to recruits. When they made that illegal, he was already one step ahead finding another way to get it done.

He really knew how to assess talent—he was one of the best in the game. He did his homework. He was very diligent—he kept coming. He would show up at our high school—this cat was everywhere. While he was not a coach, he still made things happen—he knew all the right people in your city.

He watched gobs of high school film year-round. He knew your stats, family dynamics, if you had a girlfriend, your likes and dislikes—he was profiling people before it was a thing. He knew how to click with a player. Whatever you needed, he made it look like Notre Dame had it.

Then he became one of the top personnel guys in the NFL with the San Francisco 49ers and then with the Washington Redskins. You aren't going to be successful without the talent. To assess it and then get those guys is what it was about.

He made kids want to come to Notre Dame—he sold the institution. You have to sell yourself and your program to that athlete. We did not have the greatest passing game, but we were pulling in some of the best receivers and tight ends in the country. A lot of that had to do with Cerrato and getting players to see Notre Dame as the best fit for them.

He was integral in terms of Notre Dame's success in the late 1980s and early '90s.

* * *

I did not have the opportunity to play for Ara Parseghian, but I did have the chance to get to know him as a person. He is an absolute legend, and I am honored to have known him through his players and how he lived his life—in every regard he commanded respect.

He had a larger-than-life presence. He was not a loud person—actually soft-spoken in many regards—but he was a presence nonetheless. He came across bigger than who he was. The conversations I had with him at the national championship team reunions really gave me a perspective in terms of what those locker rooms were like in those times.

He was responsible for one of the biggest turnarounds in college football history, coming from Northwestern to Notre Dame in 1964.

Hugh Devore had been 2–7, and Parseghian came in, took over, and went 9–1. That's really all you need to know. To make that type of leap and finish No. 3 in the country—with the only loss coming by three points at USC at the end of the season—he so easily could have won a national championship in his first year.

It was John Huarte's Heisman season, and passing was not as prevalent as it is now. In one year they were so very conscious of the changes Parseghian made. Huarte had great guys to throw to, starting with Jack Snow, and it shows you Parseghian's ability to assess talent and put them in the best position. Huarte was not the starter the year before and was not considered all that highly. But there was a level of trust and belief in what Parseghian said in the winter and spring. It was about putting guys in new positions across the board.

That 1964 roster had some dominant players—Dick Arrington, Jim Snowden, Norm Nicola, Nick Eddy, Nick Rassas, Bill Wolski, Joe Kantor. Snow was an amazing receiver in that year—and a lot of it was due to Parseghian assessing the talent and getting them in the right place. Snow had caught six passes the year before and he went to 60 in 1964. That's a coaching job like no other.

The roster was not that much different from the year before. To elevate, you have to have buy-in, and I'm not sure you can articulate how dynamic of a change it was. He changed the psyche of the team to build a one-loss program when you did not yet have time to bring in your own guys. He got guys to understand what it was to have a winning mentality. When you have a strong mind-set it affects everything. It's more mental than anything else to get guys to understand this is who you are.

You can change schemes, but the players have to believe in what they are doing. With the Frank Leahys, the Knute Rocknes, the Ara Parseghians, the Lou Holtzes—the success comes from getting the players to understand and buy in to what needs to happen to be successful. You have to understand how you fit to make the system work.

In conversations you would have with Parseghian—and he was a serious student of the game—it was clear that he got to know the guys he played with. Where did they come from? What was their value system? This is where you are going to be most successful. When they've never been a linebacker and you are going to ask them to be a linebacker, that's a tough shift to make. You get them to see their success from a different angle when they are not necessarily comfortable with it—not just individually but for the team as a whole.

During those reunions he would walk in the room, and to see these grown men relate to him, almost falling at his feet just to see him speak, was impressive. It was a sight to see—there was a reverence for him and his wife, Katie. It showed me how important he was to them, not just as a coach but in helping them grow as men, as fathers, as husbands. He did not just develop them as football players. They came to reunions just to see him and catch up with him and see how he was doing—this was decades later, and he still had that kind of impact.

The level of care and love was amazing. It showed that successful coaches are more than teachers of Xs and Os. It's respect for hard work—and they saw the guy at the top expressing the same values that they had in their own lives. There was a consistency with how he dealt with people—his value system was how he lived. He showed people that he cared—he was there for his players.

Years later he was still there to support those guys. In 2016 there was the 50th reunion of the 1966 national championship team. The dinner the night before the game was packed wall to wall—there were more than 400 people. Parseghian held court, and it was amazing to watch. I will cherish that always because he was inspiring to be around. "What can I do for you? How can I be a blessing?" That was his approach.

His record at Notre Dame speaks for itself. His worst season was in 1972, when they lost three games—he was consistently winning 8, 9, and 10 games a year. Joe Yonto was the defensive coordinator back then. In 1964 they only gave up single digits in scoring. It's tried and true even to this day—defense wins championships.

In 1966 when they won the national title, they gave up fewer than four points per game and scored more than 36 points per game. Think about that. For three straight years they gave up single digits in points. It was a down year when you gave up 12 points a game in 1967. They finished 10–1 in 1970, and maybe they could have won a championship—the one loss was to USC. That rivalry during Parseghian's time was probably the best in the country.

They gave up a little under 10 points in 1970. In 1971 they gave up eight points a game—the 1973 championship team gave up just over eight per game while scoring more than 34 points. You remember some dominant defensive players who set the tone in 1966—Jim Lynch, Alan Page, Tom Rhoads, and Dick Swatland. Then in 1973 you had freshman Ross Browner, freshman Luther Bradley, Mike Fanning, and Townsend.

His teams succeeded because of their outstanding defenses and outstanding defensive players. It always goes back to keeping things old-school, and he was an old-school guy. Tom Pagna, Boulac, Kelly, Yonto, Mike Stock, and the other assistant coaches—they revered him as a person, even more than as a coach. His success came from his humility—he was one of the most unselfish individuals I've ever come across. His humanity made him an icon and his legacy lives on not just for his success as a coach, but as a human being and his care for others.

Notre Dame people look at him—on the athletic side—almost like another Father Ted Hesburgh.

* * *

One of the most critical positions for any football program is the strength and conditioning coach. That person has to understand how to prepare young men to be successful and buy into a regimen like no other. It's a mental game as much as a physical one.

Notre Dame has had some of the best in the game in strength and conditioning. During my years there, Jerry Schmidt was a short, powerful dude who was committed to doing things at a high level. That buy-in is critical for success. When you walked in that weight room, he owned it.

I remember going in for 6:00 AM workouts in the winter—the most critical time of the year because it had such a profound effect on us going into spring ball. I remember walking across campus in the dark in January and February for those workouts—if we were there at 6:00 he had to have been there with his team at 4:00 AM to get prepared and have everything ready to go.

He was a tenacious guy—he would show you the drills with the expectation that you would do the drills and do them right. He knew how to maneuver with guys. The conditioning you would do even with weightlifting was more about muscle endurance.

Being tired was not an option. He went around getting guys going—he was high energy. He was built for that role. He was able to get you pumped up that early in the day to put the work in. You would make one weight, and you'd come in the next day and he's kicked them up. He'd get you pumped and then you came back in the afternoon to do the runs.

Winter conditioning was the time to get us ready for the season. He was one guy you could also go talk to, even about personal things. He would lend you his ear—and that's a fine line. He could help you through some difficult situations. No doubt he was the best I've been around—and he's still doing it to this day. He won national championships at Notre Dame, at Oklahoma, at Florida, and now he's at Texas A&M.

You wanted to be around him and work for him. We were around him a lot when the coaches could not be there. In the summer, he would get the best out of you. He had a great system to get you to peak at the best times—for the spring and then the fall.

He would give you weight sheets when you went home for three weeks before summer school. And he knew who was doing the work. He was good about preparing you so you would be ready to tackle two-a-days, which were brutal because of the physical pounding. He prepared you for that in the winter and the summer to maintain strength. He was big on maintaining strength during the course of the season.

He talked to every guy. He knew your skill set and knew your body and helped you to understand your body to be successful. These are things you do not see on the football field. His success speaks for itself—guys played for him just like for their head coach.

We enjoyed being around him. It made a big difference for us. People did not see what happened behind the scenes at that point. Now there's a lot more focus on guys in his role, especially with the NCAA time restrictions. People see them with more prominent roles.

* * *

The next guy who was very similar was Matt Balis. I remember walking over by the Gug after Coach Kelly made a lot of changes on the staff after the 2016 season. I'd run into Jerry Tillery after one of their morning workouts, and he'd say, "That's the hardest workout I've ever had."

What stood out to me was that it was so visible—the change was so tangible to the student-athletes in terms of how they were affected. Balis immediately had a huge effect on the team, and yet it was long before that next season got going. I had multiple opportunities to speak with Balis, and his philosophy was much the same as Schmidt's.

There was a commonality that I could reflect on and understand, and it helped me see things. It was going to be fun to watch. It was a different day. People talked about Notre Dame running out of gas in November and not finishing the season strong. You saw that changing. It registered that it was a little different. To see that happen over the course of the winter was not earth-shattering. But when you hear a player say it was so difficult—and they were not offended by it or upset by it—it was almost relief. We thought, "This is what we need."

To go from a record in 2016 of 4–8 to 10–3 the next year, that dramatic change occurred under Balis and how he changed how these guys worked. It was so familiar to me how he shifted the narrative and the mental attitudes of the players. For it to be so tangible so soon was telling. It encouraged me in terms of the future of Notre Dame football.

You have a desire to win and you need those key components to bring it out of you. Balis could do that—top players were excited to work out with him. You want to work because you see the value that will come from it. There's a connection there. How he did it told me a lot about the players' work ethic and commitment.

They were hungry. And you never want to be in the category of just being satisfied. There's always a chance to get better—in the weight room, when you are running. It's the motivation to always do a little bit more.

He's a high-energy guy, easy to talk to—and he's been able to tap into what gets the most out of the young men. The success Coach Kelly is having—a portion can be attributed to Balis' ability to get the best out of the kids and have them sustain that through the season. It's a continual loop of maintaining those gains through the year and doing it at a high level.

Both those guys—Schmidt and Balis—are very much responsible for the success of Notre Dame football, no question about it.

* * *

Another key coach was defensive coordinator Mike Elko coming from Wake Forest starting with the 2017 season. He brought a defense that really fit our guys. And the guy he brought with him as his linebackers coach, Clark Lea, was a huge addition to the Notre Dame defense too.

You think about the transition from 2016 to 2017. There were two key factors for me—the strong defense and the fact that the linebackers were studs. It was the same as back with Alvarez—DuBose, McDonald, Jon Autry, Ratigan, and McGill.

VanGorder had some stud linebackers like Jaylon Smith. I always wonder how much more successful Jaylon Smith might have been in an Elko-Lea defense. Joe Schmidt understood angles—he was the key to getting guys lined up in a complicated defense. He knew the front- and back-end coverages, and he was a key to Jaylon Smith's success because Jaylon Smith was left free to make plays. Schmidt communicated the calls and assignments. People wondered why he was on the field—he was there because without him that defense did not work. His football IQ was off the charts. He got guys lined up and where they needed to be.

Then the switch to Elko's system was huge for our guys—Elko was only here for a year before he went to Texas A&M and he still made huge strides with that group. You go from giving up 27 points in 2016 down to 21 points in 2017—that was significant. Guys had struggled to get on the field, getting lined up was difficult, they were constantly thinking—then you saw the change almost immediately in 2017.

The linebacker corps went from being a question mark to being the heart of that defense. Add players like Tranquill and Bilal becoming leaders—and Martini, who was a nonfactor before that switch. In 2018 the defensive average went down to 18 points—and then in 2019 to 17 points. The defense continued to get better.

What were we going to do when Elko left? Well, I've gotten to know Lea—he knew the defense just as well and he understood the different levels of the defense. He knew how to prepare and evaluate these guys. The same guys who struggled and were confused started to make plays. Lea helped the transition from 2017 to 2018—and you saw how guys developed. They make it to the CFP in 2018 with Coney and Tranquill and Love.

Now we had Drew White, Jack Lamb, Shayne Simon, Owusu-Koramoah—a lot of young players. Tranquill and Coney had taken 90 percent of the snaps in that 2018 season, so I thought the linebackers might struggle the next year and be the weak link. How were they going to manage that? They lost a lot of experience. With Khalid Kareem, Julian Okwara, Tagovailoa-Amosa, Daelin Hayes—at least there would be a strong defensive line and a good secondary with Pride, Gilman, and Jalen Elliott.

Watching the metamorphosis of the linebackers was a thing of beauty in 2019. They just made plays and stepped up—and that was all Lea. His players love him to death. You do not want to let him down. He has maintained a great level of connectivity with the guys he coaches. At the basic level he is a coach—he can put together a game plan, make great adjustments during the game, and coach his guys now. You see Simon, Bo Bauer, and White all stepping up and making plays.

I value him as a coach and a person. Your players will let you know the kind of person you are dealing with. They have a real love for Lea as a person—as someone who cares for their success.

I visited with him at one event and he talked about social justice and how he could be better at communicating with his players. How do I help my Black athletes acclimate better? How do I make Notre Dame better at providing for my Black athletes? It came out of the blue, him trying to be a better recruiter. How do I help guys be successful at Notre Dame?

It was never a Black and white thing. He just saw something that needed to be addressed and he wanted to be better and to afford his guys better opportunities. He has a holistic approach to his team and how to build community—that's where the success comes from. It's not just about having good players. He wants to elevate his game and elevate his guys to be better. That's transformative in this society.

Sometimes white people dance around conversations about race, but he was very straightforward and open to learning. That's the coach in him—he's coaching himself to get better. That's something to build off of.

I know the guys he coaches will have a lifelong connection with him. The success goes beyond Xs and Os—it's about doing the little things, and he does that every day. It brings out who you are beyond the game. He's now the head coach at Vanderbilt, his alma mater, and there's every reason to believe he'll make a great impact there.

* * *

Gerry Faust was one of the most amazing individuals I got a chance to know at Notre Dame. His enthusiasm was off the charts and he absolutely loved Notre Dame—he wore it on his sleeve. But his years as head coach in the early 1980s were difficult even though he lived and breathed Notre Dame.

There were some great players who just never had the success you might have thought they would have had. Those guys struggled at times, and it became really hard for them to get all the pieces to fall into place. There were multiple guys with NFL-level talent, but it all never materialized.

In 1981 there was amazing anticipation going into the year—Phil Carter was a captain. Blair Kiel was the quarterback. You had an All-American at linebacker in Bob Crable, plus Dave Duerson, Stacey Toran, Mike Golic, and Tom Thayer. But you just saw them having a tough time over the course of some of those seasons.

Faust had had tremendous success at Moeller High School in Cincinnati. And there was little question about the excitement level at that time. But it never came easy for this Notre Dame team. They beat LSU in that first game, and it looked like they were off to the races. People thought they'd be unstoppable.

In later years you had Allen Pinkett, Greg Bell, Mark Bavaro, Larry Williams, Steve Beuerlein—a lot of guys who had success and longevity in the league. But it just never really worked at Notre Dame. That staff recruited Tim Brown—I give them credit for that.

To his credit, Faust kept some guys from the previous staff, such as George Kelly and Joe Yonto. It still was probably unfair to think someone with no previous college coaching experience could do this. But Dan Devine had announced that 1980 was his last year and that team lost only once in the regular season, was ranked No. 1 at one point, beat Alabama in Birmingham, then went to the Sugar Bowl and had a chance against an unbeaten Georgia team. And there was a good group coming back in 1981. But it was just hard.

After that LSU game they went to Michigan the next week and it did not go well. Tim Koegel started that season at quarterback and ended up showing up on the cover of the *Sporting News* after that game—unfortunately for the wrong reasons. But that's how visible things were at that time.

I'm guessing a lot of those guys wish they could go back and try to do it all over again.

They did go to a couple of bowl games—they actually beat a Boston College team led by Doug Flutie in the Liberty Bowl. As Faust always said, they just could not get over the hump.

They had some amazing wins—they won at LSU against the odds and Faust ended up on the cover of *Sports Illustrated* the next week with the headline, "I'm Gonna Make It." But it did not happen. They lost four straight games to Air Force. Pinkett did some impressive things as a running back, but it just never quite translated to winning games the way everyone wished it would.

CHAPTER 44
THE IRISH HEISMEN

I had the distinct pleasure of getting to know five of the seven Heisman winners from Notre Dame. Growing up playing football in the backyard, I never thought I'd be recruited to play at Notre Dame, and having the chance to get to know some of the legends who played there has been kind of surreal.

Notre Dame once was just this far-off place to me. My dad talked about some of these guys, but to engage with these individuals emphasized just how special Notre Dame was. The constant thread from those interactions was the similarities in perspective—their will to win and the genuineness in these individuals. They were distinctive people in their own right, but there was a commonality among all five.

* * *

You hear about John Lujack's game-saving tackle of Doc Blanchard in the 0–0 tie against Army in 1946. Yet, to this day, he's still just Johnny. He does not view himself as a mythical entity, a first-round NFL pick, or a very successful businessman. What stood out was him as a family man and as a teammate.

The Leahy's Lads who played for Frank Leahy would come back for reunions and it was great to see those guys reminisce about old times. They had come full circle, and you could sense the level of leadership based on Lujack's interaction with the other guys. He was the man. All the Heisman guys had this brotherhood—there was a level of reverence for those individuals who stood out.

His teammates saw him as a leader—the guys were willing to follow him. He had a charisma and personality that drew people to him. A lot of it was that he made guys feel like, "Hey, I'm one of you." Yet Lujack just presented this level of invincibility and guys had a confidence that someway, somehow, we're going to be successful because this guy is leading us.

You hear the stories of this guy and you get a sense of how he endeared himself to so many because he brought out the best in people. But you felt a sense of awe in his presence. He exuded this quiet confidence. He always made me feel like I was his friend. He was so easy to talk to. You could see how he could bring that confidence to a team.

He led through action. You had to play both ways back then, so he was a star quarterback and the star defensive back too. He was there the first two seasons when Notre Dame did not lose a game from 1946 to 1949. Three national championships and they never lost—I've always marveled at that. How do you get guys to play at a high level for all that time? He was one of the orchestrators of all that. He played in 1942 and 1943, left to go off to the war, and then came back. In 1946 you had lots of guys coming back to South Bend from overseas.

We celebrated some of the guys from that 1949 team in 2019. Only a couple of guys made it back, but it was great to hear their stories. They had been off to war—it was not some sabbatical. Walt Grothaus remembers the intensity of those Army games, but also how measured and calm Lujack was. It was a marvel for those guys to see.

He embodied that Notre Dame family perspective as a dad and a grandfather. It was neat to see him around all his family members. The success he had in business was based on his team. He did not get back to campus as much in later years because of his health, but when he did he always came with his family. There was a humanity there that was impressive. He was dignified but very lighthearted. You could sense the intensity in his conversations, yet the setting was always relaxed even when he was being honored. He could make you laugh. He always acted like, "You're on my team."

It did not matter how much time had elapsed, that Notre Dame mind-set was still there. He helped build that spirit based on what those teams in the 1940s did. He was back for a game a few years ago and I was with him on the sideline and I caught his eye—and it was like we were old friends. That's a guy you are going to follow.

He is what a true leader is—he did not talk about himself. He talks about you and his values and his family and his principles. He could always put a smile on your face, but you still knew he was tough as nails.

He was the man in 1946 and 1947. You had to be willing to get in there and be part of the fight—and that was Lujack as a Notre Dame man.

Lujack was also a great speaker—he was very much at home in front of a microphone and he could really be a storyteller. I remember Bubba Cunningham telling me once about a night when he sat across from Lujack at a dinner in South Bend, and Lujack just told story after story, funny line after funny line. Cunningham had some notecards in his pocket, and he started scribbling down some of the jokes Lujack was telling—by the end of the evening he had enough comic material to last him a long time. Lujack was just an entertaining guy to be around.

* * *

I often interacted with John Lattner at tailgates outside the stadium—those were some of the best times I've had at Notre Dame. He was a rare form and that was something to behold. He'd talk about his Chicago upbringing—he stayed very close to his Fenwick High School connections. I got along with him really well. I definitely was a fan of his for a couple of reasons—he was a running back and he wore No. 41, which was what I wore before I switched to 40.

He was quick-witted, had an amazing sense of humor, and always had a comeback. He would bring his Heisman Trophy to tailgates, and it would be out there in the middle of the parking lots. People would come up and take pictures with it. It made me think, "Dude, what are you doing?" But that's who he was. Pomp and circumstance were not who he was. He just wanted to share this great honor with everybody else. And he often used his Heisman Trophy at charity events to help raise money for some great causes. That was Lattner.

He did not have a long pro career, but he had great success in business. He had that Irish-Catholic mentality. He'd get you going—always quick with a joke. He loved to have fun—from the tailgates to any dinner or function or reunion. He was the life of the show. You would gravitate to this guy. He was self-deprecating—always cracking jokes about himself. An Irish, outspoken, energetic individual.

Every time I saw him, he was the life of the party. He enjoyed life. He was a regular back at the Heisman events for a long number of years. They told jokes. They imitated Frank Leahy. They were hard-nosed guys, but they made practice fun.

He, like Lujack, was very much a family man. Seeing his funeral service at Fenwick, you could see the connections he maintained. He was such a lovely guy—he wanted people to enjoy life as he did. That's who he was. He injected life, comedy, joy, and inspiration. That's how he treated people—he made you feel like you were part of his family.

Everybody in his family went to Fenwick—if you went to Fenwick you were his friend. I always felt at home around him. He was just a great person—so down to earth. He never looked at himself as someone important. He would come to some of the Monogram Club activities—but he really wanted to be out in the parking lot at the tailgate. He loved life and he was a Chicago guy through and through. He was a prince of a guy.

* * *

I was a huge fan of Paul Hornung as a football player—he threw the ball, ran it, caught it, and was both the punter and kicker. One of the best all-around athletes you would come across as a player. He was out-spoken—always said what he thought. He stood his ground, and I can appreciate that. He was never one to back down from anything—he owned it.

We started to do these events at the Super Bowl with former Notre Dame players until his health began to diminish. The year he won the Heisman he was a part of a team that had a losing season. So that tells you how good he was as a player in a 2–8 season. That would not happen today. A lot of that had to do with how complex he was as a player—he rushed for more than 400 yards. He did it all—he could almost win games by himself. I marveled at his ability to do all those things because you just do not see that anymore. He was a fierce competitor. He was the go-to guy. What he accomplished on the field and off was impressive.

He had a great persona and swagger—very different from a Lujack or Lattner. He basked in that limelight. He had a great amount of confidence—a huge, dominating personality. He was a force—you knew who he was. He was going to be who he was. He was one of the best athletes to ever play the game.

He would call and let you know about high school players in the Louisville area. He wanted to make sure guys in the Notre Dame recruiting office knew who those really good players were. He would pick up the phone and let you know you should be talking to this guy— he always wanted to help the football program.

* * *

John Huarte is a great story—one of the great transformations in Notre Dame history and very much the work of Ara Parseghian. And Huarte absolutely will tell you how instrumental that coaching shift turned out to be for him. Those changes Parseghian made set the course for that 1964 season.

When you look at the 1963 team that struggled mightily, you see some of the players they had, and you had to wonder what happened. But it was all different that next year, and Huarte was right in the middle of that. There were some great football players who weren't in spots to be successful. To see the changes from one year to the next were amazing.

Parseghian at that time started bringing in both offensive and defensive players—they weren't going both ways anymore. The tweaks Parseghian made had a profound effect. They went from scoring 12 points a game to more than 28 in 1964. Defensively they went from allowing 17 points to fewer than 8. Huarte went from throwing for 20 yards to more than 2,000. I think the NCAA recognized that 1964 Notre Dame team as the most improved in the country from a numbers standpoint, coming from those two wins the previous year.

The leadership qualities were always there with Huarte—you just needed the right situation to bring them out. Parseghian put him in a position to flourish, so you can imagine the relationship those two had. The system allowed Huarte to excel as a player and brought that team within a minute of being the national champion. They made the cover of *Sports Illustrated* and the cover of *Time* magazine. And that was coming off one of the toughest stretches in Notre Dame history, so you could see the national appetite for a Notre Dame comeback. It was a great story.

It was a tale of two players, as far as Huarte was concerned. His connection with Jack Snow featured one of the best single seasons of production in Notre Dame history. Huarte lights up when he talks about what Parseghian did to enable all of those players to meet their potential. Some of the younger guys on that team set the stage for what would be a national championship team two years later in 1966. The temperament and the system were perfect right then. They had a dominant defense, and it took some synergies to pull the offense together—Huarte was the perfect guy for that. He was like having an extra coach on the field. Their success required every guy buying in and being committed. And let's be honest—it usually doesn't turn around that quickly.

Brian Boulac came back as a graduate assistant in 1964—he always talked about how Parseghian set the tone and then Huarte elevated his game. The relationship those two had was the start of something special at Notre Dame. They synced up quickly and got it going as if they'd been doing it at that level for years. That created a lot of buy-in all across the roster, even among guys who weren't playing all that much—and that says a lot about why those Notre Dame teams in the years to come were so successful.

Huarte is an everyday person—a really enjoyable individual to be around. I always sensed he was just so thankful for the experience he had at Notre Dame, especially that last year. It was one thing to be provided with an opportunity. It was another thing for him to take advantage of it as well as he did—and to do it on a national stage with the whole world rooting for you.

* * *

The first time I met Tim Brown was the Sunday after a Notre Dame game against Stanford. My parents and I were waiting for my brother—both my brother and Brown lived in Stanford Hall. Brown had had a great game the night before, and he was very engaging and cordial and polite—it was so refreshing. He was the star of the team, so the time he took with us spoke volumes. It was very uplifting.

In another game against Michigan State his senior year he returned two punts for touchdowns—he was like a magician with the football. I was a senior in high school then. How did he get out of that collage of potential tacklers? You go from seeing that on the field to talking to him the next day, and he was so unassuming. You would never know what he just did the previous night.

Sometimes it was tough to imagine myself at Notre Dame. But Brown had talked to my brother about me maybe coming to Notre Dame. He also told me why he came to Notre Dame—it was really more about the education. He was from Dallas and I was from Oklahoma, so there was a level of connectivity there.

In some ways, his situation was similar to Huarte's in terms of what happened when there was a coaching change. It was the impetus to his rise to stardom. Brown certainly had some success, but, as he tells it, he just figured he would get his degree and move on from Notre Dame. He had never thought seriously about professional football as a legitimate option. But then Coach Holtz came in and essentially created the flanker position at Notre Dame to fit Brown and to be able to get the ball in his hands more often rather than thinking he'd simply catch two or three passes a game.

The coaching switch changed Brown's trajectory as an athlete at Notre Dame. Similar to Huarte and Parseghian, maybe Brown would not have won the Heisman if Coach Holtz hadn't come to Notre Dame. Brown talked about how he gained so much more confidence under Coach Holtz and got the ability to take on a leadership role. Also similar to Parseghian, Coach Holtz made a number of position switches in 1986, and those changes paid great dividends. Brown's change was subtle, but it was all about taking advantage of all his skills and getting him the football. Obviously his kick return abilities played a major role too.

Brown was a great communicator and had a great voice as a leader. He took young guys under his wing and talked to them about their responsibilities to keep moving things forward. There were a good number of freshmen on that 1987 team who learned under Brown's guidance and leadership who went on to play major roles a year later on that 1988 national championship team. Coach Holtz made sure we all understood how important special teams were to the success of the team, and Brown's kick returns were a major part of that. He was a special talent and guys wanted to block for him—guys who were starters wanted to make sure Brown had a chance to do his thing.

Tim Brown accepts the Heisman Trophy in 1987.

When I came back to Notre Dame and focused more on getting former players to come back, Brown was a key guy in that initiative. Some of the pro guys had fallen away in the absence of connections. He'd always loved Notre Dame, and it was just the point of acknowledging that with him. We needed to build back those university relationships with guys like him. He came back because we reached out. He became more of a spokesperson, and that was important as a guy from Texas who also was a Hall of Fame player at both the college and pro levels. As we embraced him, he embraced the university. It's about reembracing what brought them to Notre Dame in the first place.

Brown was a superstar, but more importantly he was a friend. It was great to be able to go to Canton to see him and Bettis inducted into the Pro Football Hall of Fame in the same year—and it was even better to celebrate with their families when they came back to be honored on campus that fall.

CHAPTER 45
MORE IRISH QUARTERBACKS

Tom Clements was the national championship quarterback in 1973, but he was also the quarterbacks coach my senior year in 1992. He was quiet and low-key, but he was extremely intelligent. He came from the law community and obviously did not need the coaching business, yet he made substantial contributions to Notre Dame football in the time he was on the staff.

Clements never had gaudy numbers when he played, but he was a real leader. They leaned on him in a lot of respects. The quarterback position is one of great prestige at Notre Dame, and he handled it better than most in terms of his demeanor. He got better every year he was at Notre Dame. He wasn't a big guy from a physical standpoint, yet he went to the Canadian Football League and really lit it up. He was thoughtful and reserved in a lot of ways. He knew the game—he had a high football IQ. He won multiple championships in Canada and it fit him because it had a more wide-open style.

As a coach, he had a great handle on the game. He carried himself in such a way that you had to respect him. Guys like Dave Casper think the world of Clements. He was not a big conversationalist, but, boy, could you count on him. You believed in him. You don't hear a lot about him as a player from those on the outside. But with people connected with those teams, he was as well respected as anybody I've come across.

For one of the last reunions of the 1973 team—and he's always had a tough time getting back to campus because he has been coaching in the NFL so long—we finally got him to come back. I had the utmost respect for him as a coach at Notre Dame. He was mild-mannered—he did not have a personality that said, "Look at me." He was the ultimate team guy—introspective and thoughtful in his approach.

He had great success in Green Bay with Brett Favre and Aaron Rodgers—and now he's in Arizona with Kyler Murray. I can tell you Mirer loved him in the single season they were together at Notre Dame. I've always been a huge fan of Clements. I'm not sure he's gotten the recognition he deserves for all that he has done at Notre Dame. Part of that may be because I don't think he really cared about media attention, even though he was a bright guy who could express himself as well as anyone.

His understanding of the game and his ability to work outside the game have made him who he is. I never saw him get particularly animated. He was very precise, and he wanted to make sure you understood the ins and outs. He was a calming influence on us as players on the offensive side.

* * *

When you talk about Notre Dame quarterbacks and their success, Tony Rice was a flat-out winner, period. He was not your conventional quarterback, but he was a winner.

He was the life of the party, but yet one of the hardest working players during those grueling practices. When you got to a game, he exuded such confidence, and you just knew if he was under center you had a chance to win. He always had a smile on his face, even after the toughest workout.

He would not wear the red jersey, and the hits he would take in practice were ridiculous. Why are you doing this to our quarterback? Why would we beat the crap out of him? His toughness resonated. But he was everyone's best friend. He could hang and engage with anyone—upperclassmen, freshmen, walk-ons—he knew no strangers. That was a key to his leadership. He lost one game over the course of his junior and senior years, and we played in some tough places.

No. 9 was the guy everybody leaned on. Even with all the star power on those teams, Rice was the man. He was always upbeat, and I marveled at it. Guys would run through a brick wall for him. He instilled a toughness I've never seen.

He did not have gaudy passing numbers, but he would beat you in any number of ways. He was a running quarterback, so he was taking shots. The media kept asking how Notre Dame was going to win games if the team couldn't throw the ball any better from week to week. But Rice's record as a starting quarterback was the ultimate answer.

No matter what happened, he'd give you a smile. Even in the middle of two-a-days, he was all cheerful when there was no reason to be cheerful. He was getting pounded on and talking about what a wonderful day it was. He took everything in stride and just kept on moving. He always found the bright side to any situation.

He elevated the quarterback position at Notre Dame. He dealt with the Proposition 48 situation and never let it show. He lifted other people up and made them feel better. He was a big brother to me and remains a friend to this day. If he needs anything, I'm always there because that's what he did for so many guys.

To me, Rice was the best quarterback at Notre Dame. He empowered the people around him to be better as players and people. He always could say the right thing at that right time to keep you pushing on. He never got an opportunity in the league, but I do know that he was a winner. He was going to find a way to pick the team up and carry it to the win. Because he came out and did the little things. He was going to make it happen.

The 1988 team always has a special place in my heart. When we had reunions, Rice was always there—he was a big personality, a big people person. Everyone gravitated to him because of his inner strength and leadership. He was like a rock star when we went on the road. Rice hung with everybody—it did not matter who it was. Terrell, Zorich, Ryan, Brown, Eilers—Rice was the guy who could be anywhere with anybody and make you feel like were the only person he was there to hang out with. Yet he was very comfortable with himself—he did not have to present himself as someone that he wasn't. He could connect with anyone.

There's a reason Notre Dame went 24–1 in his final two years as a starter. Rice was on the cover of *Sports Illustrated* three times during that 1988 season. Maybe that's all you need to know.

* * *

Brady Quinn was the most prolific passer in Notre Dame history, and he was part of that resurrection under Coach Weis. He just progressively got better each year, not just as a passer but as a player and teammate. He grew into that leadership role that you thought he was just made for.

He was here as a freshman in 2003, and I came back to Notre Dame in 2004, so I got to see his interactions. What stuck with me was his humility as a player—he was a team guy. It's hard to be a normal student as the Notre Dame quarterback, but he cherished that normalcy as best he could. He always got better. From the time he played as a freshman in 2003 he had a tremendous drive to be the best.

When Coach Weis came in with the pro-style offense, everything took off. Those two were a perfect match in a lot of ways. That was one of the more prolific offenses I've seen—with Jeff Samardzija, Maurice Stovall, and Anthony Fasano. They really came into their own in 2005 and set things on fire. They scored 12 more points per game in 2005 compared to the previous year, and Quinn's numbers increased exponentially.

Guys just flourished in that system. Samardzija and Stovall were both big, physical receivers. They had big numbers in the passing game, but also a strong running game with Darius Walker. But the leader on that team without a doubt was Quinn. He was one of the more confident guys, but it was not brashness.

He was polite—always open, always willing to sign autographs and make himself available to the people around him. That was his personality. People just gravitated to him and responded to him. I am saddened that he did not have more success at the next level. But he always went out and competed. He was a tenacious competitor.

At the USC game in 2005, he was a huge part of it, even though USC technically won the game. Notre Dame got robbed. The pep rally was ridiculous—it was held in the stadium and Joe Montana was there along with all kinds of other great players. Quinn led an amazing drive to the touchdown that looked like it would win the game.

That was one of the more enjoyable games to watch, even though it was exhausting. I would have loved to have him get one more shot. It was a great USC team, but Notre Dame went toe to toe with them and had them on the ropes.

The energy that weekend was off the charts, and Quinn was as cool as a cucumber. It seemed like everybody in college football was there that day. USC had to feel like they escaped that time. That would have been the game—we had 'em.

Quinn exuded class, and he always presented himself that way. He fought, he competed, and yet he always kept that blue-collar mentality.

He had all the qualities you want in a quarterback. There's a reason he holds all the records at Notre Dame, and I don't see them being broken any time soon.

* * *

Joe Theismann was another one of my favorites, not only because he was a Notre Dame guy but also because he was a Redskins quarterback, which was where I played. He returns quite frequently to Notre Dame for various events and helps out—he's always a great spokesman for Notre Dame at football banquets and Notre Dame Day. He played at a high level in both college and the pros. Throwing for 526 yards in the rain at USC in 1970 was one of the most amazing performances in Notre Dame history.

He was always a gunslinger—a guy who players enjoyed being around. He had great stories from his playing days. Tom Gatewood tells all the stories about their time in the late 1960s and early 1970s. You can argue that they should have won the national title that year. They went 10–1, but they lost to USC, and that's always a tough pill to swallow. But they went on to beat Texas in the Cotton Bowl. Theismann and Gatewood were so in sync as players.

When Tom Carter and I were drafted by the Redskins in 1993, Theismann was one of the first guys who came to the complex to seek us out and offered his help if we needed anything. It was that Notre Dame network in action. He was a Super Bowl champion, and he still made himself available to us.

He was so engaging. He can charm the socks off of you. He just had fun with whatever he did, and he was comfortable in any setting. When Notre Dame coaches would invite him to come to speak at a pep rally or a football banquet, it seemed like he always answered the call.

Those guys who played with Theismann tell great stories about him and Parseghian and some of the magical times they had together. Theismann was definitely a flashy guy in terms of his personality, his style of play, and his leadership qualities, and it all really clicked. Over the years he has been as visible of a representative of Notre Dame and Notre Dame football as anyone. He wears Notre Dame proudly on his sleeve, even with all his success, and that means a lot.

* * *

The Notre Dame quarterback position is probably the most coveted spot in college football. Even for those who have had success, at times it comes with a cost. The pressure, the accessibility—those who handle it well have a greater chance for success. Everyone knows who the starting quarterback is at Notre Dame. It comes with a lot of positives, but there's more to it.

Tony Rice, Rick Mirer, Kevin McDougal—I think about these three guys and all the experiences they went through. Because they were the quarterback, they were in the spotlight all the time. How do guys find the right way to handle that? They relish in the hype to some degree.

A Notre Dame weekend can be a high-pressure, high-stress deal. Lots of expectations. If we lost, you had to be gracious. Rice always had a smile on his face. And then you had to deal with the media—you would walk around campus and all kinds of people wanted to take pictures. There was nowhere to hide. It was a constant spotlight. I always wondered how the guys did it—if the team isn't having success, it comes back to you.

The quarterback is always front and center. Clements had great success, yet he was very reserved and that certainly was interesting. Joe Montana and Steve Beuerlein were other guys who had great success. But it was never easy when you lost. When you win it's one of the most prestigious positions to be in. But when it does not go well it can be a little lonely.

Think about all the expectations for Ron Powlus and all the ups and downs for him. The guys who had success rose to the occasion and brought strong leadership skills to the table. You want the spotlight, but you find out it comes with responsibility.

Tommy Rees dealt with a little bit of everything. He helped Everett Golson to some extent because Golson didn't care about it all. Golson was never excited about dealing with the media—he'd be the last guy out of the locker room, almost as if he thought he could avoid it. Kizer enjoyed more of the pageantry. He liked being the Notre Dame quarterback. It's tough to live up to the expectations, and all of those guys found their own way to handle those.

It's even more complicated now with social media and the Internet. You have to stay within yourself and not get too caught up in it all. You're thrust into the spotlight, but you have to make sure you don't get blinded by it and move away from who you are. Some guys flourish in it and some struggle a little more. Montana did not have a big arm, but he had a presence about him. He defined the role as he went through it as opposed to the other way around. You have to maintain who you are.

Guys naturally look to the quarterback for leadership. Terry Hanratty never allowed the moment to consume him or to get too big. Some guys never settle in and get comfortable. You've got to have some thick skin to deal with it all. The guys who have the most success find a way to keep from feeling the pressure, even if it's there.

Be who you are—be confident in who you are. The position requires that, along with self-awareness. Don't let the role become too big for you. Lean on your teammates and don't try to win the game by yourself. Your teammates take care of you to do your job. You cannot do it by yourself.

The guys who had the most success at Notre Dame did not go out to win the game—they took care of their own responsibilities. Mirer talked about how no one guy was going to win the game. There was a reason they called Montana "Joe Cool." It's about maintaining a confidence in your teammates to know that you can count on a Ken MacAfee or whomever to make a play. Mirer had Derrick Mayes and Adrian Jarrell and Tony Smith.

Guys did it in different ways—but the successful guys had confidence in themselves and confidence in their teammates.

CHAPTER 46
AND EVEN
MORE IRISH

A couple of my other favorites were actually fullbacks. Back in the 1950s the best running back in the Notre Dame backfield was Neil Worden, an explosive downhill runner. I had the utmost respect for him. John Lattner won the Heisman in 1953, but Worden was an awfully good player himself. He was one of the most humble and gracious individuals I've met. He would tell me how much he enjoyed watching me play. I still get starstruck with some of those guys my dad talked about. Worden had a hard-nosed style of play—four yards and a cloud of dust.

I knew about the Texas and Oklahoma teams, but it was my dad who introduced me to Notre Dame, and Worden was one of the guys he would tell me about. He was on that 1953 team, winning nine games with Ralph Guglielmi as the quarterback. Worden was the other guy, besides Lattner, who ran the ball. They played six ranked teams and tied Iowa. Worden was lethal between the tackles—just a bullish guy plowing through defenders. That was not my game, but I was always impressed by his style. He was right up there with the best at Notre Dame. My money was on him.

* * *

My all-time favorite was not a big name coming out and did not have great stats, but Rocky Bleier was hands down my favorite running back. He was humble and so glad to have the opportunity. He persevered through going to Vietnam by always staying positive. I read his book and marveled at the attitude he had. He was part of the 1966 national championship team—not a star, but one of the toughest team members and best blockers.

He would say, "I was not the fastest or strongest, but I was not going to let anybody outwork me." He went around with a chip on his shoulder—"I'm going to prove myself." That work ethic was established very early. He jumped at the opportunity to come to Notre Dame. He did not expect anyone to hand him anything—he worked for everything he got.

In 1966 with Nick Eddy and Larry Conjar, Bleier gained 280 yards and was a receiver and a special teams player. When you would talk to these guys and see them get together and talk about their experiences, Bleier talked about the 10–10 tie with Michigan State being the most physical game he ever played in.

He always said they were a running team—that's what they did. Michigan State had a top-tier defense just like Notre Dame. He was a wrung-out, wet noodle at the end of it. He was always fighting—always there to say, "I'm here for you no matter what." A great teammate at every level, he did the dirty work. And you can imagine what the practices were like against those Notre Dame defensive players—trying to block Page and Mike McGill and lots of other guys of that caliber.

He was a hard-nosed dude—he loved contact and you could see why he became a champion. He was a starter and leader on multiple Super Bowl teams in Pittsburgh—and that was no accident. He's still as active and vibrant as anyone you will see.

* * *

One of my all-time favorite teams in Notre Dame history is the 1977 national championship team. I have a real fondness for those guys. They were an interesting bunch, to say the least—a really eclectic group. And they have a strong bond that transcends time.

Montana, Kris Haines, Jerome Heavens, Vagas Ferguson, Ken MacAfee—just a few of the names on offense. And Dave Huffman and Ernie Hughes on the offensive line. On defense you had Ross, Jimmy Browner, Luther Bradley, Bob Golic, and Dave Waymer. This was a real mixture of guys from different areas of the country—one of the tightest groups I remember.

It was a great backfield with Ferguson and Heavens—two blue-collar guys who did not take themselves too seriously. People talk so much about Montana, but he was really a regular guy. He was the starting quarterback at Notre Dame, but he did not have crazy statistical numbers. But guys rallied around him and believed in him, and he made some really key plays to help win games when it was all on the line.

He became such an unbelievable pro star with the 49ers after he left Notre Dame that it was hard for him to come back to campus. He just wanted to hang out, walk the campus, watch the football games. But it became so difficult because everyone recognized him.

When these guys come back for reunions, they know how to have fun. You could tell the level of camaraderie based on the way they interacted.

The 1966 guys were a little more buttoned-up—more formal. The 1977 guys didn't want to have a dinner—they wanted to tailgate. That's the way they rolled. You see the dynamics between these guys now and you see a glimpse of what their locker room was like. They had fun.

You quickly knew who the leaders were, either by example or by who the spokesmen were. Joe Restic was certainly one of the leaders of that group—he had an ability to connect with people from different walks of life. He later was on the Monogram Club board.

This was a really blue-collar group of guys. They played hard, played with great passion—and you sensed that they enjoyed every minute of the experience.

Those guys talk about the early loss at Ole Miss—how hot it was, how after that game they kind of recommitted themselves to each other, and how that was a key to their resurgence the rest of the season. They came in ranked No. 3 and let that one get away. It could have cost them a chance at a championship. But they didn't let that happen. They didn't let it go off the rails.

They learned to get along with each other. They thrived with guys like Terry Eurick, Dave Mitchell, Steve Orsini, Tom Domin—those role players who provided more than what you saw on the surface. Orsini was the guy who organized so many of these reunions—he was a captain, and he was a Pennsylvania guy like Montana, so those two were very close. Orsini and Eurick really contributed a level of leadership—forget about their statistics. They played big roles in this team's success. They were voted captains, and that says a lot about who they were—especially given the star power on that team. They set the tone in meetings and practice—"We are a family. We are a team." And that continued years later—very much a reflection of this team.

Their Cotton Bowl victory in Dallas over Texas was one of the all-time great finishes for a season—and this was against Earl Campbell the year he won the Heisman Trophy. It was almost unheard of that a team could come into a bowl game ranked fifth, already with a loss, and somehow end up No. 1. But that's how impressive the effort was in that game in Dallas.

At the end of the day this was not a rigid, stuffy group. They truly enjoyed being around each other.

* * *

Notre Dame has had a series of tight ends play at an outstanding level. Statistically the best one to come through Notre Dame was MacAfee. He was a little before his time—he didn't have a long NFL career. Some of that was because he made the decision to become an oral surgeon.

He was Montana's safety net—that was Montana's description of him. He had more than 1,600 receiving yards and 14 touchdowns at Notre Dame. Montana also told me MacAfee would have had a huge football career if he had stuck with it. But he chose a different path. That's why guys choose to go to Notre Dame—not just for the athletic opportunities.

John Carlson, Fasano, Kyle Rudolph, Tyler Eifert—there is an amazing list of names at tight end. MacAfee's life took him in a different direction—he took advantage of a different opportunity.

Eifert was an Indiana guy, and he was just a matchup nightmare—6'5" and 260 pounds—he could line up in so many different places and hurt you. He was not a glitz and glamour guy, but he's still playing to this day.

He was quiet and reserved—he was physical and had speed and power, yet he was very unassuming. He also played basketball, as his dad and brother did at Purdue. There was a decade or more in there where Notre Dame churned out some awfully good players at that position. Eifert had more than 1,800 receiving yards at Notre Dame. He was the total package.

All those guys made it to the league, and most of them played professionally for a good number of years.

Carlson was a tremendous player. Fasano played with Quinn and they had a great rapport. Rudolph has been a force for a long time.

Coach Weis had a play called "Pass Right," where Quinn would throw the ball to Fasano early in that 2005 season. The play came from a young man who was terminally ill with an inoperable brain tumor, and Coach Weis told him he could call a play in a game. That was really a touching thing for him to do.

It was the first play of the game against Washington, and Notre Dame had recovered a fumble and was on its own 1-yard line. Unfortunately the young man—who was named after Montana—died the day before the game. But Coach Weis kept his word and still called the play, and Fasano caught Quinn's throw for a 13-yard gain.

And Fasano and Rudolph still have foundations that do some great work and help a lot of people.

* * *

Notre Dame has had some dynamic running backs come through its doors over the years.

I was part of an era when the running game was at its peak—a lot of yards and a lot of excitement. That's what made the Coach Holtz era tick. It would be interesting to see how teams would play us. They would stack the box, and we would still find a way to run the football. I'm a firm believer that for Notre Dame to be successful you have to be able to run the ball.

In 1953 you had John Lattner and Neil Worden—they combined for about 2,700 yards.

The 1964 team had Wolski and Eddy combining for 1,600 yards.

You get to the 1970s and have a great duo in Heavens and Ferguson—2,200 yards and 12 touchdowns—Mr. Inside and Mr. Outside.

You had Jim Stone and Phil Carter, a balanced backfield, in 1980.

You can go on and on through the years. When you have a strong running game, you've got a great chance for a winning record.

I had a chance to be part of that with Bettis.

In 2015 the next best combo was C.J. Prosise Jr. and Josh Adams—on one of the more prolific offensive Notre Dame teams, especially with DeShone Kizer at quarterback.

When you look at trios of running backs, in the 1990s you had Bettis, Rodney Culver, and my brother Tony.

Another great threesome was Randy Kinder, Marc Edwards, and Autry Denson—2,700 yards and 30 touchdowns.

Notre Dame has always been a rushing team—go back to the Four Horsemen.

Allen Pinkett had some amazing seasons in terms of gaining yards.

When you had perennial top rushing teams, it made a difference.

When Notre Dame is at its best it has a strong running game. And that's the case in 2020 with Kyren Williams and Chris Tyree and C'Bo Flemister. Running back by committee works pretty well.

When I played, there was no animosity. Whether it was Bettis or Culver, you were happy when the other guys had success.

There's a brotherhood, a camaraderie, that supersedes any feeling that one guy had to be the man.

The success comes not from beating your chest, it comes from understanding the needs of the team. That doesn't just happen on Saturdays—it starts during the week when you demand more from each other and lift each other up.

I had a deep respect for Bettis when we played together, and I feel like I know his heart.

Heavens and Ferguson are two of the most genuine people I've ever met.

Ryan Grant and Julius Jones played together in the 1990s. These things go beyond the football field.

Wayne Bullock, Eric Penick, and Art Best—that was another great combination in the early 1970s.

Watters and my brother Tony were part of the same class in the late 1980s and early '90s. They were big-time competitors who both felt they could be the featured back.

Don't forget some of those fullbacks—Anthony Johnson, Edwards, Ray Zellars, and Jonas Gray. That position has disappeared a little bit, but it sure was a force during my years.

You see these mixes of guys, and lots of times these are different personalities. You find a way to incorporate those personalities into the meeting room so everyone develops a level of respect.

CHAPTER 47
PAGE AND CRABLE—TWO MORE OF MY FAVORITES

A person I have such great admiration and respect for is Justice Alan Page. I was never a big fan of defensive linemen, and he was one of the toughest, most vicious defensive linemen to play the game. But he is so soft-spoken—his cerebral, compassionate personality is not what you'd expect. He was a sack machine. And he's a great, gracious family guy and so committed to education based on the things he's done with his foundation.

When he played in the 1960s there were very few people of color on the Notre Dame roster. But he handles everything with such grace. He made his own way and that was never his focus.

We need to hear more voices like his. He is such a caring person, and he understands that young men and women of color need to have more opportunities. His mentality has always been to overcome whatever disadvantages you have. He has been a change agent. How do I make this country better for those who have the least opportunities? He created opportunities for others.

He was all about working hard and being a better version of yourself. Make your community better. Be better for all mankind—broaden your perspective. Understand the impact of your actions on others.

He may have been the best defensive player to come out of Notre Dame.

But his career beyond football told you even more about him—he got his law degree while he played for the Minnesota Vikings.

With Page, it was about getting better each day. I will reach out to him even to this day for guidance. He has such integrity.

He and Bleier, from that same 1966 team, have been such an inspiration for me, especially for the things they have done off the field. They really care—and that's what Notre Dame is about.

* * *

Another person I love is Bob Crable, the all-time leading tackler in Notre Dame history. I had this image of him—how tenacious and vicious he was as a player. He would knock your head off. He did not say a lot—but he spoke with his actions.

To see him as a person, he embodies that humanity. He's had games when he made 26 tackles, and he's had another five games with 19 tackles each and another game with 20 tackles. That type of success does not just happen.

But his personality is something different—he's a guy you'd love to sit and have a beer with. He's a relaxed, blue-collar guy—kind of laid-back compared to what you see on the field, where he was really intense.

When he went into the College Football Hall of Fame, he was so grateful for the entire experience. His family all came to New York, and we held a reception for him at the New York Yankees Steakhouse on 51st Street across from Rockefeller Plaza. All the Notre Dame connections in the New York area made for a great evening.

He is not about pomp and circumstance. He just wanted to have fun when we were in New York, and he wanted everybody else to enjoy themselves. He valued his teammates and his family—they are the people who were most important to him.

Crable was recruited by Dan Devine and Brian Boulac, and then he ended by playing his last couple of years for Gerry Faust, who was also his high school coach at Moeller High School in Cincinnati.

He has great stories about trying to tackle Herschel Walker in the Sugar Bowl against Georgia when Georgia was No. 1. He did not see Walker as this insurmountable player—for Crable, he was just the guy he was supposed to tackle. He wasn't worried about all the hype. He just had fun playing the game because of the challenge involved. That's what it was all about.